GOD L/

MW00514381

Rob Falgiano

Printed in Canada
First printing – August 2014

Copy editor: Kristy Mangel
Additional editing: Carol Bella

Special thanks to Stephen Katz for perfecting the book title.

"Non-conformity is not the adoption of some pre-existing alternative sub-culture." - Julian Assange, reportedly from his internet dating profile, before Wikileaks

"How we treat the vulnerable is how we define ourselves as a species." - Russell Brand

"No man is more different from another man than the same man at different points in time." - Me

"Love is the Answer." - Todd Rundgren, via England Dan & John Ford Coley

CONTENTS

ONE: ATHEIST TICKLED INTO SUBMISSION

I was 9 when I stopped believing in god. I was physically forced to reconsider atheism at 26. As witness to years of small miracles, I've become a firm believer in much more than this life. Something contradictorily cosmic and beautifully absurd. Life has meaning, everything is connected, and spirits are real. We stay in touch, and you can too.

I was brought up loosely Catholic in the suburbs of Buffalo, NY, USA, Earth, Universe or Virtual Reality (apologies to Kurt Vonnegut), and attended weekend religious education classes at St. Joseph's in North Tonawanda. Tonawanda is a nice Native American word meaning "confluent stream," named for the Niagara River which flows past on its way to Niagara Falls; but, lazily tacking the adjective "north" to the front is kind of lame, something that palefaces would do. I'm white, so I'm allowed to say that.

My mom didn't push organized religion; it was about being a good person. When my parents split mom was angered she could no longer receive Communion at church. She felt unwelcome and stopped going. (St. Joe's eventually closed.) I don't know how good the Catholic Church is at alienating divorcees today, but they excelled in the 1980s. Soon after, mom honored my request to stop attending religion class because I was missing my favorite Saturday morning cartoons, especially *Spider-Man & His Amazing Friends*.

That's not when I quit god though. It was about a year earlier when my parents were still together. The Tooth Fairy's responsible. Mom was ours. (It's always mom, isn't it?) When my brother or I lost a tooth, our T.F. was slick and would come with cash before bedtime, the same evening it was placed under the pillow. Mom later explained this was to prevent a midnight wake-up discovery. Our Fairy left notes in calligraphy with sea shells.

One evening mom was out somewhere and dad was watching my brother Steve and I. I lost a tooth, which I dutifully placed under my pillow, expecting quarters long before bedtime. It was morning before I got paid and I suspected these circumstances were related. The little detective at work.

Mom was combing her long auburn hair in the bathroom the next day when I asked if there was really a Tooth Fairy. She asked if I was sure I wanted to know. I said, "Yes." And she said, "No." Then I said, "And Santa Claus?" A fraud. "The Easter Bunny?" Scam. I didn't ask, "And Jesus, too???" But surely I thought it, for in my peanut mind all spiritual entities hung out together. If you prayed to Santa then Jesus would know too. The Easter Bunny was like talking to god's magical pet, who would relay updates to god, perhaps telepathically. I remember pondering this concept once while sitting on the toilet. The Tooth Fairy toppled Jesus.

Like the Tooth Fairy, our Easter Bunny was special. Mom added a sheen of magic by leaving three-fingered flour paw prints all over the house leading to plastic eggs filled with money (I hate real eggs), including at the foot of our beds. Some footprints stopped at a pair of sneakers which E.B. wore around the house. The magic dust would fade over the course of the day. You had to enjoy it while it lasted.

In the late 1980s, my high school years, I became increasingly skeptical of religion during the Ronald Reagan - Jerry Falwell – Moral Majority era of self-righteousness. Arrogant fingers pointed at us, telling us how to live, but without the humility of introspection. (Simultaneously, Richard Pryor hailed the rise of Reagan as the "end of fucking," and encouraged everyone to get their last jollies in.)

I became an antagonistic atheist. I couldn't stand the closed-mindedness, judgment, and false modesty, though I mirrored the intolerance I perceived in my loud opposition to it. My high school notebooks were plastered with pictures of Reagan and Falwell, with big newspaper headlines taped around their faces shouting, "LIAR!" My French teacher Mrs. Versailles (an alias) sneered at me while spying my sarcastic collage. No words were exchanged. I repaid her for the snark by skipping the awards ceremony where she would have presented me with a Fleur-De-Lis pin for highest grades in her French classes. Later that week she asked me to stay after class, to coordinated oohing from my peers, and gave me the pin from her desk without comment. It's still in my dresser drawer.

Fast forward to March 1997, nearly two decades after the Tooth Fairy debacle, and almost one since high school. Thirty-nine members of the Heaven's Gate cult of San Diego committed suicide at their isolated group compound because they believed they needed to release their souls to rendezvous with a spaceship waiting for them behind passing comet Hale-Bopp, on the other side of the moon.

On a sunny winter afternoon, within weeks of their deaths, I sat in my bathrobe on the couch of my North Tonawanda apartment flipping through TV channels. The TV isn't on much (exploitative daytime talk shows make me feel sad), but I happened to stop on an episode of *Maury*, or someone like that. All the guests on this particular episode were claiming to have had near-death experiences.

One woman said that ever since her event she regularly blew out computers. Fried the hard drives by being in proximity to them, both at work and home, as if surrounded by an electrical field or aura. Another guy said that flashbulbs often popped and lights flared when he walked into a room. As he spoke the studio lights flickered, which obviously could have been faked, but I watched without judgment, surprised to find myself interested.

None of the guests on the show seemed insane. I silently said to myself, "I wonder if there really is an afterlife." Immediately after this thought, I heard or *felt* the name "Justin." Then I had the sensation of being tickled all over my body by someone or something unseen. I was completely surprised but not the slightest bit afraid. I fell to the floor laughing, and amazed. I didn't see anything; no wispy white apparitions. It was all feeling.

The tickling continued intermittently and playfully for the next 90 minutes. An overwhelming feeling of joy swelled in my body. It was the cleanest, purest, surest happiness I've ever felt, to this day. There were tears of pure happiness running down my face (I wish I had thought to bottle them). I had to ask my "visitor" (it felt singular, not plural) to take a break so I could catch my breath. The tickling immediately stopped. The presence felt respectful.

It was the middle of the afternoon and beautifully sunny; the setting helped to make it less of an uncertain or scary experience. When it started it seemed like the most natural thing in the world. The presence remained with me as I walked around the apartment, tickling me until I'd laugh so hard I had to ask for a time out again. It was excellent company. I was buzzing and high, but clearheaded. Excited to be breathing, alive, and having the experience. Grateful.

I finally got my day started; it tickled me in the shower. More laughter as the water ran down my face. "Okay, okay!

I get it! Give me a break!" (Seriously, who gets tickled by a ghost in the tub?) It tickled me in the kitchen while I drank a glass of apple juice. The giddy playfulness sticks in my mind: perfect in its innocence. Beautifully clear.

I phoned my mom. She believed me without hesitation because she's had experiences with spirits over the years, as has my brother, though we are far from spaced-out hippie mystics. I come from a grounded family and we eschew pretense. (Except for the use of the word "eschew.") We've resisted embracing a constructed, artificial identity that suggests specialness on our part. I think humility is a key to life, and maybe the reason why some secrets have been revealed to us and others, like yourself perhaps. Or in the future, if you seek it.

Justin was my mom's second child, born three years after me. He was severely premature and died hours after birth. My brother Steve came three years after Justin, also very premature, resulting in cerebral palsy. Steve is unable to walk and uses a wheelchair.

Steve went to a terrific special needs school in downtown Buffalo when he was young and our family spent a lot of time around kids with all kinds of disabilities, many far more severe than his. The experiences inevitably color my perspective on life and vulnerability.

I can't be certain it was Justin who visited me, but someone did. The event was way too concrete to dismiss as a hallucination. It was grounded, physical, and unambiguous, not to mention lengthy. If it hadn't happened to me I might doubt this story. Hopefully you'll find me to be a credible messenger.

I have to laugh though when I catch a ghost hunting TV show and everyone's freaked out because maybe a door slammed all on its own. Once you've been playfully tickled for 90 minutes by an unseen presence your only options are to decide it was real or that you're delusional. (Truthfully, everyone's a bit insane. From there it's a matter of what type, and to what degree. My insanity's a standard strain.)

I love to get spacey creatively, mostly when writing music and contemplating the great unknown, but I'm otherwise pragmatic, and don't do drugs. Amazing Belgian beer is my delicious vice. I believe that scientists and spiritualists are searching for the same thing, investigating the mysteries of the universe to try to understand the relationship between math and magic. A belief in something greater than this world doesn't invalidate science, or vice versa. It's ironically beautiful that neither side is able to definitively prove its case as to the existence or absence of a grand designer, who may or may not still exist or care about the universe. It leaves more room for what we each believe, and whether there's a deeper meaning to life, though I'm convinced there is. A lot has changed since the Tooth Fairy was debunked.

TWO: BOBBING FOR ANSWERS

A few years after the 1997 tickling incident its vividness receded. When it happened I realized that the feeling was so powerful and special it would be nearly impossible to recall the same way later. I stepped out of the shower that day, looked in the mirror, and said, "Don't forget this is the purest joy you've ever experienced." I felt there might never be an occurrence that intense again, perhaps until I die.

I didn't immediately transform from an atheist into a "believer," but the experience necessarily percolated. The meaning wasn't absorbed for years, and it's still subject to review. Not the fact that it happened, which isn't in doubt, but whether there's anything specific I should do with the knowledge. It's a tricky thing. I need to be careful not to go around trying to indoctrinate other people like the religious extremists I disliked in high school, but I'm thrilled at the discovery and want to share it.

Intermittent events followed over the next several years. The next big thing was a method of communication with the other side which I call "head bobbing." Unseen visitors usually arrive when I'm close to waking or falling asleep, early in the morning or late at night. I need to be somewhat relaxed to get a connection, and I'm usually lying on my back in bed when it begins.

When a spirit is trying to communicate I sense its presence. There's intense pressure in the middle of my forehead, where the "Third Eye" supposedly resides. (I've not read much about chakras, but my experiences seem to match things I've heard.) The visitor gently moves my head. It feels like they're inhabiting the front of my brain. Once they've announced their arrival this way I try to figure out what kind of visitor it is.

I only feel presences, not see or hear them, though many times it's seemed like a face would emerge from the wispy, grey shapes that float in my Third Eye. (I think this is because I'm not sure I *want* to see them. Unseen visitors aren't frightening, but I haven't worked my way up to full visions.) I've seen the chalky white outlines of faces and eyes in the darkness. The images change quickly, like passing cloud-shapes collapsing and forming. Sometimes the brief images appear cubist in that the same facial outline is seen from multiple, overlapping angles at once. More recently the clouds turn colors, most often between metallic purple, green, and blue. The tones are muted and dark, like in the days of movie film.

I stumbled on the idea that I could ask my frequent visitors questions and receive non-verbal answers. To communicate I ask a question aloud or in my mind, and answers are given as either a "yes" or "no," via the gentle movement of my head by the visitor. If my head bobs up and down the answer is "yes." Side to side means "no."

Each encounter begins by asking if the spirit visitor is well-intentioned. This weeds out most of the unfriendlies because they're poor liars. I say/think something like, "Have you come with good intentions, and through the white light of god?" Friendly forces have a light vibe and answer questions quickly, without hesitation, like an honest person with nothing to hide. They provide unambiguous assurance.

If there's an awkward pause during the "screening process" it usually means the visitor is up to something. An unfriendly might try to lie and give an up and down headshake, but a weak affirmative almost always slips into a side to side motion indicating "no," or after a few more questions.

Anytime the feeling is uncertain it's best to break it off. The connection is easily cut. I tell them to run along and play elsewhere, open my eyes, or sit up in bed. Spirits don't have much power in this realm unless we allow them to influence us, or, over a long period of time, to court and seduce us.

I prefer the term "unfriendlies" to "evil spirits," because some unfriendlies are not necessarily evil, just mischievous. Some like to play tricks and mess with your mind, much like the confused, screwed up people we've all come across.

13

People like this are likely to be much the same in the next world unless they work to improve. It's part of the journey of the soul.

Once a visitor seems trustworthy, we chat. I ask about life and spiritual ideas, or whatever comes up. I refer to the encounters as "picking up spiritual traffic." We're surrounded by spirits and intelligence at all times, and can tune into it like dialing a radio station. Visitors usually approach me to start a conversation but, more recently, when I ask if there are any presences around, there almost always are. One hundred billion people have already lived on the planet; that's a lot of potential spirits floating around, though they're not confined to Earth. More on that later.

The afterlife, heaven, the other side, the realm of spirits, or whatever term you prefer, is overlaid directly on this world, but exists at a super-high vibration and is otherwise imperceptible. It's not a separate place in the clouds. When you're spiritually aligned, you can communicate more consistently and reliably.

Several times the friendly head bobbing has turned into a full-body shake, with vibrations travelling all the way down through me. I've been playfully rocked back and forth like a carnival ride. On a few occasions the vibrations have been so intense that I've been flipped over in bed! Tossed like a salad while laughing in surprise.

Being thrown around has been too joyful to be frightening. It's like when you play-fight with your dad or grandpa as a child, and he picks you up and pretends to roughhouse you, but drops you gently on the couch. You never feel unsafe even though he has far more strength. It's all the excitement of danger without any fear, because there's trust.

I never expected to have these experiences. It was a shock to find my beliefs changing, but to ignore the events would've been a denial of reality. Scientists rely on proof and testable hypotheses. For my family, physical evidence has been provided, but it's not a game. These are deep secrets. I want to be respectful of things I can't fully understand.

I don't know if there's such a thing as a single god, or maybe a collection of omnipotent creators, or whether the universe itself is god with us inside of it, or if it's some kind of quantum computer and we're all little bits of information running on the grand hard drive, or something else entirely.

I hesitate to use the word "god" to describe the infinite because it's loaded and has been co-opted by many groups of supposedly religious people whose behavior is more sheepish or cult-like than spiritual. "They've forgotten the message (of Jesus), but worship the creeds," according to songwriter Matt Johnson. Without charity, love, empathy, and forgiveness as its foundation, religion squanders its promise. But, as a form of shorthand, and to communicate with others on the subject, I've grown accustomed to calling it "god." Whatever it is it belongs to every living being in the universe.

When people of faith and hope, of any religion or no religion at all, pray, it's to the same higher power. God loves everybody and doesn't take sides. You don't need to be formal. It's not even praying; it's simply talking to god and good spirits. You don't need to be on your knees or in a church. No specific rituals are required. Those things can get in the way. Your intentions matter most. Your honesty and humility are required.

You can sit in a chair and ask, "What's up, god?" "Can you hook me up with some of that sweet love and joy?" "How's it hanging in heaven?" I bet you could make god laugh if you come up with a good zinger. The god I believe in finds cornball humor funny, when it's not mean-spirited. I think god appreciates ridiculousness because he/she/it knows existence can be extremely hard on mortals and life is absurd, just as the total absence of life would be absurd. The god I believe in laughs at dirty jokes. Hell, god probably tells the best ones.

THREE: STEVE'S VISIONS

My younger brother Steve has had more detailed communications with the other side than I do. It seemed very natural to him when it first happened. He never sought it. He gets beautiful full-color visions. He's left his body and wheelchair and travelled to fields of flowers under sunshine and describes the colors as heightened and unearthly, with a reddish tint. Steve often speaks with our deceased brother Justin. One time Justin's face was indistinct and cloudy, and Steve asked him if he could improve the image. His features sharpened like someone had adjusted a lens, and Steve could see him clearly. Justin looks like Steve and I, with thinning brown hair and the same Italian cleft chin. He wears a gold necklace when he visits Steve because it's the purest metal, forged in the largest stars, and unfriendly imposters have difficulty imitating it when they call disguised as him.

(If you're ever beseiged by unfriendly spirits, it helps if you calmly ask for the white light of god to envelop you. Think of bright light as truth and purity, or god's flashlight. Unfriendlies have trouble withstanding the light because their existence is based on deception, and they hide in pockets of darkness like rats. An angry response to an assault by unfriendlies won't help you. Believe me, I've tried, and I detail it later. Don't imitate the priest in *The Exorcist*. The most powerful resistance comes from the calmest frame of mind and spirit.)

I believe Steve gets more detailed visions and can engage in verbal conversations with visitors because he's one of the most decent people I know. He rarely gets angry, and is almost always smiling and laughing. When I meet pretentious people I might imagine kicking them in the metaphoric crotch, but Steve practices restraint while sizing them up, and is deeply perceptive. He lacks casual cruelty or pettiness. Surely spirits and the moral universe are aware, and keep track. Everything matters. There's no hiding in the end.

We learned about another way spirits can communicate with the living. It involves vibrations, which we'll get into shortly. Steve is a reluctant medium. His modesty prevents him from thinking of himself as one, or claiming a title, or trying to profit from it. I'm like this, too, to a less saintly extent.

We possess bits of a gigantic puzzle of unknowable, possibly infinite size. I don't expect to acquire all the pieces while human, or maybe ever. That's probably how it should be for anyone reaching (impossibly) to comprehend creation. The universe plays by some physical rules that can be discovered and measured, but the sheer vastness encourages humility.

Gina, a friendly psychic I met last summer in Fort Erie, Ontario, told me that mediums are in demand by spirits because they're one of the few means by which they can pass messages to loved ones here. Mediums can easily become overwhelmed because there's literally a waiting line of spirits trying to get their attention and enlist their help.

Steve learned this first-hand. Deceased relatives of family, friends, and acquaintances drop in unannounced, literally when he's brushing his teeth or trying to sleep, asking him to contact living relatives. The information Steve's been given about family pets, or inside jokes that only the recipient would understand, are things he'd have absolutely no way of knowing otherwise. More proof that we're not imagining things.

Unfortunately, forwarding messages has occasionally bitten him in the ass. Several years ago Steve attended a local church. It was more of a social activity, to make new friends, not to support a specific faith. Though he attended Saturday evening youth activities we would still make fun of overenthusiastic holy rollers and make references to "Jebus" (Homer Simpson's moronic mispronunciation).

Steve received a message from the deceased grandmother of a young woman named Brenda who went to church. Steve passed it on, but Brenda didn't believe him. Then she ratted him out to the whole church, and one of the youth leaders wrote him a letter of concern. Steve felt ostracized and sad. Mom and I were mad and ready to crack some skulls, as is our hot-blooded nature. Brenda's grandmother returned to apologize to Steve, and told him she was disappointed in her granddaughter's behavior.

Consider the extreme fucking irony of a bunch of people, who claim to believe both in god and his immaculate magical son, who walked the Earth performing miracles 2,000 years ago, not believing an innocent messenger like my brother when he delivered accurate news from their dead relatives. What a crock of shit!

These phony Christians were more interested in being a narrow-minded wolf pack than in seriously considering the deeper possibilities of spirituality. Steve stopped going to church. It wasn't fun for him anymore, even though all involved eventually apologized after mom blasted the youth leader with a letter from her Sicilian pen. It's their loss, and I get angry remembering how they made him feel.

- - -

More than a decade ago mom helped Steve transition to a comfy handicap-accessible apartment in a nice complex near her house. He was hesitant to leave home, but has grown to love his own space. Most of the retiree tenants look out for him, and know Steve by his given first name, Samuel, or Sammy, after our Grandpa Falgiano. (Steve is his middle name.) But a few of the "crusties," as Steve jokingly and affectionately refers to them, are cranky.

Lately Steve has been having dreams which accurately predict future events. The night before a mildly annoying exchange with a senior tenant, Steve dreamt that Mildred would give him grief about purchasing a ticket for a summer cookout occurring later in the week. Mildred had decided, without advance notice, that the cutoff for buying the $3 ticket was 48 hours prior to the event, and Steve was past her deadline. In Steve's dream she leaned over and put her hands on his wheelchair arms, violating his personal space, standing above him in intimidation. He couldn't hear what she was saying, but he felt the intent.

The next day the real-life exchange played out exactly as in the dream, but, since Steve saw it coming, he wasn't rattled. He maintained his composure and informed her that she hadn't given any notice, but that that was fine, and he wouldn't attend. Steve looked in Mildred's eyes, amused that she had no idea he saw her coming a mile away. A woman named Elsie overheard their exchange and volunteered her extra ticket, which Steve gratefully accepted. Later he left an envelope with $3 inside Elsie's mailbox, but she returned it to him.

At the cookout, another senior named Patti invited Steve to sit with her and her friends. As you know, seniors love gambling, bingo, and raffles. Patti purchased several 50/50 lottery tickets for the luncheon from Mildred, and gave one to each of her friends at the table, including Steve. He said, "I never win, but if I do I'll split the pot with you." Sure enough, Steve won the $60 prize and gave half to Patti. Of course he did, I thought. How could he not?

I told Steve I was looking forward to heaven because I will point my finger at Mildred and remind her of her pettiness, how shamefully she behaved. That's the petty, vengeful side of me, but always on behalf of the honest underdog. Seriously, don't bully my brother or anyone else. You don't even know what you're messing with spiritually. I said if Mildred knew what we know about spirits and eternity she'd probably be kissing his feet instead.

FOUR: FLOWERS FROM DUST

"Hey Casanova," said Uncle Bill, his habitual greeting to my brother Steve. "Please tell Annie I'm okay, and that I love her." In 2008 Uncle Bill visited Steve within days of his fatal heart attack. He had been mowing the lawn at his home in Dunmore, PA, at the time. Our aunt found him outside with the mower still running. While alive, Uncle Bill never told Anne he loved her. Steve passed the message on to mom, who phoned her sister. Anne was glad to hear this because she said she always wondered if he really did.

One of Steve's other unusual visitors at the time was a cocky guy with a 1950s look who smoked cigarettes in a black leather jacket while dispensing bad advice about women. He once told Steve he'd bag a certain girl like a sack of groceries.

Steve's other visitors have included famous and less famous artists who've died, including, we believe, actor Heath Ledger, and a singer-songwriter we admired named Josh Clayton-Felt, of the alternative rock band School of Fish. Clayton-Felt died of cancer in 2000, aged 32. A few years ago Josh visited Steve and told him he was working on his next recording on the other side, titled *Flowers From Dust*. Great album title.

(Stars themselves form in great clouds of dust and radiation. As the cloud collapses a dense core forms, and gathers more dust and gas. Some of the material becomes the star, and the rest mostly becomes planets, asteroids, and comets. When stars go supernova they seed the universe with the heavier particles that eventually lead to more complex life forms like us, plus every tree, animal, insect, ocean, mountain, and gold deposit. It's true that flowers are from dust because everything is from dust.)

I have an embarrassing connection to Josh. In the winter of 1996 my band played a gig at a college bar in Oswego, NY, about 3 hours from Buffalo. I'd just purchased my first 4-cylinder stick-shift truck. Hatchbacks like my previous car, a tiny 3-cylinder Chevy Sprint that our first drummer dubbed "the roller skate," had gone out of style and I needed something big enough to cart musical gear.

My S10 was one of the early light-duty trucks, prone to fishtailing in icy conditions due to a lack of rear weight, though I didn't know that yet. It was also the era of top-heavy, flip-prone family mini-vans. Off-road cartwheels at no extra charge. That's not funny, except when it's not you.

The streets into Oswego were icy. Coming down an incline I slid into another vehicle at a stop light, but there was no damage. It was my first set of anti-lock brakes, and the truck glided much more than my hatchback, which made me nervous.

That night we performed for a mostly indifferent audience of boozy college students, except for my friend Corinna who also put us up for the night. The next morning we had breakfast at a local diner, made up of a mix of "townies" and college students. Some of Corinna's friends mocked the rural locals. I don't care about anyone's social status, wealth, or appearance. Everyone's equal until they prove otherwise. I generally trust people who work with their hands more than number-crunching schemers in towers.

I drove home with Ron, our drummer. The other guys went in a second car. I put in Clayton-Felt's first solo CD, *Inarticulate Nature Boy*. I had seen a video for the song "Window" on *MTV's 120 Minutes* and was blown away. Mom's then-boyfriend, now second-husband, John used to videotape the show for me at his house every week since we didn't have cable. Every once in a while they'd show something truly unique, like unusual New York City art-band Hugo Largo, and Clayton-Felt. "Window" was funky, melodic, thoughtful, well-played, modest, and inviting. So, of course, the record was destined for failure, much like my own recordings.

We were listening to the second or third song when I hit a patch of ice and started to lose control of the vehicle. I was fiddling with the stereo and had just put on my seatbelt at Ron's insistence. Did I have an unconscious death wish or was I just stupidly young and cocky?

The intense fishtailing began. My inexperience at handling the vehicle didn't help. I felt slow-motion fright like in a movie, with a heightened awareness of critical fractions of seconds determining our fate. When I knew I wouldn't be able to control the truck any longer, it was simply a matter of where we would crash. There was enough time to yell, "Hold on!" We crossed the dividing line and started spinning backwards. The truck clipped the edge of a ditch on the opposite side of the road, flipping the truck on its passenger side, facing the direction from which we'd come.

The passenger window was smashed, and the entire side of the truck was crushed, but we were uninjured. We climbed out the driver's side window, now facing skyward. "Oh my god! Oh my god!" A woman from the nearest house ran out screaming. We were unintentionally nonchalant. "It's okay. We're fine!" An ambulance quickly arrived and took a look at our eyeballs. We were genuinely appreciative but didn't seem to need any help.

We called a tow truck to upright the vehicle and pull it from the ditch. It started up fine. We drove to a gas station to buy duct tape, covering the window entirely so that it would be less cold. The rest of the drive was uneventful. We weren't somber; we were making jokes. We were lucky! Or we just weren't meant to die that day. Within a few weeks I had the truck repaired and it was as if it had never happened, though mom says she will never forget the stones jammed around the tire rims.

Josh visited Steve a few years ago, at least a dozen years after the accident, and said the reason I wasn't killed was because I had more music to make. In Steve's vision Josh held up a copy of my then-current CD, *Red* (recorded in 2005), smiled, and said he liked it. I don't consider his message proof of future notoriety. He was right though; I'm

23

still writing songs. Josh probably just wanted to be kind and encouraging, as I imagine he was when he lived, based on his lyrics.

Josh's final record, *Spirit Touches Ground*, was released posthumously by his friends and family. It has some amazing songs about change, transition, essence, faith, and love that seem to anticipate his departure from Earth. In the song "Waiting To Be" he sings: "You're waiting to be what you already are / You're the only one left in your way." Steve and I were also deeply moved by "Too Cool For This World:" "You're too cool for this world / You realized a long time ago / You've got so much in your heart / You don't even want to start / You don't want the whole world to know / Nothing seems good enough / It's so hard just getting up / But the world will be here when you rise." It still gives me chills.

"Dragonfly" is the stunning closing ballad. "If your road has reached the ocean / But your legs still want to go / And if they taught you how to doubt it / But you know it isn't so / And if the moments seem to miss you / And if your partner isn't there / And if you know you could reach the treasure / But you keep coming up for air / If you want to get through to the other side / Let the dragonfly come and give you a ride / Every day you're born and every night you die / Let the dragonfly come and give you a ride." Sometimes when I listen to it I feel he's with me, providing guidance and reassurance.

We can't be certain it was really Josh who visited Steve, but I choose to believe. Maybe I'll get to hear *Flowers From Dust* on the other side, and we can sing some songs together.

I haven't thought about the truck accident in many years, likely preferring to block it out and believe I couldn't have

24

been so stupid. Don't we each have at least one story like that? There's such a thin line between life and death. It makes me wonder how much is fated and why some people get luckier than others.

FIVE: GOOD VIBRATIONS, AND TUNING INTO UNIVERSAL RADIO

All matter in the universe vibrates at specific frequencies. The particles that make up your body resonate constantly. The Earth has a super low frequency hum that's imperceptible to the human ear.

From conversations we've had with the other side, Steve and I learned that when a person dies their consciousness does live on. (This also implies life is a virtual reality of some kind. More on that ahead.) We'll call this the soul, for convenience, but, again, the name isn't important. Our contacts confirm that the spirit world exists on top of this one, but at a higher vibration, so it's unseen and largely unperceived by most people. Heaven isn't a separate place. It's right here, almost in grasp. "Sensitives" are more, well, *sensitive* and perceptive, and feel aspects of the greater reality more consistently.

Immortal, disembodied spirits vibrate at a much higher frequency than the matter which makes up the visible universe we know. The more "enlightened" the spirit, the higher its vibration. Spirits with lower vibrations cannot communicate with, or visit the more beautiful, purer realms of higher spirits until they achieve a degree of enlightenment that raises their vibration. However, high-vibration spirits can slow and lower their vibrations to visit and communicate with lower spirits and living people.

We believe that spirit vibrations are related to the authenticity and goodness of a person while alive, though how exactly this is measured, and who does the measuring, is hard to say. If the universe is essentially moral, then perhaps the calibrations are built in somehow, like a karmic calculator. Most people know what they're really like in their heart, even if they hide it from themselves and others. My brother will be a high vibration. Higher than me, and probably my mom as well, because he is more purely good, innocent, and less conflicted.

My friend Mike Rorick is a recording studio engineer who's worked with me on my last two CDs. He shares an interest in spirituality and we often start our recording sessions swapping new ideas over morning coffee. Based on his understanding of sound, Mike speculated that when we meet others with whom we have an instant rapport, it's because there are sympathetic frequencies at work. Sympathetic frequencies - sound waves - create harmony in music.

Similarly, when we "get someone's vibe" we experience a pleasant feeling of connection in their presence. The phrase itself implies "good vibrations" are at work, like the Beach Boys song. A harmonious relationship might be felt in our bodies before we even know exactly why we like someone, which is why it's important to trust your instincts. Perhaps a gut feeling is your cells resonating harmonically or dissonantly in the presence of others' vibrations, trying to tell you something important about them, good or bad.

- - -

I suspect that people with anti-social maladies, yet incomprehensible brainpower, and/or the ability to perceive complex patterns and systems, are also closer to the other side. Many geniuses, prodigies, great artists, and individuals with autism spectrum conditions seem somewhat removed from the "real world" that most of us understand. For example, how does a savant like British architectural artist Stephen Wiltshire recall and paint entire city skylines in intimate detail from memory?

We all exist in the same physical space, but perhaps their intelligence and/or afflictions elevate their awareness and interest away from this vibrational plane. They have greater powers of perception that appear, and perhaps are, supernatural. Does extreme brainpower inevitably impair one's ability to socialize "normally?" Is it possible that the essence of god, the most unfathomable intelligence, is madness?

In the last few years scientists have made interesting genetic discoveries related to intellect. As part of the Human Genome Project, mapping the entirety of human DNA, they discovered three duplicates of a gene called SRGAP2, which is involved in brain development. Humans are the only animals known to have these extra copies. SRGAP2B and SRGAP2D are essentially junk, but SRGAP2C greatly improved the growth of brain neurons when it began showing up in our ancestors 2.4 million years ago, the same time their brains significantly increased in size.

It's common for genes to be duplicated by mistake, but, to some scientists, a duplicate gene that's responsible for greatly enhanced intelligence suggests intelligence itself may have been *accidental*, a genetic quirk that turned out to have a huge evolutionary advantage. The first mutated humans to possess this gene would have appeared vastly more intelligent, perhaps superhuman or alien, to their peers. When they mated they passed on the mutation, eventually leading to us.

A damaged SRGAP1 gene (from the same protein family as SRGAP2) can lead to developmental problems and seizures, and researchers have identified several genetic variants that are common to people with autism. Scientists are now trying to determine if mutations in SRGAP2C also lead to brain disorders, leading me to wonder if high intelligence can be considered a "disorder."

As we get closer to genius do we necessarily get closer to madness? Perhaps, as one nears the all-knowing aspects of god, balancing a multitude of concepts and differing perspectives, and especially *contradictions*, one is also closer to grasping the quantum state of infinite possibilities. It's bigger and more cosmic than most people can handle. (Is god the ultimate contradiction because, by embodying all creation, god is both absolute good and absolute evil, and everything in between?) I think of the biblical notion that to look into god's eyes is to be overwhelmed by the impossibility of perceiving all of existence, the entire universe, at once. How could a limited human being stare into an all-powerful paradox and not be driven at least partly mad?

I'm apparently not smart or crazy enough to pursue the thought further, as much as I might like to, though perhaps I should be thankful that my understanding hits a wall that prevents me from going fully bonkers, or at least for now. Ha ha. However, a correlation between genius and madness doesn't make it okay to think of oneself as Einstein just because you're really smart and don't play well with others. As David Sedaris said, there's a thin line between Asperger's and assholism.

SIX: RESPECTING POWERFUL FORCES

Spirits have higher vibrations than the living, so when they want to communicate with us they must lower their vibration. A medium like my brother Steve is someone with enough purity of spirit that he can raise his vibration to communicate and meet with spirits in the middle space between realms, where they overlap.

Some spirits who visit Steve and try to talk to him are incomprehensible. When they speak the words sound like they've been sped up. Spirits have to practice lowering their vibrations so their speech becomes intelligible. Steve has heard their voices change in pitch mid-sentence when they arrive, from unintelligible to audible words, like a record playing too fast finally sliding into the proper speed. Imagine a "Chipmunks" vocal that keeps dropping until it sounds like a normal speaking voice.

It's important to respect these forces and not treat communication with spirits as a game, because what's being tapped can't be fully understood. Even people with experience like us can be manipulated by unfriendly forces, as you'll see.

Some people deliberately or accidentally attract dark spiritual forces because there are seductive elements, but they inevitably end up being used. This idea is explored in David Lynch's creepy, fascinating movie *Lost Highway* and also the best TV show of all time, *Twin Peaks*. Almost all of Lynch's work deals with the battle between the ancient, eternal forces of good and evil via surrogates on Earth. It's one of the reasons his projects are so resonant.

In *Lost Highway* Robert Blake plays an extremely intense character dubbed the "Mystery Man." He's a malevolent, manipulative incarnation of darkness. At a pool party attended by some young, attractive L.A. socialites of questionable character (they're peddling drugs, pornography, and murder), the Mystery Man confronts Bill Pullman's character, a talented but troubled sax player named Fred Madison. Madison eventually murders his wife Renee (portrayed masterfully by Patricia Arquette), and it's implied that the Mystery Man is his dark spiritual enabler and accomplice.

Madison, already in league with the Mystery Man, but in denial as to the degree to which he's been seduced by darkness to commit murder, says to him suspiciously, "Have me met?" The Mystery Man smiles and laughs ominously. "You invited me in (to your home)? Don't you remember? In fact, I'm there right now." Madison is creeped out, phones his own home, and the Mystery Man answers at Madison's house, while simultaneously smiling at him at the party.

Madison invited dark forces into his life because he is angry and suspicious that his wife is having multiple affairs, and is mixed up with the wrong crowd, filming snuff pornography. Madison forgets murdering her, as if under possession. He's arrested, and while imprisoned, his inability to accept what he's done fractures his mind and personality. Lynch pushes things further into surreal territory. Madison literally transforms into a different person, played by a different actor, because he can't cope. Unfortunately, his imagined second self still can't help him avoid his fate.

Robert Loggia's character Dick Laurent is another shady fucker – a gangster who uses other people to satisfy his perverse appetite. He's one of Renee's lovers and pimps. He prostitutes her in porn flicks, and her indulgences and deceptions infuriate the jealous Madison. Laurent is also in league with Blake's devilish Mystery Man. Near the end of the movie the Mystery Man and Madison murder Laurent. Just before he's killed, Laurent says to the Mystery Man, "You and me, mister, we can really out-ugly the sumbitches, can't we?" At which point Laurent is dispatched from the realm of the living by a bullet from the Mystery Man's gun. Laurent uses, and is used by, something dark and twisted, and he's eventually discarded by it, just like Madison. Do not let this happen to you in real life!

The infamous New York City serial killer David Berkowitz, "Son of Sam," recently claimed in an interview with the *New York Daily News* that he believes he committed his crimes while possessed by evil. I think this is possible, though it doesn't excuse his actions. Spirits only have the power over us we allow them to have, when we "invite them in" like Fred Madison and Dick Laurent.

Son of Sam doesn't deny his crimes, and now advocates for the restriction of gun proliferation. Berkowitz claims to have given himself to god and spends his life sentence at Attica counseling other criminals. He says he committed his crimes at a time in his life when he was lost, tormented, and confused.

When he was arrested Berkowitz claimed that his neighbor's dog had ordered him to kill. Looking back, he now says, "I tell you, I felt like I was under demonic possession. I don't even recognize that person. 'Son of Sam' represents evil and satanic things. That person is like a total stranger to me now. I have regrets more than words can say."

Berkowitz isn't seeking pity. "I'll be the first to say that I don't deserve to have my life spared, but I believe God spared my life to do the things I'm doing now. I want people to see my God is a God of miracles. If He can save someone like me, he can save anybody."

I believe his words with all my heart. Anyone can be forgiven for the terrible things they've done, and no one is beyond redemption. I also believe he's where he should be, locked up for life. His relationship with god is his business, and it doesn't erase the consequences of his actions. None of his victims' families are obligated to forgive him, though doing so would be an incredible spiritual feat.

There's no way to know if Berkowitz was possessed when he became a serial murderer, but it feels likely. I can definitely believe that a powerful dark force took advantage of his anger and alienation and helped twist it into a self-righteous justification to transgress and take other people's lives. Berkowitz says he felt powerful for a time, but that was a false impression and part of the delusion that evil spirits are good at perpetuating.

Please be very careful if you try to tap into spiritual traffic. Some people wisely prefer not to engage it because they don't trust themselves to act responsibly. Question your motives before you begin.

My mom once got herself in a bit of trouble by being insufficiently respectful of Native American spiritual traditions. A few years ago she told me about seeking out her animal spirit guide. She ended up having a "vision" where she found herself riding on the back of a wild horse that just kept gaining speed. It thrilled her for a bit. But she became frightened because she couldn't get off, and didn't know how to break free or make it stop. That was her last time dabbling with animal spirits, which is best. Her intent was innocent enough, but she'd experimented with a tradition that wasn't meant for her. It's likely some tricksters decided to have fun at her expense, teach her a lesson, or provide a warning. She was sick for some time after this, as if made unwell by the experience. She said it was creepy, but she recovered, and escaped wiser.

SEVEN: BIG SECRETS DON'T COME CHEAP, BUT HUMILITY HELPS

There will continue to be amazing scientific discoveries and technological innovations that challenge an already blurring line between science and spirituality, and which may force us to reconsider the nature of reality.

In 2012 particle physicists discovered the existence of the long-sought-after, extremely high energy particle, that gives other particles mass - the Higgs boson. The CERN Large Hadron Collider, an atomic particle smasher in Geneva, sent hydrogen protons through 17 miles of underground tunnels at more than 99.99 percent the speed of light, smashing into each other. The collision generated temperatures 100,000 times hotter than the sun for a fleeting moment, imitating the conditions just after the Big Bang, and creating the Higgs for a fraction of a second. It's an enormous achievement, and as with many great discoveries, it simultaneously opens the door to new questions.

Our powerful telescopes, microscopes, wave detectors, and other high-tech instruments can see down to an insanely small level of detail. A new surprise for scientists was to find that the smallest bits of matter in the universe, much smaller than an atom, appear *pixilated* when magnified, as if we're living in a detailed computer simulation, a virtual reality. Other data suggests we're like 3-D holograms living on the Holodeck of the *Enterprise*.

Technology is advancing so rapidly that in the future we'll create virtual realities that rival this one in detail and sensation. Who's to say that our reality isn't another civilization's virtual reality experiment? And, if so, did someone else create our creators' reality? How will we ever know if we're in the "original" reality, if it exists? What if our intellect and consciousness can survive this game of life?

The universe does a good job of keeping many secrets, including the original moment of creation. We gaze backwards nearly 14 billion years with telescopes to see the beginning, but hit a wall because the Big Bang is shrouded in super-hot, opaque plasma for hundreds of thousands of years before cooling sufficiently to form the first stars.

Perhaps god knows that if we were to actually land on the final answer to the ultimate question of existence, like the number "42" in *Hitchhiker's Guide to the Galaxy*, we could only grow deeply unsatisfied, because there would be nothing truly important left to ponder. All sense of wonder would be lost. Either that, or having reached full enlightenment, we'd merge back into god and start over again from nothingness.

One of the beautiful and maddening things about life is that as soon as you think you've got your mind around a big truth, language often fails you. The closer you get to that profound magical answer, the more the words seem to gum up in your mouth, contradicting each other, or being misunderstood by others, as they stumble out. It's like the Tower of Babel. By trying to build an enormous temple that would reach god, the Babylonians overreached. God stymied their efforts by causing each to speak a different language while attempting to finish its construction.

I've cited the Bible, but *it should be obvious* it's not to be taken literally. It wasn't written by god, but by men. The historical record, as detailed in an interesting book called *Don't Know Much About the Bible,* implies that the gospels of the New Testament weren't written until at least 100 years after the life of Jesus. It consists of stories passed down through many generations which were finally transcribed onto scrolls. How many attempted clarifications, additions, and alterations may have made it into the stories over hundreds of years? The Bible has been translated across a half-dozen languages before we get to modern English, which leaves more room for alterations in wording and meaning.

The Bible and all religious texts are fragmentary books filled with amazing passages, and contradictory irrelevancies. The Sermon on the Mount is a beautiful set of thoughts on compassion, mercy, and love. I'm moved without needing to know whether Jesus really existed. *Someone* wise and loving transcribed or composed it, and its lessons resonate.

I haven't read the Koran or the Torah, but the suspicion is the same; that having been written by men (and always men, never women), and not god, they're imperfect philosophical documents. Of some extracted value, but far from absolute. If god exists and wanted to provide a set of rules to live by, he/she/it could have literally dropped a golden book from the sky that reads itself to you and leaves little doubt as to its magical, divine nature. There are probably many good reasons why this has never happened, including the limitations it would impose on intellectual curiosity, speculation, and individual beliefs.

It is likely that a man named Jesus lived 2,000 years ago, dispensing wisdom and guidance for leading a spiritual life. Short of observing a miracle first-hand, how would anyone have distinguished Jesus from a lunatic? If someone like

Jesus lived today he'd probably be persecuted just the same, and possibly hounded to the grave by a bunch of narrow-minded Christians, like the ones at the church my brother used to attend.

Did Jesus actually say he was the immaculate son of god in his lifetime? That idea might have grown after his death instead, when he became more myth than living being. In truth, isn't each of us a son or daughter of god? Aren't we also miraculous and divine? We were each sent here, or chose to come, as an eternal spiritual being, to have an experience in a temporary physical shell. We're messengers like Jesus when we embody generosity of spirit.

Knowledge is a mixed blessing. Perhaps we're meant to realize that, despite all we know, the limits of our understanding help us reconcile to half-wisdom, to accept existence as it is, moving humbly forward with an incomplete picture. Then we can enjoy the ambiguities and cosmic weirdness, while continuing to learn new things. The answers to life we come up with remain subject to doubt, and that's okay. Civilization advances on partial answers to practical and existential matters. So my book of truths, as I understand life, ultimately has to fail, at least partly. These ideas are no more absolute than those in any religious text I fault, and that's the only way it can be.

Celebrating the mysteries of the universe is not to defend ignorance, or to suggest that one shouldn't seek answers to big questions. Close-mindedness is a drag, and worse are people who know little but act like they know everything, and railroad others with their lack of logic, thoughtfulness, and curiosity. You have to be vulnerable and brave to admit there are things you don't understand, and to seek answers from those who may know more. This is how knowledge and courage are built. Modesty seems to be the only way to gain access to life's secrets; it benefits your cellular health and raises your vibration.

Whether we were created by a god or we live nestled deep inside a fractal series of virtual realities, if a creator exists surely it's hoping for signs of intellectual and spiritual progress? If my consciousness and intellect can survive death, or get promoted to another level of the ongoing "game of life," then I'd like to maximize my chances by being open minded and loving. I want to be interesting, both for my own satisfaction and fun, to intellectually stimulate others and be inspired in return, and to live up to the potential given by creation.

This cliché is true: the best things in life are simple. Joy, honesty, generosity, laughter, empathy, and trust. If you lose your way in complicated head games with damaged people you can always start back there. If your friends and family don't value these qualities, there's something wrong with them and they may not all be worth keeping. If you've become too jaded to any longer enjoy the simple, good things, you probably need to do some soul searching to get back to elegant simplicity, as I sometimes must.

Those who put too much value on their social status, career, appearance, and wealth, and believe in their own infallibility, are in for an eventual karmic shock. Pretense leads to self-delusion. Self-delusion is like living with a bag over your head. Living with a bag over your head is a great way of not experiencing reality. Reality is necessarily a mixed bag of beauty and horrors, but the beautiful parts are exquisite. Arrogance and pretense are cancers to the body, spreading like black poison in our cells.

Pretense and formality are veils that keep us from communicating more honestly. I have some edumacation but no interest in an overly intellectual, yet emotionally distant, academic approach or arty farty vagueness to life. Wealthy, educated classes sometimes rely on pomp and protocol to keep the focus off actual ideas. Some are sinister characters, and there are intelligent sociopaths in positions of great power. Be very careful if and when you wander into their world. They don't play by the same rules as anyone who was raised with any degree of respect for others.

Those with wealth and an entitlement mindset like to feel superior, to effectively enslave their perceived social inferiors. They value exclusivity and access to others with fame and wealth, who they perceive as their peers in a special club. They're simply afraid to be real, or have no idea what the world is really like, removed from the daily struggles of the majority. Anyone who tries to elevate himself above others, and envisions himself as brilliant is, of course, quite stupid. Raw intelligence and/or multiple degrees don't necessarily lead to wisdom.

Most of the truly profound ideas in the world can be communicated with language that a teenager or smart child would understand, though it should be noted that less educated people have collective affectations, too. No group of people is immune. The affectations of the wealthy and powerful are more twisted and dangerous because, in positions of authority, their actions negatively affect far more people when they behave badly.

- - -

Another big challenge of being human is trying to reconcile the innate needs and desires of the body with the conscious mind's knowledge of what's best, and the spiritual yearnings of the soul. Balancing 100,000 years of evolution and competitive survival with notions of decency, restraint, and community is a tall order. Many people aren't good at it, or for periods of time. Body, mind, and soul in collaboration and conflict, with differing agendas. We get confused sometimes and struggle to understand our own behavior as it relates to what we consider our values.

On a biological level, all nature desires is more of the species, and the continuation of life. I sometimes wonder if the main function of parents is to advance the next generation. Once they've fulfilled the mission, perhaps nature is indifferent to the emotional needs and continuation of their coupling. It necessarily becomes about taking care of the kids.

An animal must do certain things to survive, competing and killing for food, and extending the species through sex. We're animals and spiritual beings who possess enough intelligence to be self-aware. Cats and dogs aren't introspective, but still spiritual. If you're kind to most pets they will reward you with loyalty and love. Affection and companionship are key to the wellness of most animals, including people.

African elephants are loving creatures. They nurture each other, but pack life doesn't always protect them from poachers who kill them for their valuable tusks. The animal fights for survival and sometimes loses, just like a person. Violence can be unavoidable, but love is still the powerful force that gives life meaning. The cells of the body register it like sunlight, an energy that fosters health and well-being. It can never be meaningless to love, even if your fate in this life is "defeat." Loving is its own end, an inherent victory.

Perhaps when we leave our bodies and no longer relate to a physical shell we won't be consumed with reconciling our animal desires with the lofty intentions of spirit. Existing as spirit might not be superior to mortality, though. They seem like such different experiences as to be incomparable. Reincarnation seems possible and potentially desirable because, once you've been dead and immortal awhile, it might get boring lounging on a cloud every day, polishing the sky (thanks to songwriter Paddy McAloon).

Is the playground of disembodied spirits all of history? As spirits will we not only be able to travel anywhere in the universe, or even outside it, but also to any time? Could we peek in on events on Earth and other star systems hundreds and billions of years ago? Will we carry what we learned in this life into our next mortal life somewhere, some-when else?

You might decide to try Earth again, even though you know how tough life can be. My mom feels like she's been reincarnated many times. For whatever reason, I feel this is my first and last life here. There are so many other galaxies to try, you know? And maybe other universes, too.

EIGHT: FIRST EYEWITNESS

In 2007 my ex-girlfriend Jane got a first-hand account of one of my head-bobbing visitors. We'd been dating for three months and I'd recently told her about my ghost experiences. Jane's one of the first people I ever told. I trusted her and felt believed. It was nice.

We were lying in bed, waking on a Sunday morning. I felt a presence - the familiar pressure in the middle of my forehead - and told her we had company. She was startled and a little afraid.

When I sense a visitor the best way to communicate is to relax. I've learned that they access us closer to sleep and in dreams because we're more at ease and less naturally defensive. The visitor began to slowly and subtly move my head in an oval pattern. My eyes were closed and was I talking quietly to Jane at the same time.

The circular, orbit-like pattern was unusual in its precision. The rotation was so perfectly mechanical, slow, and controlled that I knew I wouldn't be able to imitate it later. In my unscientific opinion, it was a more perfect oval than any human being could have faked. "Does the circular motion look perfect?" I asked. "Because that's how it feels." It was convincing to Jane; she said yes.

We asked a few simple questions, including if the visitor was simply passing by to say hi. It said yes. (My head bobbed forward.) I was very surprised to receive a spirit with someone else present. Jane saw it with her own eyes. It had never happened before, but I was happy to share it. Since then a few other visitors have arrived with guests present.

Jane later told me one of the first things she felt when the visitor arrived was, "Why not me?" As in, why didn't she receive it? Again, spiritual connections are available to everyone, but they tend to manifest more with people who are at the right place and time. Connectivity comes and goes. Possibly once we've become more enlightened and our vibration is up, we can access it more consistently.

There are periods when I'm more and less open to reception, like a manual-dial radio going in and out of tune. The happier I am, the more resolved within, the more synchronous in my thoughts, feelings, and actions (like that song by The Police), the more I align with spirit. And when I write about it, too.

Although it didn't happen *to* her, Jane was a witness. She was meant to see it at that point in her life for a reason. She could explore it too, though I don't believe she's pursued it. You still have to be careful how you go about inviting it in, though. For every friendly tickler and head-bobber, there are just as many unfriendlies, and they like to cause problems for hobbyists.

NINE: DEVIL SAYS HOWDY

Speaking of the downside, a few years ago, while lying in bed at the end of the day, a powerful unfriendly visitor was eager to converse with me. There was a more intense energy in my forehead. I usually dismiss negative visitors quickly, to avoid potential manipulation, but there was something different about this one. Perhaps I could gain insight about the "enemy," to counter it better in the future. I cautiously asked questions though I felt its restrained dark weight.

As we communicated I realized, despite my faults, I'd like to help people understand themselves better and feel more fulfilled, if I'm able. I want to "spread the good word" and positive feeling, but not like a missionary. Being preachy is a turn off and can have the opposite effect. If more people were connected and felt free we could share that openness. Is that too idealistic?

My dark visitor revealed wild things about the nature of evil. The primary goal of dark forces is to increase and further spread *suffering*, which pains god's creations and god. The unfriendlies want to extend sickness, make things difficult for decent people, and recruit more defeatists. They'd like to dominate creation with despair, but they don't want to end life. They'd prefer to pull you down to their level and make you believe that the logical point of view is cynicism and the only reality suffering. This is a lazy, garbage philosophy.

As the universe is god's creation, he/she/it could pull the plug on the experiment any time. Dark forces want to provoke god, but only to a point, because if god decided there was too much suffering to allow life to continue it would also mean the end of the unfriendlies. Terminating the universe would be an admission of defeat by god that they'd enjoy, but only fleetingly, because they too would be obliterated.

Unfriendlies and tricksters present themselves as tough and powerful so that others will buy what they're selling, but, in truth, they're cowardly and fearful. This is their main weakness and it can be exploited. They're unhappy, jealous, and manipulative, but mask their insecurities with aggression and hatred. (People are like this as well. The more antagonistic they appear, the weaker they actually are.) When you embrace these feelings you align with them and add more negative weight to the world. Honesty and good intentions are difficult for them to counter because these energies are pure and incorruptible.

Unfriendlies are also weak in that their closed-mindedness limits imagination. They expend most of their energy looking for flaws in perfection. It blinds them to inspiration, beauty, and creative ideas. They spend so much time judging life instead of experiencing it that they become dim-witted and slow. The brilliant run circles around them.

I don't believe suffering is the truth of life, as hard as it can sometimes be. I believe in love. It means we're strong enough to be open. Unconditional love may be rare, but it's very powerful.

If you think love is for suckers one day you may change your mind. I felt that way until I realized I had all the love I'll ever need from my family. My well-being is rooted in it, even if I still make jokes about how romance and marriage are for saps. Pure love's a raging joy that wants to explode from your chest. It's available to all, even if you've had a life chock-full of rejection, and most of us have had at least some.

When you operate from hope love emanates from you, and resonates inside, which makes it as good for you as whoever/whatever you're directing it towards. No love is ever wasted, even if it doesn't always land on target, or isn't fully requited. More love in the world increases the overall supply, and the world will always need more because there's much suffering.

The tricksters have another serious weakness; they have no real allies, even among themselves. Their entire network and philosophy is based upon deceit, and I suspect they squabble among themselves and leverage each other politically for greater status and perceived power. The entire foundation of their power is darkness, and the higher up (or rather, *lower down*) that chain you go, the more compromised and lost you become. Evil is the ultimate nightmare bureaucracy. Spirit is wild and free.

A life in darkness is competitive and rife with backstabbing. The entire pursuit seems damn awful and lonely. Some unfriendlies must eventually choose to switch sides and come over to the light. The hopeful and decent are always glad to have more allies. Ultimately, both spirits and humans get to choose a side. Will we be loving in the face of savagery, or will we be weak or, even worse, hateful?

Decency and courage are rare enough that these qualities have their own mystique and intrinsic value. Generous people are like gold or diamonds. Precious by their scarity; their true nature unchallengeable.

The popular depictions of demons and devils as charming seducers or rebels against oppressive sanctity are probably incorrect. My experiences have convinced me that there's little or no humor to them at all, only bitterness and anger. They sometimes try to act carefree, but it's a façade, and they crave attention.

The truly rebellious spirit is open, generous, irreverent, friendly, thoughtful, unselfish, empathetic, and maybe even a bit mischievous, in a playful way. Surely god is cool with us enjoying life, having some drinks and getting stupid, waving your panties running down the street, making dumb jokes, whooping it up, dancing, singing, making hot monkey love, and having a great time so long as nobody gets hurt. Being loving doesn't mean you must transform into a saintly weirdo and give up your spark. You can remain the regular weirdo you've always been, just more tuned in.

TEN: GROWING UP HAPPY

I loved mom's 1970s vacuum. It was soft pea green with white trim. The body was thick, rectangular plastic, with a long shiny metal tube. Like most machines of the era, it was awkward to wield and weighty, and probably worked better because it didn't shake itself to pieces out of the box. (My reconditioned vintage Whirlpool washing machine will likely outlive me.)

We had wall-to-wall carpeting in our cozy home on East Stenzil Street in North Tonawanda. The vacuum had a two-inch circular vent to expel excess heat. As a child of 5 or 6 I followed mom and the vacuum room to room, focused on the vent, crawling to position myself next to the warm exhaust, which would be brief since she'd only stay in one area for so long. This may be why I connect space heaters,

45

fans, and other motorized blowers like air conditioners with childhood comfort and security. Is this common?

The warmth relates to another sensation I used to get intermittently when I was a kid and teen, though less often now. When an adult would pay special attention and take interest in something I enjoyed, like my comic book collection, I'd get a pleasant, tingling sensation that travelled up the back of my neck, spread into my shoulders, and around my head like I had my hand on a science museum electrode. Not dissimilar from goose bumps, but warm and comforting. A child instinctively knows when an adult has genuine interest.

When it came I'd try to live in that moment as long as possible, though it would usually last only a minute or two. I wanted to stay where everything felt perfect. Every once in a while, I'll get a hint of that old feeling when the cleaning woman takes a few minutes to vacuum my office at work, which makes me smile.

Last week I read that other people get this sensation too, and it's come to be known as Autonomous Sensory Meridian Response. I thought I was the only one who experienced it. According to Ohio State University professor David Huron, ASMR is "strongly related to the perception of non-threat and altruistic attention."

Mom thought the tingling sensation was cool, but, after their divorce, I made the mistake of trying to explain it to my father and his young girlfriend from the backseat of the car during an evening ride to his apartment. My deeply-felt experience, and my vulnerability in sharing it, was greeted by dad's chippie with a vulgar joke about the tingling sensations I'd eventually experience with women, and some form of half-laughter at her joke mixed with a non-response from my father.

I never shared anything like that with them again, though my brother and I drop hints on dad that the spirit world is real. He usually doesn't know how to respond, even though he goes to church and thought *The Passion of The Christ* was profound. (I never saw it.) There's still hope, though. At his 2013 Father's Day dinner we ended up discussing my book and, when I looked in his eyes after an hour detailing an abundance of inexplicable events, I saw the teary glimmer of recognition and possibility. The evening ended with a light rain, followed by a gorgeous sun halo outside, which everyone at the restaurant gazed at in wonder. Steve told me later that the last time he'd seen a full rainbow was after he and mom had been discussing our recently deceased cousin Gigi, who I'll tell you more about later.

My father gummed up our brains when we were young and impressionable, by taking no position whatsoever with regard to our needs versus those of his young girlfriend. Fortunately, as adults, our relationship has improved even though communication is sometimes awkward. His heart is in the right place, but he's buried or repressed a lot of his memories and feelings regarding the distance during our upbringing because he feels guilty that he wasn't really there. (I believe avoidance can actually cause brain damage over time.) It took a long time for me to stop carrying that anger around, but it has dissipated and we show love more openly. I see the ways in which I am selfish and desirous of attention like him, and it's partly why I've avoided marriage and kids, though I wouldn't rule it out as I grow and change.

Artist types are often selfish anyway, nearly of necessity. We spend endless hours improving our skills and investing in the creative process. If one is a singer, then mental, physical, and vocal health are interrelated. (I do voice exercises every day, even when it's the last thing I feel like doing. I swim and bike to try to maintain my weight, strength, and lung power, especially as I age.) We mine ourselves for emotional content and then share it with the world, sometimes instead of the people closest to us. It's a bit messed up when you really think about it. All your favorite performers are probably at least partial narcissists who need you, the audience, more than you need them, though they're unlikely to admit it. I've tried to keep myself grounded, but haven't always succeeded. Time and experience have humbled me. I'm closer to serenity.

When I was 10, prior to my parents' divorce, we used to take an annual summer vacation at Buckhorn Lake in Ontario. My dad paid me quarters to massage his big, knobby feet. Then I'd run down to the general store to buy comics. I caught many sunfish on the lake. There was a primitive trampoline with a pit beneath it that all the kids loved and that my mother nearly broke her neck on one year. The adults played cards in various cottages in the early evening heat. There was a tiny beach, and afternoon games of competition for kids like me, racing from end to end, running like crabs. There was a small cement shuffleboard court halfway down the hill between our cottage and the lake. My mom gave me raw bacon to fish with sometimes, and I ate half the bait in quarter-stamp-sized servings. Luckily, I never got sick.

Being the little ham-bone I was then and now, I'd perform each year at the campfire talent show. My act in those days consisted of nearly any joke from the wildly popular first two Steve Martin vinyl comedy records *Let's Get Small* and *Wild and Crazy Guy*. I listened to the records constantly, learning every bit, even the dirty stuff, which my parents would have me do at their parties even though I didn't understand the jokes. "Grandpa bought a rubber!" What's a rubber? It sounded funny anyway.

I somehow knew which jokes were okay for a group of 7-year-olds and which ones you kept for adults. Mom made an "arrow through the head" by bending a coat-hanger into shape and affixing a cardboard tip and tail with drawn-in feather ridges. (A good prop helps get you into character.) The big hit at the campfire was when I sang "King Tut" and did the accompanying choreography, and for the remainder of the week I'd be on call to do it by any kid or adult passing by.

My father gave me an important lesson in humility when, while receiving praise from a parent after my set, I tipped my head back to drink a soda at the same time she spoke. Dad told me to knock it off while this woman was being complimentary. I felt embarrassed and immediately knew I was wrong. And never forgot it, obviously.

Parents should crack the whip on kids when hints of arrogance creep in. If you don't check it when they're young they may imprint the belief that such behavior is acceptable, and then one day you've got Justin Beiber and it's too late. There are enough people with a sense of entitlement walking around as it is given the last hundred years of American prosperity. No one's above anyone. Kids should learn that young.

- - -

My mom's an incredible human being. She was raised Catholic and went to an all-girls Catholic school until high school, when she admits she went boy crazy and never opened another book, yet somehow still graduated.

That's not what makes her incredible, though this might be. In 1953, when mom was 7 years old, she attended her sister Joni's wedding reception at Washington Hall in downtown Buffalo. Mom was fascinated by a young disabled girl with a huge smile on her face and a spiritual glow. The girl, Anna, was innocently beautiful. Mom said to herself that she wanted to have a child like that when she got older, and this did occur. My brother Steve was born extremely premature with cerebral palsy, which prevents him from walking, but he's a lovable, hilarious, intelligent, and deeply decent person. I love them with all my heart.

I was born first. My mom's second son Justin died just after childbirth. Steve was born three years after that. Justin is with us all the time. Mom and I have the same small tattoo on our shoulder of a sliver moon representing her, and three stars for her sons, with two on one side and one on the other. We got the tattoos together, around the time of my original tickling event in 1997.

When my parents split I was 10 and Steve was 4. Mom had the bulk of the job raising us. I don't think she ever saw it as a burden, though it was a huge challenge, and cost her emotionally and physically. The love and gratitude I feel is enormous even though there were conflicts and tough times, as in any family.

What I really remember is how much laughter there was. My mom was wisely permissive. To make each other laugh and cringe, we swore around the house more when I was 13 than I ever did after, to this day. We made fun of everything, and still do. There were no sacred cows, and also no pretense. The lack of taboos and abundant tolerance of weird ideas meant I didn't need one personality at home versus outside. I got to be more or less myself all the time.

At my urging, mom took Steve and I to see Cheech & Chong's *Still Smokin'* when I was 12; my bro was 6! I'll never forget "E.T., The Extra Testicle," and the medley of wild animals humping. It was so dumb, but funny to a pre-teen.

In high school she let me dye my hair, dress like a punk, and explore my identity. She and Steve tolerated my horrible singing and years of guitar playing throughout high school as I slowly learned the instrument while trying to become a deep, tortured singer/poet in the Morrissey mold, even though I sucked. I didn't have the urge to drink or do drugs because I was busy enjoying becoming me. I felt like a caterpillar in development for my future glory in musical flight.

For dumb laughs and candy, Steve and I employed a series of chants at the kitchen table, pounding in mock outrage, like at a political rally. After dinner we'd yell, "Sweets in general!," banging our fists over and over in unison to the words. This was often accompanied by, "Chocolate in particular!" Bang, bang, bang. (It still makes me smile.) Our other running joke was passing the buck after burping. "It wasn't me, it was *carbonation*." This could be shortened to a look of angelic innocence while stating simply, "Carbonation."

We chewed with open mouths to display the chow. I had remarkable patience (stubbornness!) in this regard. Steve or mom would turn away, refusing to look at me, but I'd just stare at them unwaveringly and garble, "Look!" through a full mouth of material, perhaps with outstretched tongue, until they caved in. "You cannot escape my stupidity! I will stay like this forever if I have to," I thought. Then we'd laugh until our sides hurt.

Mom amused us in the living room with her freestyle "clogging" while I played a country-esque rhythm on guitar. My mom does not know how to clog. (Does anyone really know how to clog?) Which is, of course, what made it excellent. She'd work herself up pretty good, stomping and shuffling her feet and stubby little legs on the rug at high speeds, like running in place, with intentionally-awkward, spastic dance moves. We'd nearly piss ourselves. She'd crack herself up too.

Walking in the door after school, any one of us might say to the other, "How'd your day go, dago?"

Many late summer nights were spent in the living room listening to music in my "corner" and writing. This was my hangout from age 12 to 19. The corner was located at the intersection of our rust-colored couch and chair, positioned perpendicularly against each wall. The gap between the edges of the furniture was a few feet wide, creating a natural box shape in between. I hunched down when writing, doing homework, or listening to music with big Radio Shack headphones. I napped on my back with my feet sticking out between the chair and the couch.

The corner centerpiece was an inexpensive, but vital multi-unit stereo, with twin cassette decks, a receiver, and turntable on top. We put a speaker on each side of the stereo, flush to the walls like the chair and couch. There was a large, pull-chain lamp above the stereo, low to the ground. The wall to the left of the stereo was furry brown grass cloth, and our carpet was an inviting shaggy maroon.

All my essential goods were in the corner, around and under the stereo, speakers, and furniture. There was a cutting board that I used for artwork, to create fake cassette covers for fictional bands I wanted to be in, which I perforated and cut out of cardstock with an exacto-knife and ruler. I decorated them with an abundance of multi-colored markers.

On each side of the stereo were three-ring binders full of hundreds of lyrics, and hand-written chord charts, which is how I still notate songs. There were different notebooks for various musical projects. The larger notebooks held all the raw lyrics. I would pick a lyric from the pile to fit to new pieces of music I'd come up with. There were cassette tapes everywhere. I had multiple ceramic jars of pens; one was a big, red, blobby mug with a large "F" mounted on it, emanating sunbeams, that I made in grade school.

The nice thing about the corner was it allowed me to have a semi-private space in the living room, while also being accessible to, and part of, the family. Mom and bro would watch TV in the same room, and I could be in the corner doing my thing, then poke my head out and watch for a while with them, or see what was going on. We were together in that room a lot. Steve would often go into the adjoining room and listen to his radio. We bonded over many things, including a mutual love of music, though he didn't seriously take up an instrument.

Late one evening, in my corner, I was on the phone with a high school friend when something odd happened. Before cellphones, early cordless phones picked up a lot of other people's conversations. When lines crossed you could sometimes hear others talking without them hearing you. My friend and I were having an intimate conversation when I heard the faint echo of a male voice whispering on the line. It didn't sound like he was talking to anyone, and I heard no one respond to him. I asked my friend if she heard it too, but she said no. I heard the voice whisper matter-of-factly, seemingly directly to me, "If you can hear this, you're dying." A little chill went up my back. It didn't sound like a crossed line. There was none of the usual static. It felt like someone had jumped into the phone line to plant a mysterious, spooky truth in my head.

I was surprised but intrigued. A lot of my strange experiences are like this. Initially I might be startled, but another part of me regards strangeness as perfectly normal, as if I've always been aware of, and open to, the existence of *more*, and these are reminders and confirmation in retrospect.

If you think about it, "If you can hear this, you're dying" is as true as it gets. A reminder of the brevity of life, something I was morbidly fascinated with in high school and college. It amazed me then and now to think one day I'd no longer exist. How does one conceive of it? All we've ever known is what it's like to be here, not to be silent and absent. I was still a teenage atheist at the time.

- - -

During summer vacation I'd get out of work from Wilson Farms convenience store around midnight and rush home to watch David Letterman at 12:30 a.m. It felt like a secret, with a fabulous cast of fun weirdos, like Chris Elliott hiding under the stairs and creepily stalking Dave. I might do some writing or reading at the same time by the boob tube's blue light.

At 2 or 3 a.m. I often sat on the front porch with a candle, softly playing guitar and whisper/singing, contemplating big ideas about the world. I'd climb the tree in the front yard or walk to the curb and stare up at the sky full of stars in total amazement, like Huck Finn. We lived on a dead-end street, so it was very quiet at night. I was a stargazer, dreamer, and cosmic kid. I love impractical dreamers and I hope you're one, too. I hope you have big ideas that you never give up on if you love them. Naysayers will always abound, but usually they're jealous of the permission you've given yourself to think big. They wish they could be you, or, failing that, they'd like to drag you to Earth and make you common. Which is so dull and predictable.

Sometimes I'd stay up all night and mom would find me in the living room at 5:30 or 6 when she got up for work. "Go to bed!" she'd yell. I didn't understand why she was so angry. In retrospect it's because the early morning was *her time* in the house. The only moments to enjoy complete silence and peace, and a quiet cup of coffee before the world would come at her again. She says she doesn't remember getting mad at me, but I remember well!

I later learned we weren't living on a lot of money, but neither were we poor. Mom's part-time office job didn't bring in much, but our father paid child support, to his credit. We never felt at a loss for anything and weren't materialistic. Once I got into wearing vintage and half-shredded clothes I rarely bought new things anyway. (This is still true.) I took pride in wearing non-brand name clothes. I bought a pair of bright yellow fake Chuck Taylors in high school with no symbol in the white circle on the side. I drew in a Mr. Yuck face with the tongue sticking out and the words "LABELS SUCK." I wrote the lyrics to a Morrissey song, "Michael's Bones," down the pant legs of one of my half-shredded pairs of jeans, folded and safety-pinned at the ankles. The physical possessions that meant the most to me were all related to music: my vinyl records and cassettes, guitars, stereo, and Walkman.

My mom is loving, generous, and feisty though she was virtually ignored growing up. She was the last of five girls to be born; her father's final failed chance at a son. Mom says she never felt like she had a single ally in her family growing up, and even as an adult, especially when Justin died, yet she always knew that she would be okay and survive. She vowed to give her children everything she wasn't given. She spoiled us.

Though mom is well-adjusted, she has an Italian hot streak. There are definitely cultural differences. It's probably why I identify more with hot-blooded Latin and African cultures than tight Euro-WASPs. I like people who feel life deeply, and bring a depth of emotion to their art, music, and relationships. Give me spicy funk, jazz, tango, bossa, hip hop, and blues.

Mom said she didn't even feel like she became a real person until she turned 30. She was only 18 when she got married in 1965, a whole different era and sensibility. Many women from her generation, especially those who married young, felt like this. Young ladies, barely removed from adolescence, who suddenly found themselves with a home and family to take care of, before they even knew who they were or had time to contemplate it. Maybe this is why my grandmother failed mom growing up. It's probably also why some women who marry young suddenly "wake up" in their late twenties, or thirties, and go buck wild. I've dated a few.

I inherited my mom's fire, or partly I learned it. When she was mad at me or Steve she was explosively verbal. My self-esteem would dive. Most of our conflicts came during my pubescent years. We had an average amount of yelling at our house.

At some point during high school I told mom her attacks were harming my self-image. She was surprised and toned it down after that. My brother had the same experience. Mom

says now that she always saw life as war, and that she felt
like she spent her entire adolescence and adulthood fighting
her way out of a paper bag. I get it. I've felt this way most
of my life, too, though I'm changing for the better. I don't
fixate upon the bumps in our relationship. I remember it
mostly as loving and open, and it's grown stronger with
time.

ELEVEN: REJECTION AND REINVENTION

Our childhood and adolescence is inevitably ingrained into
who we become. Certain key events in youth make deep
impressions, burning life lessons and subconscious loops
onto the hard drive of the brain, compelling some of us to
repeat painful behaviors over and over again, until we learn
our lesson or never learn. Part of fixing yourself, if
necessary, comes from recognizing the patterns of your life
and altering your mind-set. Sometimes the passing of time is
a natural agent of change; you grow out of an earlier
unhappiness. Other people try combinations of
introspection, therapy, drugs, writing, prayer, etc. I'm in
favor of whatever works.

My life changed at 13 during an early fall walk around the
quiet streets of North Tonawanda. Two grade-school
friends were transforming into middle school jocks. Though
Alex and I had been friends and played together for years,
everything from street sports to drawing comics, things
were changing fast. He and John had formed a new
exclusive club I wasn't yet aware of.

I don't remember the words, but I became aware they were
mocking me, and that I was no longer considered an equal.
Some conscious or unconscious calculations had occurred
in their soft young skulls over the summer. I hadn't had the
same growth spurt and was apparently fair game for

ridicule, or to be their lackey. I came home confused and crushed.

It wasn't a great time anyway. I was rail thin and had bad back acne during middle and high school (because I'm an Italian testosterone machine, and there's an obvious upside), which added to my self-consciousness. Mom let me buy a small sunlamp to burn the buggers a few minutes each evening.

She knew something was wrong the moment I walked in the front door with my head low. Thinking of it now, I imagine this scene repeated in the homes of awkward 13-year-olds and their parents all over the world, every day and every year, in every generation, backwards through all time and forward into the infinite future. Maybe kids don't even need to leave the house anymore for the full humiliation. Antagonists and bullies have computers too and I'm sure the Facebook wars between teens are unreal. It's not getting easier to be young, is it?

Thank god she was there to hear me and provide comfort, assurance, and a big hug, and do what mothers do best. What would I have done otherwise? I'd be a different person now entirely, and I've encountered many people who obviously did not have the same support.

It hurt a lot but, fortunately I didn't need approval badly enough to accept humiliation in exchange for being "allowed" to hang around.

I sat in my corner listening to the radio after I got home. Like many young people at the same stage of adolescence, I heard a song that changed my life. It was when music really began to speak to me.

CFNY 102.1, *The Spirit of Radio*, an independently-owned alternative rock station in Toronto, was an amazing source for new music in the 1980s and early 1990s, and a big influence on the Buffalo alternative music scene. An unusual British band called Prefab Sprout came on. As often, I was running a cassette to capture and collect songs of interest.

"When Love Breaks Down" floored me. The lines that stood out most felt parallel to the immediate loss of my friendships: "When love breaks down / the things you do / to stop the truth from hurting you." It's on a record called *Two Wheels Good*, which I've listened to possibly thousands of times the last 30 years. Prefab Sprout were a top 10 band in Britain, but never broke through in America. They were probably a little too literate, intelligent, jazzy, and melodic. Not enough cock in their rock and roll.

The deejays on CFNY had the power to introduce new music outside of the mainstream. While Madonna, Bon Jovi, Guns N' Roses, Def Leppard, and Bruce Springsteen were dominating American radio, CFNY was feeding outsider kids The Smiths, New Order, the The, The Style Council, Aztec Camera, The Go-Betweens, Chalk Circle, The Pursuit of Happiness, General Public/The English Beat, The Adventures, Shriekback, Siouxsie and The Banshees, XTC, World Party, The Woodentops, The Lilac Time, The Blue Nile, Stone Roses, The Cure, The Cult, R.E.M., Del Amitri, They Might Be Giants, Robyn Hitchcock, Lloyd Cole, Michael Penn, Dead Milkmen, The Sundays, Love and Rockets/Peter Murphy/Bauhaus, Camper Van Beethoven, Scritti Politti, Dream Academy, Talk Talk, Fairground Attraction, Idle Eyes, Thomas Dolby, Guadalcanal Diary, Trash Can Sinatras, Public Image Ltd, Echo and The Bunnymen, The Housemartins/Beautiful South, ABC, Pixies, OMD, Psychedelic Furs, Smithereens,

Gene Loves Jezebel, Sugarcubes, Sisters of Mercy, The Mission, Hunters and Collectors, The Alarm, Feargal Sharkey, Pierce Turner, Danny Wilson, Swing Out Sister, Sigue Sigue Sputnik/Generation X, Midnight Oil, Kirsty MacColl, Phranc ("your basic average all-American Jewish lesbian folksinger"), Sun-60, Lightning Seeds, Furniture, James, Jim Jiminee, When in Rome, Pop Will Eat Itself, Bronski Beat, Erasure, Captain Sensible, Kissing The Pink, Carter The Unstoppable Sex Machine, Men Without Hats, The Church, Yello, Billy Bragg, Big Audio Dynamite, Nik Kershaw, China Crisis, Suzanne Vega, Double, Cocteau Twins, Yaz, Depeche Mode, Moev, Haircut 100, Killing Joke, Proclaimers, The Primitives, Secession, The Damned, Jazz Butcher, INXS, Mood Six, Tall New Buildings, Split Enz, Royal Crescent Mob, Dead or Alive, Gowan, Flesh For Lulu, David Sylvian, Bryan Ferry, APB, Howard Jones, Tears For Fears, Pet Shop Boys, Joan Armatrading, Images in Vogue, The Wedding Present, Platinum Blonde, Ryuichi Sakamoto, Circus Circus Circus, Alphaville, The Waitresses, The Wonder Stuff, and Kate Bush! Plus hundreds more quirky British, Canadian, and American bands of major and minor fame. The programming was innovative and driven by people who loved music. Sadly, CFNY has long since been bought out and homogenized as a rock chain station, programmed from a central office located god knows where. The love is gone.

(When President Clinton signed the 1996 Telecommunications Act, changing radio ownership laws, huge American corporations swallowed formerly independent stations, just as they swallowed newspapers. Radio changed overnight, not for the better, and has been on a steady decline since. It's part of the overall consolidation and corporatization of all formerly-rebellious American cultural institutions that began in earnest with the election of Ronald Reagan, and continues cynically to this day. Rock and roll is no different than Wall Street anymore.

The general public seems to have little idea why radio sucks now, but many are bored, turning to talk and sports stations to alleviate the repetition. Hopefully the whole radio paradigm will collapse and we'll get back to locally owned and programmed stations someday. Hell, I want to own and program my own station! In theory, the public owns the airwaves, but we've temporarily abdicated our claim.)

"When Love Breaks Down" spoke directly to me, or that's how it always feels when a young person is deeply moved by music. You feel the song was written specifically for your situation. A bond is cemented for life. The song, and many others on CFNY and local college radio, inspired a defiant re-invention of self, fueling a lifelong musical journey that freed my soul. I wish I could meet Paddy McAloon, Prefab Sprout's reclusive songwriting guru, and give him a big hug.

I experimented with my appearance. My Aunt Rosie was a hairdresser. In eighth grade she, mom, and I somehow came up with the idea of dying the front of my brown curly hair blonde. We thought it would be fun and odd, and it was. I had a gold skunk tuft on my head when I went back to junior high that Monday, in black parachute pants and a funky no-sleeved geometric shirt, possibly purchased from *Chess King*, that my mom thought was radical yet tasteful. (Ok, we mixed genres a bit and didn't quite get it right.)

I wasn't prepared for the amount of attention. Teens and adults dye their hair every color now, but *in my day* (old man voice), in 1984 at Reszel Junior Middle School, in suburban North Tonawanda, NY, population 35,000, and "Home of the Carousel" Museum, Riviera Theater, and the Mighty Wurlitzer organ, this wasn't done.

There was every reaction you can imagine. Stares with no comment, giggles from packs of girls, threatening looks and commentary from meatheads, and kids who thought I was a completely new student. (I guess I had been invisible before.) Everybody seemed to be trying to figure out what I was supposed to be, and take sides as to whether that was okay and *allowed*. Between the rear entrance doors a girl asked me why I did it. I think I said, "I don't know, I felt like it." I got some votes of support, not that I was consciously looking for them.

A student teacher in math who used to treat me as a star pupil instead gave me an uncomfortable, skeptical look handing back my paper. I probably did look ridiculous; it wasn't a subtle thing on a skinny kid, and too much weird attention for an insecure 13-year-old. The test had gone awry. I didn't understand how shitty some kids can be; I thought most were as open and fun-loving as my family. Within a few days my mom helped make the gold tuft more subtle by dying some of the hair around it back to my original color. I liked it better too, but it was one of my last concessions to other people's opinions.

Later that same year I pierced my ears. I started with the left one, then went up a couple more holes, and later did the right. Again, today this is not a big deal and young folks stretch their lobes to extreme proportions and cover every available space with tattoos (I have two), but in 1985 you were apparently planning to subvert the entire social order or bomb the school by getting a gold stud earring.

My favorite incident involved a tall, skinny wannabe tough guy, with short feathered hair, and a perpetually popped collar (douchebag chic) whose locker was next to mine. In between classes while grabbing books he made a crack about my earring and called me a faggot. Or maybe he asked me if I was some kind of faggot. "Faggot" was the focus of the exchange, the word echoing all the way down the corridors or my mind. I didn't react. Said nothing. Closed my locker door and left.

One or two years later he, and every other guy on the football team, got earrings together. Did they hold each other's hands and giggle like schoolgirls while they did it? Did he have even a remote recollection of what he'd said to me when he got his own earring? Or did he push it to the back of his dim, dull brain with all the other temporary identities he sleepwalked through with his friends?

The other major musical influence on me was another British band, The Smiths, the perfect group at the perfect time. I felt like they saved my life. My "skinny bones" understood the uncertain sexuality and oversensitivity of lead singer Morrissey. The lack of connection to the body and an accompanying fear of women, men, sex, and intimacy. The longing for an acceptable means of expressing affection for other people without being marginalized as effeminate.

The Smiths soared in the underground because they celebrated awkwardness and vulnerability, turning it into a rallying cry, somehow transforming weakness and alienation into strength. There was a love of absurdity and an obvious intelligence and literacy to Morrissey's lyrics that was uncommon then, and now. They are correctly regarded as a monumentally important post-punk band. Their legacy has been significantly entrenched in the counterculture to the extent that even those who regarded them as a "band for fags" 30 years ago now heap praise and claim kinship. As with many radical, important artists, they are only regarded as geniuses at a distance, now that they're no longer together and threatening in real time. It's much easier to get on board once everyone else has already done it, isn't it? *Where were you when it was going down?*

Morrissey's insecurities were refocused as hostility to mindless conformity, combined with the perhaps contradictory yearning to be loved and broadly accepted. In an interview he said, "I'd rather be remembered as a big-mouthed failure than an effete little wimp." I signed on for that. He helped transform my thinking and attitude. Morrissey was willing to take the enormous, relentless ridicule of the Accepted and, almost worse, their whipping boys (what Alex and John probably had in mind for me) who would never be invited to the big party, but still felt compelled to defend their socially-superior slave-masters.

In high school I probably would've committed murder if instructed by my hero. Not literally, but I needed his philosophical musings like air. It was a religious devotion and the feeling of loyalty remains even though I'm sometimes put off by his persistent narcissism. Maybe I feel he needs to grow up a little, or I do? But he's earned the freedom to be whatever he wants. I would love to survive as a full-time artist, too.

The Smiths released a persistent stream of material from 1983 until their end in 1987 in the form of multi-song 12-inch vinyl singles, full-length studio albums, and compilations of radio show appearances and alternate song versions. In just four years they recorded constantly, knocking out more than 70 songs, and the band's break-up led into a Morrissey solo career which continues to this day.

There are two Morrissey lyrics that matched up with my life at the time. A line in the song, "I Know Very Well How I Got My Name" mirrored my hair dying experiment and matched my age, too: "When 13 years old… who dyed his hair gold." I was in fact 16 years old when "Half a Person" was released as a B-side to "Shoplifters of the World Unite": "Sixteen, clumsy and shy / I went to London and I / booked myself into the Y… W… C… A." In my high school yearbook I proudly declared, "I love you mom, dad, Steve, and Morrissey". I quoted "Unloveable" next to my photo: "If I seem a little strange / Well, that's because I am."

In reality, it was everyone else I regarded as strange, even though I was excessively judgmental. I saw them as inadequate in their limited dreams and aspirations, blind acceptance of and deference to authority, lack of spine, lack of fun and lust for life, rigidity, conformity, monotonous small talk, lamenting their lives while making no effort to change, resolve to ordinary drudgery even as teenagers, mindless desire to marry and procreate, "white picket fences," unwillingness to look foolish or self-deprecate, lack of creativity, superficiality, aspirations to immediately sell out and cash in, adherence to social conventions and groupthink dynamics, intentionally dumbing themselves down, lack of courage, lack of love for truth, lack of love for love, and overall dullness. I found it incomprehensible, as if I was living in a separate, more vital world from my classmates. I found meaning in everything, though I was overly expressive and dramatic, especially for a straight young man. But the world was pulsating and alive, like Van Gogh's "Starry Night," and all the time, if you chose to see it. Why couldn't they see it? Why wouldn't they?

To this day I can tell you when and where I purchased nearly every Smiths U.K. import record, and who was with me. My friend Rob Linville, the first and perhaps only real punk rocker I've ever met, was so amused by my devotion and enthusiasm that he bought a few Smiths singles for me just to watch me literally laugh out loud while hearing them on a turntable for the first time. Which would in turn make him laugh his funny monkey cackle and point at me yelling, "Falg!!!"

My laughter was involuntary. I'd find myself so immediately, deeply moved by the songs that the abundance of feeling overflowed and spilled out as laughter. It was the joy of recognition, of being united in my strangeness with this unconventional, intelligent artist, and the happy realization that the first listens would be just the beginning of the experience, as I played the records over and over again for days, months, and years, and rolled the lyrical philosophical notions into my emboldened self.

When my best friend Tim skipped school to visit Poptones record shop in Niagara Falls, Ontario, and buy the Morrissey single "Interesting Drug," he did me the kindness of stopping home to put it on a cassette tape so I could listen to it on my Walkman during art class and lunch. Like Linwood, he wanted to make me happy. I was blissed out. I sat with my friends in the cafeteria, but I wasn't really there. I was floating, high on sound. Already dreaming of an incredible musical future, outside the narrow halls of N.T.H.S.

(Here's an aside about Tim. For my 43rd birthday this year, on February 24, my mom bought me two helium balloons. She dropped by the house while I was at work and tied them to chairs in the living and dining rooms so I'd have a laugh when I got home. The one in the living room died within a week, but the other persisted. It says, "You're How Old?," with lit cartoon candles. I decided to leave it up until it dropped.

Months passed and the balloon remained fully inflated. I thought it might fall on my brother Justin's birthday on June

26, but it didn't. Then on July 18, nearly five months after it was tied, it started to droop on Tim's birthday, staying at half-mast but not reaching the floor until the next morning. This works equally well as I think of Tim like a brother. We've made the effort to keep our friendship strong since high school even though he's lived in Oakland many years. Maybe in some other life we were blood brothers and part of a larger group, which includes my immediate family, who chose to come here together. I'm beginning to wonder if our arrival was orchestrated.)

The rejection remains a part of me, for better and worse, though I'm nearly reconciled. Being an outsider kick-started and accelerated my development, and made me hungry to become someone, if only in my own eyes, in spite of what anyone might say or think. I decided to fight my way through high school and life, and would verbally savage anyone who sought an advantage at the expense of someone who was kind or who they perceived as weak, including myself. A lyric by another British artist called Momus became my mantra: "The words were to cut down and to kill the muscle bound / The swords to fell my intellectual enemies." (In a sense, they helped make me, and I'm grateful now.)

I discovered that if you fought back it helped prevent you from becoming a victim, though I usually knew when it might be time to run. You can only mouth off so much for so long; some people are too dangerous to mess with. I probably learned how to fight from my mom, who felt alienated her entire childhood as one of the only Italian girls in an Irish neighborhood, and with no allies in her family. She could conjure a storm when enraged.

I was kind to outsiders or anyone friendly or marginalized, and mirrored what I found in others. I feared no one's opinion, answered to no one but myself and my family, and considered my friendship a privilege. It was an act of total self-respect. I openly mocked the beautiful and popular when they displayed predictable conceit. I detested group behaviors and conformity and lashed out at mindless conventions. I was on a mission. There's still fire in my heart. Hopefully I've become more empathetic and understanding. I work to see things and people from more angles, to better comprehend and accept human complexity. I feel intensely, and want to become more loving as I deepen. I'm happy and proud of who I've become. No one can take it from me. I wish the same for you.

Curiously, my rebellion and identity "makeover" in high school inadvertently made me semi-popular. By rejecting and lampooning the popular, I made them curious to know why I didn't need them. I said what I really thought and felt, whether it was socially or politically advantageous to me or not, or got me into trouble, which it did. I made enemies of idiots and didn't care, which inevitably led to accusations of arrogance. The trade-off was acceptable in order to maintain self-respect.

Some popular girls began to take an interest in me, and some were nice. Others approached out of curiosity, but would retreat if their friends told them I was unacceptable or weird. Some bitches do this to each other to control the pack. I saw it in high school and still in my twenties, thirties, and forties. The games don't change much. By senior year I felt less hostile. I began to see them as unformed works-in-progress, and tried not to judge others based on social affiliations, only on whether they were nice and seemed to have a conscience. It's still how I unconsciously evaluate people. I see most of what I need to know when I look into someone's eyes upon first meeting. Openness to life is hard to fake. I love finding it. Conversely I recognize the look of confused fear or uncertainty instantly - even in my own eyes from time to time.

TWELVE: AMBITIOUS OUTSIDERS

My suburban high school friends were influenced by punk and thought that's what we were, but history and our haircuts later informed us we were *New Wave*, like Duckie and the other misfit kids in *Pretty in Pink*, *Ferris Bueller's Day Off* and *The Breakfast Club*. One of our frequent weekend rituals was to attend midnight screenings of *The Rocky Horror Picture Show* and Pink Floyd's *The Wall* at a sketchy cinema in Cheektowaga, NY. (See? They came up with their own Native American name. It can be done.) We saw each movie at least two dozen times, and the flicks drew other oddballs from the surrounding suburbs. It was our underground scene.

I made out with a girl with big boobs under my trench coat who I met during a *Rocky Horror* showing. We were flirting across the rows in the middle of the movie, and I gathered my teenage balls and went over to sit with her. The coat went up, we smooched, and I put my hands on her cans. My forwardness even surprised me. Boldness by degrees.

She said something really dirty like, "Fuck me, Robert Smith," because I had big, curly mushroom hair, a bit like the lead singer of The Cure, though I more often got compared to Lyle Lovett, and I wanted to be Morrissey. Going to *Rocky Horror* in the summer was ridiculous because I wouldn't get home until 3 a.m., then I'd get up for my summer shift working the Wendy's drive-through at 6. There was no point in showering because working at a fast food joint is like being an auto mechanic. You come home covered in, and smelling like, everything in the place.

69

I'd start my shift whipping eggs while taking early-riser coffee orders. I worked there only one summer when I turned 16. The young staff rented a campground on Grand Island one weekend, during which I had far too much to drink and burned a *Raiders of the Lost Ark* oval into my hand by palming a scorching hot lantern on top of a picnic table. My kind compatriots advised me to stick my arm in the beer cooler ice water and drink much more to numb the pain, which worked and prevented scarring. A few hours later I vomited all over a girl's pillow and they burned it on the bonfire. Later still I ended up in a sleeping bag kissing the girl who prepared the pans of meat patties for the walk-in cooler. She was a smoker, and tasted like an ashtray. I assume I brushed my teeth in between or had gum. I'm not usually that gross.

Despite these adventures, I was naive in high school. With the exception of the campground, I didn't drink, and did well in school, graduating third in a class of 500. I met Allie, a fiery 16-year-old redhead from Lewiston, NY, at a Dirty Rotten Imbeciles punk concert in Niagara Falls at the Turtle (a huge Native American art museum that was rented as a concert hall). She let me know the score outside my friend Mike's house that summer, to my disappointment and confusion.

"You're pretty innocent," she said, leaning against Mike's red speed buggy in very high cutoffs with lots of luscious, pale teenage skin on display. Mike provided the daily carpool service to school, and transported me to boobs at *Rocky Horror*. I badly wanted to kiss Allie but she let me know why this thing we barely had wasn't going to work.

I didn't know what Allie meant; I hadn't done it yet. That memorable, awkward, and predictably brief experience came during my junior year. Young guys have little chance their first time, or their second through tenth time. The shock at how good it feels, and to be one of two people without their clothes on, doing things with weird parts, nearly guarantees an early ending. You need *practice* to get great, like playing an instrument.

I was too self-conscious. After a few tries it was easier to be celibate like Morrissey (supposedly!). I skipped it until college when I had a steady, mega-sexual girlfriend, who read women's magazines to pick up new tricks and introduced me to reverse cowgirl and other great stuff. I loved her and thought we'd eventually marry, but she moved on after a few years, possibly tired of my insecurities. I pined a long time.

Allie was right; I was innocent. I didn't do drugs - hadn't ever seen them - didn't have sex, studied hard because I feared embarrassment and failure, and was busy crafting my plan to become a famous, socially-conscious singer. I was too occupied creating myself to wreck me prematurely. The debauchery came later, though I remain disinterested in drugs. In high school the future was clear and nothing would get in the way of The Dream.

Allie ended up pregnant within a few years, not by me. I saw her again at Mike's house and she'd converted her post-birth wardrobe and look to middle-aged twenty-something mom, with unflattering glasses and bulky flannel. She was buttoned all the way up to the top, or that's how it felt when I looked at her. She shredded her old identity so easily, and substituted it with a new one to fit the new role instantly.

Like Allie, many of my friends traded identities regularly. The punk kids I found great kinship with in high school also had phases as straight-edge missionaries (which involved renouncing liquor and scrawling thick black magic-marker "X"s on their hands); skinhead white supremacists in black combat boots and red suspenders (which I condemned); hip hop aficionados with backwards ball caps and big chains; long-haired hippies in tie-dye; and dedicated alcoholics and nitrous oxide sniffers. Each group identity change was accompanied by a renunciation of the previous identity, and sometimes mild verbal harassment of those outside our immediate circle who continued to maintain an identity they'd only recently abandoned. (The socially weak bullying the weaker?)

In high school the lines between groups of like and unlike-minded people are stark in your mind (jocks, punks, metal heads, skanks, nerds, stoners, cheerleaders, etc.) and you use the perceived divisions to help define yourself, often by what you're not. The willingness to temporarily assume and then abandon new facades, especially dangerous ones, was puzzling and helped me imagine how easily terrible movements can infect an entire culture, like Nazism. During World War II, people went along with atrocities, or adopted the dominant mindset of the day, to fit in with the group and avoid persecution. Identity-swapping appeared to confirm the power of socialization and conformity, even within a counter-culture like my group of friends. That they moved in tandem like the mainstream conformists they condemned went seemingly unnoticed, while I observed from a slight distance. An outsider among the outsiders.

We went to a ton of punk concerts during high school, mostly at the dive bar River Rock Café on Niagara Street in Buffalo's Black Rock district. My friends wore T-shirts representing their favorite sweaty bands for slam dancing in the mosh pit; I'd wear a nice sweater or Smiths T-shirt and make eyes at the hot, lost girls of the scene. Jackie took an interest in me and, even though I hadn't a clue, stripped down to her white bra and panties in my bedroom one evening just as my family pulled up in the driveway. No score!

The album cover for the Dead Kennedys' *In God We Trust, Inc.*, with Jesus crucified on a cross of money, was revelatory and a bit frightening. Definitely subversive. My friends, we gravitated to punk because it offered resistance to bland suburbia as we perceived it, understanding later that our parents just wanted us to get the best education available. The North Tonawanda schools system was actually very good. I mean, *look at me now.*

The Dead Kennedys had an obvious intelligence at work behind their antagonism, and an extreme, adolescent sense of humor. During his first spoken word tour opening for the Butthole Surfers in December 1987, I congratulated singer Jello Biafra before the show for his recent hung jury verdict in Los Angeles. He'd been charged with obscenity for including an artwork called "Penis Landscape" (it looks like it sounds) by Swiss artist H.R. Giger (who also designed the creepy creatures from *Alien*) on the inner sleeve of the band's *Frankenchrist* album. Sure, it was meant to offend and amuse, but it should have been obvious as protected free speech.

I liked Jello. He questioned authority and was a smart ass with a cause. He was dressed in colorfully mismatched vintage clothes, including a loud sport coat. As we shook hands he gazed at my friend Bob's "Y.O.T." (Youth of Today) T-shirt with mild disapproval. I suspected that Jello felt, as I did, that Y.O.T. were not-so-bright skinheads, promoting a soft-skulled straight-edge lifestyle like a fascist teenage religion.

The Dead Kennedys were intentionally ridiculous, but certain songs will probably always make me laugh, like their teenage love anthem "Too Drunk to Fuck," with the priceless, tasteless lines: "You give me head / It makes it worse / Take out your fucking retainer / Put it in your purse."

THIRTEEN: EMBRACING ABSURDITY BECAUSE LIFE IS A PARADOX

Life is weird. We're a bunch of monkeys clinging to a big round rock flying through the galaxy at 67,000 miles per hour, orbiting an impossibly dense, compacted ball of mega-hot gases that took 50 million years to form and will burn another 5 billion years, and which floats among hundreds of billions of other galaxies in an ever-widening universe. That's not normal. Nothing's normal. You defy the slow but powerful force of gravity necessary for star formation every time you lift your hand to gesture or get up from the couch. That's how powerful you are.

Existence is a paradox because the chicken and egg problem of creation may never be resolved. Which came first, the universe or god? If the universe exists without a creator, how could it begin at all? Classic physics dictates you can't have something emerge from nothing. No matter can ever be created or destroyed, from or into nothingness; it must always change form.

For the sake of argument, let's say that the universe exists without a creator. Before there were days, or even time, there was no universe of any kind. Then the next day (really, the first day) the universe popped into existence by itself. If that's true we're faced with a contradiction. What sets the Big Bang in motion? How does a universe birth itself from nothing? It's a paradox.

Next let's imagine that the universe was born as the result of the death or contraction of a previous universe. How did the first, original universe begin on its own? The same problem remains. It's still paradoxical.

Conversely, let's presume god exists, or existed, and did create our reality. How did god come into existence? Who created god? If the answer is that god has always existed, that's also a paradox.

To summarize, whether god exists or doesn't exist, or whether the universe emerged from nothingness or didn't, the paradox at the heart of existence remains unsolved. It would also be absurd if there was no universe at all and a complete absence of life. How does one imagine nothing? We at least know we are *something*, for we think, and therefore we are.

If you accept, as I do, that life is inherently contradictory, then weirdness is what's really normal. Absurdity is the natural state, which is hilarious. Life is a fantastic cosmic joke.

If you feel alone in your thoughts and think you're strange, you're actually normal. Meanwhile, anyone who thinks there's such a thing as normalcy is the real weirdo. Absurdity is truth and liberation! It also means we can accept ourselves as goofy, say ridiculous things and have bizarre, illogical thoughts, because the universe is equally odd. You can be whoever you want to be, and see life however you like, so long as you're not hurting others. All the supposed rules people invent are like trying to put brackets around the grandiosity of the universe, to reign it in and make it small. An impossibility. And dull, too.

Absurdity and paradoxes imply *infinite possibilities*. The universe is abnormal, mysterious, and magical. There's no reason not to think broadly and imaginatively. I believe we can manifest altruistic dreams into reality, and there's evidence in quantum physics to support it. More on that shortly.

FOURTEEN: IS EVIL NECESSARY? PLUS, GOD'S ORGASM

Is god by necessity both good and evil? Again, assuming the existence of an omniscient designer, when I consider god creating the universe I wonder if he/she/it/they experienced both ecstasy and anguish at the moment of conception. Being pretty smart, god surely realized that the universe would embody an uncomfortable duality, a mutually-dependent relationship between opposites: light and darkness; hope and despair; success and failure; love and hate. These extremes are necessary for us to be able to distinguish between what's desirable and what's not, and to give us the opportunity to choose our path when every option is available.

We couldn't comprehend great beauty unless we also had great ugliness, and all gradations in between. Love requires the existence of hate to distinguish itself as the better choice. If god created everything that exists, then god is a contradictory being encompassing everything desirable and undesirable simultaneously. Perhaps god shattered itself into an infinite number of pieces to create the universe, and created its dark doppelganger in the devil.

Since love requires the counterbalance of hate for contrast, then good requires evil, making evil *necessary*, and the depths and heights of each must be unlimited, or god would be imposing artificial boundaries on conduct. It's hard to accept, but it means we need the most loving, angelic beings and the purely destructive in the same world. Life can't be any other way than we know it. This doesn't excuse depravity, but perhaps puts it in some context?

Evil is restless, always trying to mine new awful depths, to shock us and wear down our will and hope in other people, and to get us to believe that sorrow, suffering, and decay dominate life. Evil works hard to recruit you. But love is always at work, too, though often with more subtlety. There are miracles of generosity and beauty every day, and people so pure of intention that their example is an inspiration reminding us how good we can be, and how nice that feels. When you're able to absorb some of the harshness of life, but retain optimism, you're acting as a filter, helping to cleanse the world. It's noble and hard, but rewarding, though no one can do it all the time.

Life's duality, with good and bad hand-in-hand, is mirrored in sex and reproduction. The classic French literary description for an orgasm is "la petite mort," meaning "the little death." I think you'll agree an orgasm is an intense release. Your body shakes with the incapacitating loss of control and rush of neurochemicals to the brain. The physical intensity is often matched emotionally. The feelings you've been carrying for several days, weeks, or longer, are tied in, but condensed and amplified. You may feel acutely realized, and taste bitter sweetness, like truth. It's an act of simultaneous creation and death. You are the contradiction. You are the birth of the universe. You are everything and nothing for a fleeting moment. You know what god felt at the moment of creation.

For males, there's also the singular sensation of millions of mini-mes departing the body at 28 miles an hour, coincidentally the maximum speed of the fastest human alive, Usain Bolt. There's gratification that you finally got to fulfill your biological mission, and maybe some embarrassment at being reduced to a happy animal who got his rocks off. (Bolt could give his own sperm a run for the money.)

The release/Big Bang/orgasm is both beautiful and terrible because creation always leads to the same result: new life which will inevitably experience extreme joy and sorrow over the course of its existence. The qualities are inseparable.

When god created all of this and us, it surely knew that mortal beings would have to contend with both the most amazing, life-affirming moments and periods of such total despair we might wonder why we were born. God's orgasm unleashes the best and worst of everything. God too felt great joy and sorrow, rolled together like yin and yang, at the moment of conception, and there was no other way it could be.

FIFTEEN: THE BIOLOGICAL IMPERATIVE

This universe is geared for life. For every billion particles of anti-matter released during the Big Bang, there was one extra particle of matter, giving matter, and therefore the possibility for abundant life, an edge. Otherwise this would be a big, empty universe. No one knows why matter has the advantage, unless the universe was meant to support life, as I believe. It's also possible we live in one universe out of billions of intersecting universes of possibility, and ours is ripe, while others are not.

Creativity is the driving force of our reality. There's a bat the size of a raspberry that lives in the Andes Mountains, and a tiny worm that only exists in the lungs of Singapore lizards. The millions of species of insects, animals, and plants on Earth are a testament to the relentless ambition of nature, under challenging conditions. Likewise, artists are driven to make beautiful works of art, imitating god's boundless imagination and echoing the original creation. Being creative and contributing to the abundance is inherently satisfying. I see god as the ultimate artist. Some people want to make babies with prolific creators. Perhaps it's like making love to god.

We exist to create. Humans are wired to keep making more of ourselves until we fill every available space on the planet with flesh, bones, and blood. *The Biological Imperative* is so strong that our sexual behavior is sometimes inexplicable to us. Who we end up with, choose, or prefer, may feel encoded or inevitable.

An ex-girlfriend and I once stumbled on an obvious idea: when stimulated, a lot of blood rushes to your loins. When that happens, guess where there's less of it? Yep, up in your noggin. You might as well be intoxicated, because you're nearly impaired. Once the nether region gets a hold it doesn't want to give it up. It seeks satisfaction before release. Your groin temporarily dominates your (sexy) decisions.

Everyone should have lots of sexy fun as often as possible, and we should laugh while having sex because it feels really good, and possibly we should be eating pancakes at the same time or maybe rolling around in pancakes or pancake batter or having sex on top of a bed that is one enormous fluffy sweet-smelling powdered sugared pancake (with chocolate chips) and maybe rubbing pancakes on each other at the same time. I like pancakes and absurdity, and, as we've discussed, absurdity is the true basis of reality.

In pursuit of a romance explosion (thanks, Borat), some men forget that women want to sleep with us as much as we want to sleep with them, but they need to trust the guy they like and want. If you're the kind of person who'll tell your friends intimate details after, you've put her in a no-win, humiliating position. (Don't be that guy.)

Generally, women feel comfortable with men who help them to feel safe physically, but especially emotionally. Particularly attractive women get hit on at such a steady pace that it becomes understandably tiresome. They've heard all the dumb lines and had the creepy looks. You can better earn someone's trust by being genuine, though it requires courage to be vulnerable. It also proves you're in the real world, not deluded or overly egotistical. You haven't bought into a posture.

Sometimes I struggle, as many men do, with my basic nature. When I see an attractive woman walking by I don't always care about her personality. My caveman brain reacts before I'm even aware. I want to have her, but my conscience and intellect provide appropriate feedback guilt before I speak. It's possible she might like nothing more than to skip the small talk and get filled with hot goo (not necessarily by me, but maybe by some other guy, or a lot of guys) but there are dangers to acting on impulse and many ways to get burned.

Being good in bed and relationships is about communicating and acting as you feel. (Look at me, I'm Dr. Phil now.) When something feels really good, it usually feels equally good for your partner. But, as with many things in life, when a person's fear of failure leads to an inhibited performance, it makes both parties feel awkward. To grow, you must risk failure and learn to be comfortable with improvisation and uncertainty, whether it's singing on stage or knocking boots. Practice your blowjobs, ladies! Learn to be expressive, gentlemen!

Great sex makes you feel more connected to your body, and the whole of creation. Every cell in your body screaming, "Yes!" in rapture, like Steve Martin discovering his "special purpose" in *The Jerk*. It's *everybody's* special purpose. Sometimes sex feels so good I involuntarily laugh (just like when I'd hear a new Smiths record in high school), as if my body's saying, "I can't believe how great this is! Man, I'm lucky! Good thing it's dark in here." Shouldn't we try to curl each other's toes? It can't be cosmic every time, but effort and enthusiasm matter a lot.

Nature has laid an elaborate trap. Our bodies say yes, let's make babies, but our brains warn us if we're not ready to be a parent, hate children, want to be untamed awhile longer, have a drug problem, are completely lazy and selfish, or are chasing a career before considering a family. Maybe your childhood was messed up and you're afraid you'll pass on damage to your own kids.

Studies show that women have definite peaks and dips in their sexual desire depending on where they're at in the menstrual cycle. Researchers have discovered interesting patterns in terms of preference. During ovulation most predominantly heterosexual women prefer men with more traditionally masculine, rugged features. He-men with hard-ons. Fit, tanned construction workers in tool-belts. There's also a fantasy component, with attraction for mysterious strangers. (Beloved self-destructive comedian Gilda Radner once said to husband Gene Wilder, "Kiss me like a stranger." He used it as the title of his autobiography.) The popularity of vampires who seductively suckle your lifeblood says a lot about women too!

When not ovulating, the same group prefers men with more sensitive, perhaps even feminine faces. This may also be the reason women want their men some of the time, but not all of the time. However, for a guy, sperm production is constant, though it wanes with age. Most of us are ready to impregnate at the drop of a dress, until literally every sperm has been expelled from our testes. (No, this isn't possible, but we'd like to try.)

The semi-sad conclusion: if you're a sensitive guy, you can be in a relationship with a woman you love and who sincerely loves you back. Yet, a few days every month the kind of man she really wants is the guy who harassed you in high school. Her eggs groan for his load while she lies in bed beside you. Some women suppress this feeling, and others sure don't. Thus the milkman's baby, or the pool boy's.

It's no one's fault, or it's everybody's fault. Penises are powerful. They shoot out half the batter of life at 28 miles per hour (remember Usain), though it feels like 10,000. Boobs are powerful. They provide vital nourishment in the form of milk. That's a lot of power between boobs and dongs. If you're obsessed with either or both, you're possibly normal. You're fixated on the life-givers.

Studies suggest large-breasted women are more fertile and men with larger penises are more successful impregnators because they can get closer to the egg for special delivery. To deny the power of our protrusions is to ignore being an animal, though of course we're much more than that, too. (Well, some of us.)

Even the most happily married person probably believes it would be fun to fool around with someone other than their spouse. Attraction to others is natural. There are many interesting, vibrant people.

Monogamy is difficult. It may not even be natural, but it's socially sensible, and loyalty is beautiful. It helps prevent the proliferation of sexually transmitted diseases and unintended pregnancies. Dedicated couples pool their resources for survival and a better quality of life, and to create a stable family unit for children. If there was no such thing as sexually transmitted diseases, or children's feelings, would we continue to believe monogamy is desirable? Could we exist more communally without the specter of jealousy? (Probably not.) The traditional partnership has been under great scrutiny since the women's rights movement of the 1960s, and Madonna inspired a generation of voracious women in the '80s. I'm probably getting too old to know what the current generation's attitude is, even though I watched some episodes of *Girls* on HBO.

The problem with the concept of open marriages or friends with benefits is that it doesn't work! Or rarely. You might think you can be in an F.W.B. situation, and it may fly a short while, but it almost inevitably crashes. One person starts to have more than just sexual feelings for the other person, or hopes that a sexual relationship that shows promise as a friendship can turn the corner into something greater, yet retain its libertine bent. Or one person starts to feel underappreciated or used.

Still, can marriages survive the whole truth? My ex-girlfriend Evelyn believed in absolute honesty 24/7. Her marriage was freshly buried when we met. She was very vulnerable. In retrospect I should have thought more about whether it was a good time to become involved, but that's not how it works. We don't get to pick the sequence of events, and if we wait for the "perfect moment" we might end up alone forever.

We had a hot, neurotic affair that burned out quickly. I found my extreme edges and learned more about life, and got great material for new songs! She was a drug. I craved her and felt addicted and out of control. (I understood when singer John Mayer described ex-girlfriend Jessica Simpson like sexual "crack cocaine," even though he took a beating for his honesty in the press.) She brought me high and we got weird and I discovered I didn't know myself as well as I thought. The illusion of self-control was again revealed. In one another's presence we would sometimes shake, like atoms recognizing familiar atoms.

Evelyn said one of the reasons her marriage ended was because of all the things she and her ex withheld over the years, presumably crucial emotional information. In response to a newfound belief that withholding any thought, no matter how potentially hurtful to your mate, always creates a problem, she adopted a policy of *All Truth, All the Time*. She told me everything on her mind and about her past, in great detail both anatomical and emotional, about each of her previous and post-marriage lovers. I was more selective with what I shared.

I think Evelyn believed if I was unable to deal with this potentially off-putting information I wasn't strong enough to be with her, or our relationship would be based on lies. Perhaps she subconsciously wanted to undermine a long-term relationship, never intending to keep me. She was a magnetic handful; a creative, pretty, talented, smart 120-pound sex bomb with arched eyebrows. I tossed myself into her flame and smelled my ashes filling the air. It was sublime and devastating. We loved in a desperate, not entirely healthy, way.

When our relationship started to crumble I wondered if my own philosophy about the beauty of truth had holes in it. *Is there such a thing as too much honesty?* Maybe some things are best kept to ourselves, for the actual benefit of a relationship, though I still need to tell myself the truth about who I am.

I feel the key to understanding her is something that happened when she was a teen. Her father was a farmer and worked for a land owner who occasionally dined with Evelyn's family. After dinner one night, still at the table, the landowner wrapped his arms around Evelyn in an inappropriate way. He sat her on his lap in front of her father, who didn't object. In fact, he didn't say a word. I gasped. The lesson Evelyn said she learned was that she was worthless, disposable, and not worth defending. I believe it's been locked in the back of her mind, distorting her self-esteem and relationships with men for more than 25 years.

If I'd been her dad I would have confronted the boss on the spot, damn the consequences. Whoever her father was, whatever life he'd had, he somehow lacked the strength to defend his blood at a defining moment. Many people would fail in the same way, from fear. Look at what it cost her.

There have been lots of clever human strategies (and some polygamous cults!) that have tried to solve why men and women, and men and men, and women and women can't live with or without each other, but no one's landed on the perfect solution because there isn't one. Compromise, patience, and understanding are surely the key. I sometimes envy those contented within a long-term relationship; it's eluded me, or I've eluded it while chasing wispy artistic dreams. At the bottom of my being I fear giving myself to someone again, as I did when I was younger and more hopeful, and being abandoned for greener pastures full of other dudes. I sometimes fear I only have enough going for me to catch someone great, not keep her. I've been running for years.

But I like being by myself, too. You need a quiet personal space to make art. Maybe I'll continue to be a horny bachelor with good intentions, but questionable romantic judgment, or I'll evolve to another perspective. Like many people, sometimes I'm pure lust, though that will change in time. I'll eventually see life through different goggles, as any man who lives long enough must, when his testicles shrivel up and return to an infantile appearance and function, every chest hair goes gray, and all testosterone has been exhausted! I'll wither in bitter exile like Casanova in Bohemia. *Boo hoo*, right?

Or perhaps in my burgeoning middle age I'll revisit innocence and return to romantic love. I'll rise above the slights and unintentional games we engage in when we feel vulnerable, but the expression of insecurity is defensiveness instead. A flawed man will wake up but live the dream. I'll meet somebody who completely rocks my world. It will be obvious and fated, her face framed by fireworks when we meet. That would be sweet. Life's full of surprises.

SIXTEEN: APRIL NODS

I can trace one period of heavy spiritual traffic to 2007 because I was reading the final novel by Normal Mailer. My brother Steve and I would compare notes to discover we'd each received head-shaking visitors on the same evening at about the same time. I wondered if we were not only picking up spirits, but sympathetic vibrations of each other's experiences.

One sunny afternoon, while discussing it over the phone, Steve realized he had a visitor. She appeared in his mind's eye and said her name was April. I asked Steve if he would mind if I asked April some questions through him. We'd never tried it before, with Steve acting as a medium, and it wasn't long after my intense experience with the dark visitor who revealed that unfriendly forces are interested in creating more *suffering*. Through Steve I asked April if she could confirm this was true. She said yes.

I was close to finishing Mailer's book. "The Castle in the Forest" is about the existence of god and his angels, the devil and his minions, and attempts by each side to influence events on Earth. Mailer speculated in his personal essays that the struggle between good and evil was likely to continue into the afterlife, should it exist. I believe he was right.

In the novel Satan successfully engineers an extremely evil being via the incestuous birth of Adolf Hitler. On the night of Hitler's conception the devil is in possession of Hitler's father. Mailer's devil is not cartoonish. He's an intelligent dark force that isn't entirely healthy to contemplate. (I humbly ask for guidance from good spirits and the white light of god as I wade in. I won't stay long.)

The book was fascinating in its depiction of a war on Earth between fundamental forces while most of humanity remained unaware. Though it was fiction, Mailer touched on what I was contemplating deeply at the time, and that matched my emerging beliefs. I asked Steve to ask April if she was aware of the book and if it was true. An image suddenly intruded upon his mind's eye. It was a cartoonish Hitler face with its eyes "X-ed" out. It stuck its tongue out at Steve. He was startled and momentarily taken aback. The image dissipated. (Tricksters often try to prank and intrude on moments of positive feeling, much like sour people you probably know. We shouldn't let them spoil good moments.)

April became the dominant responder on this "open frequency," but Steve had the sense he'd only be able to maintain its integrity a short time. She replied, via Steve, that Mailer's book was an allegory. Steve didn't know what allegory meant; he simply relayed her answer. I was reassured this was a genuine communication; Steve doesn't use words he doesn't know.

We asked April about the nature of spirits. She confirmed what we already believed to be true, that to communicate with the living, spirits must lower their vibration. She said people who've died suddenly are sometimes shocked to discover themselves dead, and may linger for a great time near their homes, or the place they died, which accounts for haunted spaces. Until a dead person accepts their transition and decides to move on to the next plane, he/she can linger around the living for a long time, though nothing can change fate. Acceptance is the only option, or they'll remain unhappily stuck between worlds.

(In a related instance, Steve was enlisted by spirits to help a recently deceased, handicapped teenager who had lived in town. The young man didn't yet realize he'd died in a terrible accident at a train crossing. We felt awful. Steve was asked to explain the boy's situation to him and to tell him to proceed into the white light of the other side. We're not sure why Steve's assistance was sought as he didn't know the boy personally.)

April said the dead have better access to us in our dreams because we're more relaxed and our natural defenses are lowered. When you have a dream about a deceased loved one it's likely they've come to deliver a message.

As I'm hoping to eventually explore the universe, I was curious if it took spirits time to travel great distances, like between neighboring galaxies. If spirits are like quantum particles in string theory, they should be able to jump to other locations instantly, or through as-yet-undiscovered (though theoretically conceived) other dimensions. April confirmed that spirits can indeed travel by thinking themselves from one place to another, violating Einstein's Standard Model in which nothing we know of can travel faster than light speed.

- - -

It's time for a related tangent. Quantum physics have proven to be stranger than most scientists imagined. Unlike the school diagrams of my youth, in which electrons orbit the nucleus of an atom like planets around a star, electrons don't move in circles at all. They "pop" around inside the atom, blinking in and out of existence in seemingly random patterns, and between these micro-second appearances they disappear entirely. No one knows where they go. The electrons jump to new positions without appearing to travel, just like spirits. Some physicists believe they go to parallel or intersecting universes, then back to ours, in a multi-verse of possibilities. That's the essence of string theory, to the limited extent I comprehend it.

Atomic particles seem to exist in a state of "quantum uncertainty." In addition to jumping around in the atom, electrons do not have any fixed location until they're observed. The object, the electron, doesn't declare a position until an intelligence, an observer, attempts to fix his/her gaze upon it. Until that moment it's everywhere and nowhere at once. All possibilities.

My brain wants to connect this idea to what happens when we think about friends and family. In recent experiments using external electrodes, scientists have measured thoughts as they travel in the human brain. Thoughts are electrical impulses, requiring energy for their creation. Your body uses fuel (food) to create them. For example, a simple motor command to raise your hand measures just a millionth of a volt. Once you have that thought, or many, the energy's expended. It leaves you in the same way your body burns calories and radiates heat when you move, exercise, or even just breathe. Since the energy is released into the air, wouldn't our thoughts travel outward as we have them? If we're thinking of someone, wouldn't our thoughts travel to them as our object? I believe so.

Feeling another person's thought is similar to the sensation we get when we realize someone's watching us, but we can't see them. Perhaps they're staring at us from a distance and our back is turned, but we still feel their gaze. I suspect what's happening is no different than in quantum physics. The observer, the person looking at you, consumes energy to direct their eyes to you, the object. The observer's attention is a thought, an energy pulse, which travels from the brain to the ocular nerves, out the front of the head, literally hitting you in the back of yours! As the object, you feel their gaze even if you can't see them. The observer's thoughts alter your awareness, like a physicist's gaze alters an electron, forcing it into position in an atom.

Perhaps every time you have a thought about someone it jumps instantly through the quantum field without travel time, and arrives at its object. This makes telepathy seem much more plausible, and no more mystical than quantum physics. Whether the person on the other end feels your thought probably depends on other circumstances, like if they're busy, and whether they're receptive to this form of communication. I would think an openness to greater, mysterious possibilities matters; it determines what you receive, if anything. We can all become more perceptive, but it's not for cynics.

If you have ever thought you know exactly what a person is thinking when they look at you, even if nothing is spoken, it's entirely possible that you are feeling and hearing their thought. It might be even easier in close proximity. I've had years of instances of thinking of someone and then hearing from them within hours. I no longer consider it coincidence.

(Another side thought: What if we had technology to amplify our thoughts? Could we send messages around the world or deep into the universe? Do we have this ability already even without amplification tech? How close is that to mind control? When will the N.S.A. start using it on us? Ha ha. Kind of.)

Here's another quantum physics concept. Related atomic particles retain their relationship to one another, even when separated by great distances. When one particle flips position, its companion particle will flip at the same exact time, even if it's half the world away. The particles can communicate at any distance, instantly. No travel time is needed.

At the time of this writing there's an experiment involving Earth-bound physicists and the crew of the International Space Station. The scientists plan to separate two related particles on Earth and send one to the ISS. Then they'll manipulate the particle on the ground and see if the one in orbit corresponds. As with previous experiments, the particles will probably still relate despite the distance.

Following this logic, I've wondered whether members of the same biological family, a child and parent for example, share an atomic bond because they're derived from the same matter. If related particles in family members behave like the related atomic particles in these experiments, then it would make sense that a child might feel something that their parent is feeling at any distance. A quantum communication occurs; the child's atoms resonate in response to the parents'. This is probably why there are so many reports of a parent or child sensing when something unusual or traumatic has happened to the other.

My mom and I had something like this happen a few years ago, after Christmas. Mom was preparing for a serious surgery, but she hadn't yet told Steve or I about it. A few days before our holiday dinner, I had an unusual, unfamiliar abdominal pain. It didn't feel like a stomachache or a pulled muscle or anything I could think of or had experienced before. I could press on the spot, but it didn't hurt more or less when pressure was applied, which was odd.

After dinner mom told us that she was going to have surgery. The location of the operation was exactly the same place, somewhat below the right rib, in the middle of the abdominal muscles. I'd put my finger on it. I believe I felt mom's pain as a sympathetic vibration.

In high school a nice man named George ran a comic book shop I often visited. One weekend the shop was closed and there was a note on the door about a family emergency. Later George told me he'd woken from a sound sleep with the sensation that his mother had just died. His father woke up at the same time; he also just knew somehow. Obviously

George's dad doesn't share DNA with his mom, but George was the bridge between them genetically.

We read about couples who die of natural causes within hours or days of each other, and sometimes while holding hands. My father's mom and her brother died of old age only hours apart. What are the chances that's a coincidence? Literally, if Vegas gave the odds, what would they be? Almost zero.

- - -

Back to April. I asked her to confirm another cosmic idea. I'm not sure where the notion came from, but I believe that the universe is like an old-fashioned vinyl record. (I love my old turntable; it's reassuring to watch a record spin smoothly while listening, surely related to my adolescence. In fact, last night I dreamt of my old corner.) The entire history of the universe has always existed, and will always exist, with a beginning, middle, and end, and every moment and event which has ever occurred or will occur, exists simultaneously when one omnisciently looks at the universe from outside. But in order to experience and make sense of it you have to play it from beginning to end on the universal turntable.

We don't know if time exists outside this universe. Time began with the Big Bang and might only be a rule for this reality. I think time exists so that we can experience growth and change and reflect on what it means to age and grow wiser even as our bodies eventually grow weaker. There's a naturally long road from adolescent arrogance and the accompanying feelings of invulnerability to, hopefully, the wisdom of humility and empathy through experience. Given the challenges of life, I also wonder if, once we die, we have the option to take a break from existing and go into cosmic hibernation, to rest the soul.

Years prior to Steve and I meeting April, I wrote and recorded two different songs, which appeared on consecutive CDs from 2001 and 2003, about a girl named April. She wasn't based on anyone I knew; she was made up. The songs are called "April Nods" and "April Again," and the second song loosely continues the narrative from the first. I've written hundreds of songs, but it's the only time I've written a sequel, though I didn't give much thought as to why.

The biggest surprise of the conversation was when April revealed that she was the famous "tickler" from my first big spiritual event in 1997, and not our brother Justin. There was no reason not to believe her, but I felt some disappointment that it may not have been my brother. I won't know for sure until I die, but it doesn't diminish the significance because the biggest lesson from it was that there's more to life than what we can see. There's nothing else I can be 100 percent sure of, and it's enough.

Still, I asked April why she chose to reveal her existence then. April said that I was feeling down and having troubles adjusting to my new job. She wanted to give me a lift. She changed my life. We asked if my "meeting" her was the subconscious impetus for my two "April" songs. She said it was possible, subliminally or indirectly, but not intentionally.

One of the last things April told us is that everyone has three guardian angels. We don't know why it's three. The specificity of that felt a little suspect, but we don't have any additional information, including who "assigns" the angels, if anyone.

The experience with April lasted about 30 minutes. Relaying questions through Steve was surreal and hair-raising, but felt perfectly plausible. We haven't tried to communicate with anyone on the other side in tandem since then. It was a serendipitous thing.

SEVENTEEN: MEXICAN ROOM WARP

My mom doesn't generally try to contact spirits, though she's had some interesting experiences too. Years after the death of her son Justin, a psychic told her he would appear as a child in the doorway of her bedroom at our home in North Tonawanda. It freaked her out. A few days later she called the psychic to tell her she wouldn't be able to handle that. The psychic said Justin would never do any harm and that if she didn't want to see him, he wouldn't come. It's probably why he doesn't visit her that way. She does feel his presence though.

Mom, Steve, and I have similar beliefs about the other side. We have one significant shared experience. We often meet for Sunday afternoon brunch. I always look forward to catching up with them. One Sunday 5 or 6 years ago we went to a Mexican restaurant on Hertel Avenue, which is notable because we rarely eat Mexican and we never went back there even though it was very good. I don't know why, probably because there are many other nice places closer to my house. We were talking about spirit stuff and really getting into it, laughing and carrying on as we often do, kicking a lot of positive energy into the air.

As we chatted a strange feeling came over me. The room felt like it was falling away. Mom asked, "Can you feel that?!" We each nodded. It was like a scene in a horror movie when the camera zooms in on an actor but the room appears to simultaneously drop back. The room seemed to warp behind us as if it didn't really exist, the illusion of solidity stripped away. The feeling didn't last long, maybe 10 seconds. It wasn't scary; it was fascinating. We were pleasantly surprised to experience it together.

Based on what we've learned about vibrations I think that our fun conversation elevated our vibrations synchronously, and we began to lift, floating in between connected realms. We've not been able to duplicate this moment, though my mom has rallied us to try a few times. It requires the perfect set of circumstances, including the mood of each person in the moment, and in the right setting. Trying too hard, or self-consciously, to duplicate what happened naturally and spontaneously is nearly impossible. It's important to enjoy moments of perfection, to be present, because it may never feel quite the same again. They're bittersweet in their brevity, just like life. The more we live in the moment, the more real life becomes. Yes, I'm mushy.

I get a similar feeling of peaceful connection to something deeper while performing. Sometimes the room nearly warps, or the performance has a surreal quality, like I'm both participating and observing. When the energy is perfect, an unspoken, but palpable relationship forms with the audience, and we communicate non-verbally inside an elevated bubble. Audience and artist feel like one shared emotion. Pulses slow and we relax, feeling loose and free. Minds wander to nice places, riding the sensation.

When someone disrupts the mood and the spell is somehow broken, the air changes quickly. The shared feeling was fragile and free of gravity. Once cracked you can nearly feel the broken pieces hit the floor. Someone might even yell out in disappointment, irritated that a nice moment has been shattered.

Inside the bubble our senses were heightened and we felt more alive. We crave a return to it when we're not there. We search for it in other places, people, and activities. We want to feel connected to something greater, to understand ourselves and others better, and to be ennobled and empowered by a collective spirit. We crave reunification with the deep intelligence from which we came, even if we're unable to articulate it. We get glimpses of peaceful perfection, and we know one day we'll return.

EIGHTEEN: "I'LL BE WITH YOU AT 4 P.M. ON CHRISTMAS EVE"

My mom's birthday is on Christmas. Her name is Carol. Yep, Christmas Carol, that's the joke. I've only missed one of her birthdays, and she wasn't too happy about it, either. It was the winter of 1997, the same year as my tickling incident. My friend Kate was living in New York City, at the corner of 20th and 2nd. I stayed with her for a week over Christmas, sleeping on an air mattress in her cozy studio apartment. Air mattresses aren't even vaguely comfortable, but cheapskates can't be choosers. (She eventually let me share the bed platonically. I complained my way in.)

Gramercy Park was Kate's first Manhattan apartment after living in San Francisco several years. Many of my friends left Buffalo in their 20s, but I didn't. I thought I might end up in New York too, but the urge passed. I feel like I was meant to be from here and stay for now, and like I was born at the right time.

Over the next decade Kate also had apartments in Greenwich Village (on St. Mark's Place); the lower east side; and Hell's Kitchen (smallest studio apartment ever, criminal for the price of rent) before eventually moving to Brooklyn with her husband Chris to start a family. Gramercy Park was my favorite, and I enjoyed eating at the Cosmo Diner on 2nd Avenue, which looked like it was out of *Seinfeld*. Maybe that's how they thought of Kramer's first name.

We went ice skating at the tiny rink beneath Rockefeller Center on Christmas morning. It's a glamorous story that sounds better than the reality, though we had fun. As with most activities in New York, you have to wait in line a long time to skate a short while, on a modestly-sized rink with many other people, on deeply grooved ice that forces inadvertent directional changes.

It occurred to me not long after that everything in New York City is about time and space. If you go to a club show, there's almost always a concrete start and end time because there'll be more than one performance that evening. Unlike Buffalo, you don't just get to hang around afterward. They shove you onto the street once your show is over because they have to get the next audience in right away.

Once seated, there's little room to spread out. Depending on the mood this is often charming, as one is nearly forced into conversation with strangers. At the B.B. King Blues Club in Manhattan, the chairs are packed so tightly that they could only be closer if they were permeable and occupied part of the same space at the same time molecularly. Perhaps one day someone will try so hard to cram two chairs into the exact same spot that they'll succeed and force two parallel universes to intersect and overlap, like String Theory on drugs. A spatial anomaly will develop, like in the last episode of *Star Trek: The Next Generation,* growing in size as you go backwards in time, leading to the end of humanity unless Picard embraces the paradox. I love that episode; it's the perfect analogy for embracing the mysterious unknown. But I digress.

New York is stimulating in its wild cultural diversity and innumerable intelligent, attractive people working in many different fields, though there's also self-importance and pretense to be found. Perhaps a "New York attitude" must be cultivated to handle a cramped New York life? (No, pretense is pretense wherever you go.) I read that New York has more millionaires than any city in the country. 660,000 of them! That's more than Chicago, Boston, and D.C. combined. Crazy. Who are these people?

One week prior to Christmas, while I was in Manhattan, mom had a dream about her long-deceased mother. My Grandma Bella came to her in the white waitress uniform she wore her entire life. Mom said her face was lovely, and her arms chubby and pink, unlike the frail woman who died in 1990. She did not appear to speak but mom clearly heard her say, "I will be with you on Christmas Eve at 4 o'clock." The time was specific. (This is like when I heard/felt the name "Justin" on Tickling Day. It felt silent and heard simultaneously. Telepathic.)

Later in the day, mom called her sister, my Auntie Anna, in Pennsylvania to tell her about the dream. Ann, a Eucharistic Minister, told mom she would be serving Communion at Mass on Christmas Eve at exactly 4. She planned to place flowers on the altar for their mom and dad. Ann suggested mom stop at church in the morning and light a candle for them, as they'd done as children for their favorite saints. A 7-day candle would burn until Christmas.

After dinner mom recorded the dream in her journal. The last word she wrote for the entry was "BELIEVE." As she climbed into bed that evening she began to feel a bit creepy. Our first dog Toby was the only other one in the house. Mom looked around the room and so did Toby, perhaps sensing her thoughts. When he lowered his head so did she, and they both fell asleep.

Mom lit candles at church for her parents the next morning on her way to work. It was her last day before Christmas break and co-workers were exchanging gifts. The first present she opened was a small garden stone with the word "BELIEVE" written across it. Synchronicity!

The next day mom was more emotional about her mother's visit. She thought how great it would be if all four of her sisters joined in, too. When the mail arrived she received a birthday gift from her sister Kay, a white nightgown and pair of gold earrings. Later that evening she and my brother went to a holiday play called *Greetings* at Buffalo's now-defunct Equity theater, Studio Arena.

In the play an angel visited a family via the body of their handicapped son. The young man could not communicate in reality, but when the angel inhabited his body he spoke with wisdom and insight. His family thought it was a miracle that he should speak on Christmas Eve, and his message was love. In the final scene the boy is in a room alone when an unplugged Christmas tree lights up on its own. They enjoyed the play very much. It made them teary-eyed, which made them laugh at themselves, and then they cried some more into their tissues.

On the 22nd when mom checked her mail there was a flyer from a neighbor with a Nativity scene printed on the top informing her that the block was going to light luminary candle bags on Christmas Eve at *4 p.m.* Four white paper bags filled with sand would be distributed to each house. When she showed my brother the note she started to cry again, because she felt it was the manifestation of her mom's message. She loved the symbolism of welcoming the

100

Christ Child (her words) with a public display of faith. Mom still thinks like a Catholic even though we're non-denominational.

On her way to the mall mom stopped at the home of the luminary organizer. Her name was Kathy and mom offered to help. She also shared the line from her dream about "Christmas Eve at 4 o'clock," which gave Kathy the chills. Her dog Willie was jumping all over mom. Kathy realized mom had been the one to help her son chase down and catch Willie when he escaped the day before Halloween. Mom followed him in her car over several blocks and across a major highway. She knew if she didn't succeed he'd likely be clipped by a car. With the help of another woman, the three of them finally caught Willie and she drove the exhausted boy and dog back home. Kathy took mom's hand to thank her again. Later mom remembered that her mother had died the day before Halloween, another small synchronistic sign.

On Christmas Eve mom helped her neighbors and their children prepare 300 bags with candles. It was cold and sunny outside. At 4 p.m. mom lit her bags and she, Steve, and Toby walked the block from end to end, marveling at the beauty of the lights in front of more than 70 houses. She said it looked like a runway and she imagined it as a brightly lit path for Christ, welcoming him into their hearts and homes. She had thought Christmas would be sad because I was away in New York, but her mom's gift was a wonderful diversion. When I got back she told me I'm never allowed to be away on Christmas again.

Much later that evening she sat bundled on her porch steps. The candles were burning brightly. She sang Christmas carols by herself to her mom, and embraced her memory. When she went to bed in her new nightgown she told herself the arms she wrapped around her were actually her mother's.

After Christmas, mom's sister Ann told her the angel atop her tree wouldn't light. Neither would the new one she bought. But on December 23rd when she went downstairs the angel was lit and blinking. Mom's sister Rosie, who had no knowledge of mom's dream, called Ann on Christmas Eve at 4 o'clock. Her sister Joni told mom that the strand of angel lights on her tree hadn't been working either, but came on while everyone was opening their gifts. They felt Grandma Bella had walked through the room and played a small trick.

As siblings age and start their own families, and their own kids have kids, it is easy to drift apart. Mom believes the event was meant for all of the sisters to feel the presence of her mom, to be reminded of the connectivity of family, and that they're all a part of something bigger and universal, too.

NINETEEN: GREEN CHAIR

Mom wrote the following piece for a local newspaper for Father's Day 2013, though they chopped it down and left out important parts, which have been restored. I like her conciseness as I sometimes suffer from verbosity. Maybe the wisest people in the world evolve towards near silence when all has been reconciled in mind and soul.

"Do you have a green chair? I'm seeing a green chair, a light green chair." I told the psychic that I did not have a green chair, nor could I remember anyone who did.

That evening I decided to look through old photo albums. In the last picture I had taken of my dad, on Christmas Eve 1972, he was sitting in a light green chair. He had a sheepish smile on his face, as if he knew I was searching him out. He was holding my 2-year-old son. He died the following March.

He was a very quiet man, with a heavy Italian accent. At age 14 he arrived in "America," basically alone. He taught himself to read and write. He read every one of my *Compton's Encyclopedias*. He gave me nickels from his worn leather change purse whenever I asked. I only asked him if my mother had already said no.

We had a large three-car-garage in our backyard, but no one owned a car. Two of the garages held tools, paint, stray cats, and stacks of newspapers. One day I set an old mousetrap out there. Two days later my Dad asked me if I had done this. When I said yes, he simply said, "Don't ever do that again." He never said more than he had to.

My father worked for the New York Central Railroad, starting as a water boy, and learning cement masonry. During snowstorms he would be called to work, clearing frozen train switches. For days I would watch out the window for the bus he might be on. I worried about him. We did not have a car, and he never used the phone, so I just had to wait. Eventually, days later, he would come home and I was grateful.

On Sundays we would take the train to Dunkirk, where my mother's family lived. The Buffalo Terminal held fond memories. We loved the big buffalo, and the cold descent down the steep walkway to the tracks. We went to Washington, DC, and then on to New York City one weekend. My Dad found a very inexpensive hotel, with one bulb hanging in the center of the ceiling, and a common bathroom. I slept with my sister and mother, while Dad had his own room. I thought it was a great adventure, but my mother wasn't so happy. I loved the bracelet I bought, with the dangling NEW YORK CITY letters. My friends at school could not believe I had been to the big city!

My reserved father gave himself a 65th birthday party. It was a great time dancing and eating in a banquet hall. He was such a private man that I could never quite figure out why he wanted that party. I am so glad he did.

Every once and a while, Dad would gather my mother up in his arms and dance with her in the kitchen. It always warmed my heart to see them laughing. My father surprised my mother with a wedding ring set on one of their late life anniversaries. It replaced the simple white gold band she had worn for years.

There were dark moments in our house as well. I recall a time when I heard the word "separation." I have no idea why I knew that meant someone would be leaving the house, but I decided right then and there I would be going with my father. He needed someone to take care of him. I was about 10. He never left.

My Dad never liked dogs, but he loved Porky. Porky was a huge shaggy dog, belonging to one of my sisters. She was probably his favorite daughter, actually. They had a special bond which just existed. When he was sick, my sister would know, even though she was hundreds of miles away.

Once, my other sister and I tried to run away. We heard my Dad say, "If you leave, don't ever come back." We looked at each other, and walked back upstairs. A psychologist once told me that my father was actually saying, "If I can do it (live with my mother), so can you. Be strong. Come back."

At the end of his life, my Dad spent a lot of time in the hospital. On one visit, I noticed his normally well-groomed fingernails had become neglected. I took his hands in mine, washed them, cleaned his nails, and sat with him for a very long time. He told me how good his hands felt. When I kissed him goodbye, I said, "I love you, Daddy." He replied, "I love you too, honey." I was 25, and it was the first, and last time my Dad said those words to me.

Fathers are such powerful people. Happy Father's Day to the men who hold our hearts in the palm of their hands.

TWENTY: OH REIKI, YOU'RE SO FINE, YOU BLOW MY MIND

My mom started having Reiki "attunements" after a major surgery. She's had four sessions since January 2013 and really likes it. I don't know much about Reiki so this is neither an endorsement nor critique. I'm in favor of whatever makes people feel better. Like mediums, doctors, musicians, presidents, and financial advisors, I'm sure Reiki practitioners vary greatly in quality and insight.

My mom wrote Steve an email about going. He wrote back, "Reiki Reiki you're so fine – Reiki Reiki you blow my mind. Ha ha." Fucking hilarious. So Steve.

Rose the Reiki Lady's studio is chilly, so mom lies beneath a blanket with her eyes closed. Rose hovers her hands above mom's head, neck, arms, sides, knees, and feet in succession. She employs a gentle touch, not a massage, which mom finds relaxing. There are lit candles and music playing.

In her mind's eye, Rose said that she sees her clients as stick people, with shiny silver rings around their arms and legs. The rings are fluid and soft like the ribbons gymnastics use in floor routines. Silver is the default color she sees, the most common, but my mom is the only one she sees in gold. This makes me think of how Justin appears to Steve, always in his gold necklace, the purest metal, difficult to replicate (perhaps impossible) by low-vibration spirits.

One of Rose's clients appeared to her surrounded in tiles as if she was being smothered. Rose confirmed the woman was feeling uptight and stressed. Another woman appeared in crystal, as in a person who is crystal clear, a walking metaphor.

Mom sees different colors while her eyes are closed, like the swirls you get when you rub your eyes a little while. It's a single color at a time, and Rose said this was common. Rose and my mom have experienced synchronized colors, most often purple, which mom says is the most sensitive of colors and reveals psychic power in attunement with self. Perhaps the colors are energies being released from the body, or related to one's aura.

My friend Amisha in Toronto involuntarily sees colored auras around others, varying from light, friendly colors to dark and menacing. The colors seem to match her sense of their spiritual state. People like Amisha can detect auras much the same way infrared cameras capture people in the dark from radiant body heat. Perhaps the colors in an aura are not just of the individual but of spiritual forces which we attract with our attitudes and feelings.

About a week after mom's last session I saw metallic green and purple sunburst colors in my mind's eye while lying in bed. At first the colors were small, fuzzy dots of light, like distant suns. Over a few minutes' time they kept getting closer until they eventually filled my entire field of vision. It was cool. They seemed organic and fluid like clouds, perhaps alive. Were they spirits? I wondered if the colors were a synchronous echo of my mom's experiences. I hadn't really seen colors before. Not as sustained and bright as these.

At the end of a session, Rose envisions a connecting line coming up through the top of a client's head, through her, ascending upward, presumably to god. She told mom that her connection was exceedingly bright compared to most people, as though she were lit up like a Christmas tree. This reminded me of mom's connection to her mother with the luminary bags on Christmas Eve, and her Christmas birthday.

The metaphor of god and spirits as light is appropriate. In the vast darkness of space the light of stars is relatively rare, but intensely concentrated, visible to us from millions and billions of light years away.

Rose believes that the more spiritual her client, the better Reiki works. This makes sense; someone who's more open is likely to be more positively affected. That doesn't mean people can't become more receptive and open over time, though this requires a willingness to be vulnerable and uncertain, and to risk embarrassment in exchange for growth.

In the days that follow each session mom feels more energetic, alive, and aware. This is how I often feel during and after a musical performance or session at the recording studio. Focused emotional energy is tapped, released, and shared. Energy cycles around the space, through me, and to the other musicians and studio personnel. I ride the positive wave after a performance or studio session for quite a while. If a few days in a row are like that I get pretty high, and I'm more prolific.

Mom finds Rose interesting in many ways, partly because, as a practitioner of a healing art, she doesn't seem to connect all the dots in her own life. We can easily make the mistake of believing that someone who spends a lot of time on spiritual matters would be introspective and insightfully balanced, but it's not always the case. (I definitely get out of whack.) We don't always see ourselves objectively. Rose is intrigued by my mom because "a gold stick person" has never appeared, nor with the brightness of her spiritual wire channeling up to god. This tickles mom.

Mom looked up some Reiki stuff online. A gold aura is apparently "the color of enlightenment and divine protection. When seen within the aura, it says that the person is being guided by their highest good. It is divine guidance, protection, wisdom, inner knowledge, spiritual mind, intuitive thinker."

Mom's next session was on a day she felt stressed because of digestive problems with her two dogs, Mike and Nelly. Rose felt intense heat on mom's right chest and she'd had pain there all day, which dissipated after the visit. When Rose got to her left foot she told mom she again saw soft gold rings around it, and her leg and foot were bending backwards like rubber. Mom looked nearly alien to her in her mind's eye. Rose thinks it means that she is flexible and moving forward.

For some reason, her bendable leg reminded me of our experience at the Mexican restaurant when the room fell away from us and seemed illusory. I wrote her an email speculating that since matter is vibrational and we may all be illusions of solidity, perhaps her vibration is higher than before, and closer to the spiritual realm.

During their second-last visit Rose told mom about her own post-cancer diet. Rose keeps track of her food intake in exacting detail, trying to avoid any potential trigger for a recurrence of cancer, which she's dealt with for decades. Mom felt Rose's intensity might not be helping her overall health. (Funny enough, that's also one of my worries about my mom.) The fixation and fear could be affecting her energy. Rose said she thinks my mom is further ahead than she is in the life process.

Mom didn't know if she could be as obsessive about her diet as Rose. Regarding her own health post-surgery, mom thought, "I'm doing the best that I can." After their session Rose said, "When I was touching your right side, I was thinking about our food conversation when I heard in my head, 'I'm doing the best that I can.'" Rose heard mom's thought at the exact moment she'd had it! "That's what I was saying in my head," mom told her.

Again, our thoughts are energies like any other. They leave our bodies when we have them, traveling outward into the universe. The deeply-attuned, the sensitives, can perhaps both project and receive ideas telepathically.

Recently I read about scientific experiments in the US and South Korea employing non-invasive electrodes to read brainwaves in rats. Researches remotely connected a rat brain and a human brain with external sensors, a brain-to-brain interface, to pick up their brainwaves. The goal was for the human subject to try to make the rat wag its tail from a separate location. When the human projected the thought of the simple motor action to the rat, it was compelled to do so. Consider the interface as an amplification of an existing signal.

It seems like we're close to discovering powerful means of non-verbal communication and perhaps even collective simultaneous thought, like a hive mind, with implications both good and bad. Lab experiments are beginning to reinforce spiritual ideas. There are many ramifications. The sovereignty of the human mind will be challenged. We will need to consider a legal framework for the privacy of our thoughts, but the greater point is that telepathy is already possible without technological assistance.

When you think about someone you haven't had any contact with in a number of years you're probably receiving a signal from them, or sending one out. Many times I've suddenly thought of someone and then get a message within hours or days. Again, I see no coincidence, only evidence of connectivity and oneness with others in a meaningful, intelligent universe. More proof of More Than This.

TWENTY-ONE: GENE AND TWO CRAZY BLONDES

My first apartment in Buffalo was at the busy intersection of West Utica and Elmwood. I lived there five years, on the second floor of a large house split into four apartments. There are many huge houses downtown, reminders of the housing boom during the city's golden age. In 1900 more millionaires lived in Buffalo than anywhere else in the country. Fortunately, things are looking up. Many people have returned to make an impact and there's a lot of new construction and fun activities on the waterfront.

The first floor was divided into two units, and the attic apartment took up the third floor. There were many different downstairs neighbors. The front apartment was designated Section-8 for housing assistance. I was sorry to discover that it drew problem people about half the time.

Two heavy blondes, both insane (one clinically, fresh from the Buffalo Psychiatric Center), and who looked frighteningly alike, lived there at different times to ensure endless drama. I still support housing assistance, but some people make it hard.

Blonde Number One was a low-IQ drug user who would scream and fight with her creepy boyfriend, banging shit around downstairs at all hours with no concern for the other tenants or neighbors. One week they were at it every night, and I was coming unglued from lack of sleep. Maybe she got the attention she craved, including from the police, who visited often but never took her away. Would an evening in the Erie County Holding Center really have been such a bad idea?

Blonde One's black cat had a litter of four. One Saturday morning I woke up early to the sound of a kitten crying in the downstairs hallway. It was my little puffball Gene. He wasn't mine yet, but he was outside her door crying because she'd accidentally let him escape. I knocked on the door; no one was home. I took him upstairs and gave him some milk. At 7 weeks old cats are irresistibly cute, nature's way of tricking humans into cat adoption.

Gene stayed several hours; I returned him when she came home, but asked for him the next day. He had a little limp. Blonde said she'd accidentally stepped on him a week ago. This was completely plausible because she was a selfish bitch. What I didn't know was that she'd broken his leg, and it had already started to heal improperly.

While playing a few days later, Gene jumped off the couch and screamed in pain because he'd re-broken it. I had no idea what was happening. I tried to grab him but his pupils were dilated and he was hostile. He bit me hard. It was close

111

to midnight. We went to the expensive, all-night veterinary clinic in Williamsville. They gave him an X-ray and I could see the busted bones forming an awful "X" shape. They doped him, immobilized the leg, and told me to call my vet in the morning. I didn't even have one yet. I'd only owned him a week.

When the drugs wore off a few hours later Gene was in great pain. He cried all night and there was nothing to be done. I didn't sleep and felt traumatized. A vet on Main Street agreed to see me right away in the morning. Doctor Layton, a gentle, red-haired man-child not unlike myself, said he'd never done leg surgery on a 7-week-old, but was willing to try. There was no hesitation. We were already bonded. Unnecessary suffering makes me sick. The emergency hospital and surgery cost a grand, but it didn't matter. Somehow when you do the right thing it comes back to you.

The cast on Gene's leg was longer than his actual leg, so he learned to walk lopsided, and did so a short while after the cast came off, too. The surgery was successful. The pin in his thigh worked perfectly; he grew normally and wasn't stunted. Gene is deaf, but he's a happy, feisty cat. There is nothing better than hearing him squeal with joy and run to me (I call it his "happy trot") when I come home, and I love to hear him snore at night. One of his favorite things is to stick his head in the shower stream and quickly flick his tongue into the water while it soaks his face and head. He waits by the tub ledge for me to turn it on.

Blonde Number Two moved in a year after Number One left. When I first saw her I instantly knew I was screwed, in part because of the way she eyed me up and down with her hungry, desperate blue eyes. The fact that she looked like Number One didn't help.

Number Two had no business being in her own apartment. If her social worker had thought she could be mainstreamed and leave the Psychiatric Center they probably should have put her in a group home with supervision first. Our culture could use a correction. We spend more money jailing non-violent criminals than on psychiatric care for people with big problems. Ok, soapbox shelved.

Number Two didn't work and had plenty of time to dream up how to mess with all of the tenants. She was intentionally defiant and refused commonsense practices and requests, *like locking the front door of the house*. She insisted on propping it open all day and evening simply because we wanted it to be closed. It wasn't the worst neighborhood in Buffalo, but it couldn't have been described as safe. My apartment door was wafer thin. Anyone could have entered with a single kick, and I would have lost everything, especially Gene.

I fought to have her evicted. A dangerous person is dangerous, no matter how much it's not her fault due to mental illness. Years after the eviction, I saw her back at the Buffalo Psychiatric Center, when I was hired to perform for the residents. I've performed there many times and they're one of the best audiences around. They pay attention to everything because they're overly sensitized, and they pick up on sincerity, or a lack thereof, immediately. My own experiences with depression help me connect.

To win them over requires an A-plus performance end to end, of three 45-minute sets. I really enjoy it, and a few of the women are so kind and innocent they seem saintly. At the Psych Center, Number Two looked frightened and small, just as she had outside, but less dangerous because she had no power to randomly wield. I felt sorry for her, but not nearly enough to be neighbors again. I hope no one else has to traipse around her in fear. No words were exchanged and she didn't interrupt. There was no reason not to be gracious.

TWENTY-TWO: GABE AND THE NIGHT OF SKULLS

A year after Blonde Number Two was evicted, a conceited college girl moved in. Her cocky boyfriend was sometimes around. She was my second cat Gabe's original owner. I would see Gabe in her front window when I came home from work. He seemed friendly and lonesome. Late one night, during which I was getting no sleep whatsoever because I was under assault by flying ghost skulls in my Third Eye as I lay in bed with my eyes closed, I heard him crying in the downstairs apartment, through the heating vent.

Yes, that's right. Nebulous, wispy grey floating skulls swirled before my closed eyes for hours, one after another in waves, depriving me of sleep. It didn't matter if I closed more tightly, or opened them awhile and closed them again. Unfriendlies were mounting a full-out assault to try to drive me up a wall, and they succeeded. It was already a period of heavy spiritual traffic. I had been contemplating weighty cosmic matters in too great a depth, apparently. An abundance of unseen messengers were stopping by for a quick visit in my forehead and some head shakes.

What I think set it in motion was that I'd recently decided to use my new knowledge to try to help people more overtly. I'd come to believe that the reason a hidden spiritual layer was revealed was to enlist me as a soldier for the cause. But the danger in contemplating life as a spiritual warrior is the inherent contradiction of considering it a war to begin with. The best aspects of spirituality are peaceful, not confrontational. I found myself sliding into the strange self-righteousness that I had disliked in others who claimed to be religious, even though my intentions were good. I started to see common conflicts exclusively through a spiritual lense, small daily episodes now representative of the larger, endless conflict between good and evil. I got weird.

I know now how and why. Cruelty towards those least able to defend themselves is nearly intolerable. So much sadness is preventable. Fighting back usually surprises a predator because they're counting on your intimidation and fear. I want to atomize bullying antagonists with godfire, except I don't have any, which is best. This is obviously a carryover from my teenage experiences and growing up with my brother. A bully is a weakling and coward. Those who feel powerless and angry, yet pass on their self-hatred to others, are ultimately risking their soul. If a person finds himself on this path, he should eat his anger whole if necessary. Be the braver, better person, get psychiatric help, or consider suicide.

Frequent visits by spirits had emboldened my sense of purpose and appetite to fight darkness. In my obsessiveness, I even began to wonder if certain biblical ideas about only a select few people making it to heaven were true and whether I was obligated to fight cruelty with a form of divine counter-aggression. I'd never before given credence to any biblical idea. The more worried I got about a path to "heaven," the more paranoid and judgmental I became. This went on for a few weeks.

In retrospect, I believe I let myself be successfully manipulated by clever unfriendlies. My self-righteous anger over injustice got twisted. I may have temporarily been under a spell. My heart was set on helping others, but my means had become confrontational. Fighting fire with fire was burning me up.

At the height of the confusion sleep became elusive, and then, finally, the skulls arrived. As a spiritual novice I mistakenly assumed I could "cast out" the invaders with vigorous anger. My rage didn't make the skulls disappear, only intensify, and as the hours of sleeplessness dragged on I feared I might never sleep well again and that this was a new battle I'd have to wage every day for the rest of my life. Odd, sleep-deprived thoughts were multiplying.

As the battle dragged into the wee hours I heard poor Gabe crying downstairs. He must have been nearly right below me in her apartment, and he sounded very sad. I got out of bed, skulls swirling in front of my eyes, got on my knees near the heating grate, put my hand up to it, and started speaking soothingly down into it. "It's okay, buddy, don't cry." I reached through the fear and focused on his comfort instead of my situation. Soon after that Gabe stopped crying. The skulls were partly dispelled, their influence diminished. I finally managed to get to sleep.

I recovered from the focused assault. The spell had been broken and I no longer felt self-righteous. The susceptibility to negative energies receded. I began to understand that only positive and hopeful feelings are an adequate defense against negativity. If for some reason you find yourself in a similar situation with dangerous, malevolent spirits, try to stay calm, then ask good spirits to help. Calmly pray to be enveloped and protected by the white light of god, which helps dispel darkness. (Ironic how easy it is to slip into the biblical language I've always rejected, and how hard it is to avoid when discussing spiritual matters.) Try not to overdramatize the situation. You're not in a movie. Please remember that anger and fear won't help.

Sometime that spring the college girl decided to go on vacation and left Gabe outside. I brought him inside the common hallway of the house and set up a makeshift bed and food for the week she was gone in the event she'd made a mistake or he'd escaped. When she returned she or her boyfriend took him from the hallway and put him back outside again. I was pissed.

Gabe pathetically hung around the house for a week, stretched out on his back on the porch waiting to be petted, hoping for a friend. I couldn't stand it anymore and took him in. He was a mess. All bones. He'd been eating garbage. I put him in the spare bedroom, where he proceeded to shit the most foul smelling feces for weeks. Gene was mad that there was a new cat in the place.

Gabe had fleas and ear mites which spread through the apartment and had to be fumigated. Dr. Latson, Gene's surgeon, cleaned him up good. He became my cat. Gene got used to him. They hang out, they fight, they play, and they fight. Gabe is now seriously overweight and he probably overeats to compensate for his week of starvation. He fears the food will disappear or that he'll be abandoned. Psychologically it's so obvious and human.

Selfish assholes get pets and then abandon them because they "can't handle it" when it doesn't work out exactly as they planned. To which I say, "Fuck you, handle it." You took on the responsibility for this life, now take care of it.

Recalling the Night of Skulls, writing it down, it sounds bonkers. I never imagined my life would take a Shirley MacLaine turn, but who can predict the future? It's hard to vouch for one's own honesty and sanity, but I'm not a bullshitter. Friends and enemies know I can be painfully direct. It's okay if people don't believe, though I'd prefer they did.

When politicians and religious leaders claim god has spoken to them I consider they may indeed have had an encounter with spirits. George W. Bush thought that god told him to run for President, and House Speaker Nancy Pelosi said she once felt the presences of suffragists Susan B. Anthony and Alice Paul at the White House. Ronald Reagan believed in ghosts. He and Nancy had a White House psychic they consulted regularly before making big decisions, and guests who've stayed in the Lincoln Bedroom report seeing the ghost of the Emancipator. (By the way, Lincoln dreamt of his own assassination three days prior to his death.)

Politicians have big egos, which makes them susceptible to troublemakers. Dark forces have little power on Earth unless we enable them, but any politician who's more interested in power than public service could be manipulated. Clever spirits use flattery to influence and deceive. If there's a covert spiritual war on Earth I imagine the most skilled and powerful spirits are employed to both positively and negatively influence world leaders, for a lot is at stake.

Please keep in mind, if a spirit tries to communicate with you, you can't be sure what it's after. Some skillfully misrepresent themselves at first; it takes experience to discern intent. Steve and I would never claim we can't be fooled by a clever visitor, and no one should. Sometimes I think it's a good idea to forget about this spirit stuff entirely and just live. It doesn't need to be the full-time focus of anyone's existence, and can lead to obsessive behavior, as I've detailed. An awareness that our choices have a moral component may be enough.

Gene and Gabe came into my life through less than ideal circumstances. I never planned to get one cat, let alone two, but they're a trip. As I write this, Gabe is trying to take over my left leg so that I'll scratch his head and belly, which I'm managing while typing one-handed. He's transferring massive amounts of white and black fur to my blue pants this very moment.

Over the years, as his boldness has grown, Gabe has learned to wake me between 2 and 4 a.m. to fill their food bowls. He lightly touches my face with a paw, claws retracted, until I wake. Gene watches the proceedings from the dresser above like a detached accomplice. Sometimes they camp at my face until I wake up. Gabe will come when called, because he knows what "milk" is and he knows about petting time. It seems like pets who get more attention are more stimulated and aware. I imagine it's vaguely like raising children. The more you engage them the more curious and alive they become.

TWENTY-THREE: GENE ESCAPES; SPIRITS GUIDE HIM HOME

Several years ago I bought my great grandparents' house from my father and aunt. Built in 1890, it's a big colonial in the Allentown neighborhood of Buffalo. Like many old houses, it needs constant work. When he retired a decade ago, prior to my interest in it, my father did extensive renovations of the exterior and lower apartment. Later my deceased grandparents came to my brother Steve in a vision to tell him they'd wanted my father to get the house in better shape for my eventual arrival all along. Since the purchase, both of my parents have been a great help in continuing the second floor renovations, room by room.

119

A few summers ago, in a moment of carelessness while working alone at my place, dad failed to close my apartment door, and Gene escaped. My father had no idea he'd gotten out. When I got home from work I couldn't find him anywhere and panic soon set in. My poor deaf indoor cat was on his own on the mean downtown streets! I felt sick. My brother Steve soon received a visit from our brother Justin letting him know Gene would be found in two days, but it didn't much console me. I wanted to believe it, but I was distraught.

I told my neighbors and put up posters on the block. My neighbor Rose has taken care of many strays, and believes in spirit stuff, too. She and her boyfriend John sing and play in a jazz group. Rose had a few helpful suggestions. The first was to get a small animal trap and stock it with tuna to lure Gene in. My father borrowed one and we put it out for a day. Her second idea was to scatter used cat litter around the perimeter of my house so that Gene might be better able to recognize it by scent if he wandered near.

On the second day Gene was missing, a hot Saturday, Rose phoned because she thought she'd spotted him and his big ears between houses. I ran to the location and saw Gene in a patch of weeds, about 20 feet away, but I was in silhouette and when I approached he ran away, climbing a high wooden fence. That night I heard him crying somewhere nearby. It sounded like he'd gotten into a fight with another animal. Being deaf, he has no idea how loud he is, and his voice is unmistakable, a distinguishing feature. It was torture.

At 4 a.m. I was sleeping lightly with my bedroom window wide open. I heard the loudest sustained crying outside, like an announcement. Somehow Gene was just below my window in my neighbor's driveway. I threw on a pair of shorts and booked down the stairs, practically tackling him. He was dusty and thirsty, and ran to the water bowl when we got back upstairs. Justin's message had been true, and I think Gene may have had some help getting back home.

The next nice summer day when we went out on the second floor porch Gene was different. Instead of exploring the perimeter, and ogling birds he hoped to devour but could never catch, he looked all around without moving from his comfortable place at my feet.

TWENTY-FOUR: LET'S BE LIKE JESUS

It's not hard to imagine that a man named Jesus lived two thousand years ago. He nobly wanted to help mankind, preached about love, charity, and humility, and was murdered for it, leaving aside for the moment whether he was sent on a mission from god or rose from the dead.

Jesus was persecuted for telling the truths of life as he saw them. He challenged the established order, those with an entrenched financial and political interest in the status quo, the powerful patriarchs and religious leaders who spent their lives climbing the social ladder, supporting and empowering those above them in the hopes they too would be buoyed by social subordinates. A sustained pyramid scheme in pursuit and support of entrenched power. Do you think these people were going to let some penniless philosophical hippie tear down their empire in favor of the dirty, stupid common man? Who does this man think he is to tell us how to live?

Those who persecuted Jesus built their lives upon corrupted religious, social, and political institutions. They had the most to lose should the falsehoods of that order be revealed by him, especially as he'd gained a sizeable following and couldn't be bought off. The paradigm might have flipped and they'd be shamed and ostracized, or worse. They perceived Jesus as the very real threat he was and conspired to engineer a downfall. Jesus probably anticipated this would happen and prepared for his fate as a martyr.

Jesus told truths which the powerful perhaps knew in their hearts but could not afford to admit. Instead of considering his message, the fearful authorities decided he must be discredited, slandered, killed. If Jesus came back today I fear the same thing would happen again. Radical Christians and Muslims would probably be most enthusiastic for him to fry. He'd tell them to stop being closed-minded and judgmental, and, more critically, to stop perverting religion for power and money, territory, social status, and the subjugation of women, which are contrary to empathy, generosity, compassion, and love.

(Countries with repressive, autocratic/religious governments are about *control*, and always patriarchal. Armed thugs want to dictate how people live. They want to govern the sexual behavior and reproductive choices of women, mostly so that they have a better chance of mating with them, or at the least, are able to prevent perceived rivals from doing so. An excessive desire for control is the unhealthy root of much mental illness and delusional ideology. The ultimate loss of control is the inability to prevent one's own death. It lies beneath all other obsessions. But no one controls life except god.)

Unfortunately, once any set of ideas, even great ones, becomes codified, they're always susceptible to manipulation. Over time, Jesus's teachings have been co-opted and exploited by many of the kind of people who helped get him killed. Most of those who really do "god's work on Earth," helping the less fortunate and treating their fellow man with respect, operate under the radar. Humility prevents them from seeking profit or influence simply for doing right. They're averse to the falseness of fame. I'm not this pure. Fame is unimportant, but I've long hoped to become a financially independent full-time artist after decades of 9-to-5, mostly so that I can live an art-centered life all the time. And maybe write another book!

I think of Jesus as a messenger, and feel there's crossover between his role and that of an artist. Each has a calling and is compelled to share what he knows, speaking the truth as he understands it, despite potential consequences. A good artist would be a bit like Jesus, trying to help himself and others become more realized and joyful. Still, it's valid to question any messenger/artist's motivations. Some posture for egotistical reasons, to cultivate fame more than anything. Some artists aren't really artists at all.

An insightful messenger/artist also helps us to see that great leaders - those we look to for inspiration and guidance, and often place on pedestals – began at the same starting point as you and I. Everyone starts from nothing, as no one. We create ourselves in time by accumulating experiences and knowledge, and maintaining an open mind. We're each responsible for claiming our own voice, even if it begins with the smallest bit of self-respect. It's *never too late* to become who you want to be. To change we need to own who we've been before we break ourselves down and start rebuilding.

Honest, idealistic loudmouths often end up as artists, be they musicians, writers, or comedians, or as political and social activists, or some combination. They stir things not simply to rile, but to, hopefully, encourage us to reflect and ponder the world more deeply, to help us become more real. To embody a way of life that doesn't require muting one's voice like the faceless kids falling into a meat grinder in Pink Floyd's *The Wall*.

Those most fearful of authority sometimes resist those willing to challenge mores, even when the goal is to advocate for greater equality and justice. The majority dislike being lied to by the rich and powerful on a regular basis. However, it's telling that what they also can't stand is someone who won't go along with the charade. We deeply crave authenticity in a fake world, but we don't always celebrate it when we discover it.

To some, the truth is offensive because it's impolite. Bigmouths often lack subtlety and come off preachy, which can alienate. It's hard to remain emotionally balanced when talking about how our entire genetically-modified, hormonally-injected food supply has become suspect. We don't know whether the government has been bought off by Massive Corporation of America or has always been run by a rich cabal. Banks scam us and make us pay for their greedy mistakes with our tax dollars. George Bush cynically infected important American regulatory agencies with cronies who ignored science. They abdicated their role as watchdogs to protect the public. His tenure felt like a sick victory of ignorant ideology over reality.

America's in a strange place. We hate our fake, corporatized culture, but we're addicted to it (thus the success of Amazon, McDonalds, Facebook, Coke, Wal-Mart, Apple, etc.), and resist change. We're used to being lied to every day. Advertising is based on emotional manipulation, and we're bombarded constantly by false messages of inadequacy. Other omissions seem intended to preserve polite civilization and keep you from questioning the social order, and those who benefit from it. It's not necessarily a sinister conspiracy, but sometimes it feels orchestrated.

There's nothing wrong with entertainment and distractions from the daily grind, but it's like candy. If it constitutes your entire diet you will get fat, lazy, and sick. If we don't exercise our brains sometimes, and debate difficult issues, then intellect will atrophy.

Even with its faults, American culture is still moving towards more honesty. If we compare the simple morality tales of 1950s family TV shows to what we have now, the contrast is amazing. There's much more nuanced writing, mostly on cable TV, with greater moral ambiguities explored.

Perhaps there isn't much honesty in public discourse because speaking certain truths can get you fired from your job, ostracized, jailed, harassed, or killed, depending on what you say and where. Russian journalists keep turning up dead when they write about the government sliding back towards an autocracy under President-For-Life Putin. In 2012, the Russian all-female punk rock band Pussy Riot were sentenced to prison for two years for conducting a musical protest against Putin and the Russian Catholic Church, which have been in league since he came to power.

Every social movement begins with a small handful of people who won't go along with an immoral status quo. Slavery, suffrage, the American labor movement, and Vietnam protests all started with idealists who acted from a belief in a higher moral law, as Jesus did, and paid a price for bucking the system. Tidal social waves begin small, but grow over time to a tipping point, forcing politicians to respond.

Oscar Wilde lampooned the elaborate pretenses of the powerful in his sharp-tongued plays, and, in turn, they used the justice system to incarcerate him for homosexuality, breaking his spirit. John Lennon, an honest, irreverent, and contradictory artist, was nearly chased out of the country by U.S. Immigration under Richard Nixon because of his peaceful bed-ins and loud-mouthed opposition to the Vietnam War. Lennon's F.B.I. surveillance and political persecution lasted five years, during which time he became understandably paranoid, and made no new records. Shortly after his return to music he was murdered by Mark Chapman.

At a Dublin concert in June 2004, my adolescent hero Morrissey announced the death of former President Ronald Reagan and said he would have preferred if then-President Bush had died instead. Not even I've wished death upon Bush or Reagan, and it would pointless to wish it on Dick Cheney since he's a cyborg. Morrissey's confrontational, though legal, remarks about Bush resulted in a visit from the F.B.I. He was also interviewed by British authorities for his anti-Thatcher song, "Margaret on the Guillotine."

- - -

When you're young the lack of honesty and substance in the culture can be offensive. It doesn't help you figure out who you want to be. Being young is about knowing little, but feeling everything. You haven't lived long enough to grasp how things work and don't work. In time, you'll become more comfortable with the fact that there are many awful things you'll never fully understand. You'll figure out enough to thrive. It's not just the young who don't understand why they don't understand the world, but young people have less experience and are less equipped to cope.

If you practice examining what you really feel about things, as opposed to how you *think* you should feel or how others react, then you'll be more aligned with your nature. The

126

further you get from your core, the less you'll be able to access and trust it. You'll be lost at sea by your own doing. Hope is the key to life, and joy the goal. It sounds fluffy, but it's true. Once you don't mind whether anyone thinks your ideas are sentimental or challenging, you're on the path to freedom. Belief is very powerful, and magic is real. If you recognize you deserve to be fulfilled, your thoughts will absolutely influence and steer your life towards that reality.

Trust your gut! Peer pressure is powerful, and groups often behave strangely, but if something doesn't feel right, then it's not, even if you don't know exactly why. You're not obligated to explain how you feel to anyone, though some will nosily pry. The tingly feeling of unease might be your cells sensing danger or ill will before your brain does, sounding an alarm you should heed.

Many young people aren't imaginatively cruel enough to conceive of the cynicism that corrupts others. People who lash out at us are damaged and lacking in self-esteem. When they mock you it's their fear or self-loathing they're projecting, or jealousy of your self-respect. Many (supposedly) heterosexual men avoid expressiveness because they associate verbosity and thoughtfulness with femininity. They fear association with those whose friendship might call their fragile sexual self-image into question.

No one with love in their life would try to make another person feel bad. The universe is moral. Assholes eventually get smacked by life, or in the next world.

To have some of your innocence stripped is unavoidable, but if you're able to maintain youthful idealism – that vital, hopeful spark – you'll live joyfully. Deep secrets unfurl for those who live with good intentions.

Jesus reportedly said, "How you treat the least among you is how you treat me." When I was a boy I hated when kids would gang up, as they inevitably do, on someone with a mental or physical disability. I observed that very few kids would object to the harassment of a weaker peer, even when they knew it was wrong, because they too feared being singled out or losing status in the tribe. There's little difference with adults. If we're not strong enough to defend the weak then we're failing the decency test.

A few years ago my brother was railroaded by a deceitful manager at his part-time job at a pet store. Perhaps she perceived him as an easy target. We thought about suing the company, but let it go. The process of retaliation would have added negative weight to our lives; how could it have been worth it even if we "won?"

You can choose to forgive screwed up people who mess with your livelihood, though some may incorrectly interpret your empathy as weakness. You'll notice repeated behaviors among the lost, see that their problems have nothing to do with you, and realize you're not obligated to try to fix them, figure them out, talk about them, or waste time contemplating them. You owe them nothing. Move on.

When you're young, it's hard to understand all of your own inclinations and actions as a spiritual being in a new, rambunctious animal's body. Your desires are natural, even the weird ones. Don't feel guilty about what you perceive as inappropriate feelings, but please be cautious about which you act upon, what you share about yourself, and with whom.

It can take a long time to see patterns in our lives. Some of us are self-destructive for years or decades. (Sadly, some never learn in this lifetime.) You may have to fully pass through a difficult stage and look back from a distance to understand why you felt and behaved as you did. I've done some astoundingly stupid things I can only partially explain. Forgive yourself for being dumb, and when no real harm is done. Apologize if necessary. Choose to learn from your mistakes.

It's easier to stay positive when you pursue what makes you feel alive. A lot of people stuff themselves into emotionally-stunted boxes because they're afraid or have internalized defeat. If you allow yourself to become yourself, you might have a longer road. Others often want you to be what serves them best, threatens them least, or makes them comfortable. They almost can't help themselves. Don't give up your essence and self-respect for nothing. We can become uniquely beautiful creatures who no longer seek or desire praise, and give up our animosity towards those we consider unenlightened. That's an evolved mindset I'm still working towards.

Mom says many people are "asleep." On our spiritual journey we've tried not to judge, but we don't always succeed. I don't know whether anyone is qualified to judge anyone else without compromising karma. Yet, to exist, we have to gauge intent constantly, if only to protect ourselves. We're bound to judge, and make mistakes when doing so, and we learn to live with it because there's no other way. Maybe when we die we end up judging ourselves.

There's only so much we can do to make life better, or are obligated to give. If we become more open, while simultaneously toughening up, it will flow naturally from us into our circles of influence. A single person can contribute a lot. Our positive impact on the lives of others may be greater than we'll ever know, even if built upon a small stream of courtesies, and seeing ourselves as part of the human race, neither above nor below anyone else.

Even someone as selfless as Mother Teresa was overwhelmed by her efforts to ease suffering. She said in all her years of service in Calcutta, and her constant prayers to god, she never once felt his presence. I don't know why, unless a lifetime of assisting the poor and ill exposed her to constant darkness. She tried to act as a filter, to absorb suffering and provide relief, but maybe it was too much. Did she feel she had to overcome it all by herself? Perhaps she eventually feared that suffering was the dominant human condition. Any of us fortunate enough to be able to feed ourselves, have shelter, and some material comforts should probably thank our stars for where and when we were born. And perhaps some responsibility also comes with that good fortune?

To focus on the negative is like staring into the abyss trying to reason with blackness. But to ignore it entirely is to live in a fantasy land like my nice, but deluded, Rush Limbaugh-loving cousins. Surely there's a balance. It's impossible to ponder darkness without being cooed by it. It's seductive because it seems to offer power. It strokes your ego, encouraging you to see yourself always as the center of existence, entitled to have your wants and needs addressed above others. Your focus, where your thoughts lie, is where you live in your mind. What you think and feel is what you are.

Courage is like a muscle. It gets stronger with persistent practice. It's a lifelong endeavor. Fear is a powerful inhibitor, but if you work at building your courage you will know what to do at the critical moments when someone really needs you or you're up against a bigger challenge. Practice courage. Any day is the right day to start.

TWENTY-FIVE: SEX GHOST

This is embarrassing, but true! One night I awoke from a realistic sex dream in an inspired state. (This has happened to you too, so cut me some slack.) Men know that once the blood has routed south the only options are to wait for a slow dissipation and reunification with the rest of the body, or to take matters into your own hands. (Or just your right hand.)

As I neared the finish line I realized a presence had been in the room with me the entire time! Yes, a ghost hung out while I buffed the banana, and perhaps helped set it in motion by spiking my dream content. Crazy.

In the home stretch I felt a female visitor's presence in my Third Eye, which heightened the sensation. At the summit a round of super high speed "head bobbing" began and I felt the teasing, giddy energy of the spirit. Sex Ghost's manic playfulness vaguely reminded me of my original tickling visitor, but the naughty aspect was damned odd. I didn't know spirits were interested in sex. Why would they be? They don't have bodies, do they? Or maybe my visitor wanted to make me feel good or have weird fun. I was too shocked to ask any questions afterward, and I've not had a visitor like that since.

(Later I wondered if spirits can enter the bodies of the living in order to share what we feel. Can ghosts surf our souls for a vicarious thrill? Apparently the answer is yes. In late 2013 I had a CD release show at a downtown Buffalo club. In the middle of the performance mom and Steve became aware of Justin's presence. Like our Mexican Room Warp, Steve felt the room shift as if it wasn't entirely real. Mom said, "Justin's here." Steve saw him "emerge" from one of the blue stage lights as if a small door had quickly opened and

131

closed, and felt a tap on his shoulder. Mom felt a light jab in her side. When she turned towards Steve she saw a white, shadowy trail, like an arm, between he and her. Justin asked Steve if he could watch my performance through his eyes. Steve said yes, and Justin jumped in, which freaked mom out when she heard about it later. Steve said Justin also sat at one of the tables near the front of stage, in an unoccupied chair.)

I didn't literally have sex with a ghost like in the movie *MacGruber*, which, by the way, is underrated and hysterically inappropriate, but supposedly pop singer Ke$ha did.

On a gross related note, mom told me she often felt watched by the presence of an elderly man in their bedroom when my parents first got married. The previous tenant was an old guy who'd died in the apartment. The bedroom creeped her out for years. Yuck.

TWENTY-SIX: OUT-OF-BODY TOMFOOLERY

A few summers ago I met a sassy 30-year-old woman after corresponding for a short while on an Internet dating site. We decided to meet for coffee downtown. She had a pretty, nearly intimidating face, and was well aware of her appeal. The spot was close to her apartment, but she was plenty late in the way self-absorbed, attractive people think they can be because they're confident you'll wait or they don't care if you don't. I'll allow a reasonable amount of time for anyone, but past a certain point you better be Penelope Cruz. Mmmm, *Penelope*.

Our emails had touched on a mutual interest in spiritual stuff. We jumped right in. Danielle expressed absolute confidence in her ability to manifest wishes into reality. Though she'd recently moved back to Buffalo, she claimed that a few years earlier she'd made her way to Florida on sheer will. She didn't have money, but she believed that putting her wish into the universe would get it answered. Someone eventually loaned or gave her enough to move, and she found odd jobs to do on an older guy's off-coast island, living lean in the sun. I'm not entirely sure if this constitutes influencing reality so much as the persuasive power of young female biology.

She may have tapped the other side, because anyone can. Anyone can muck it up, too, especially if they treat spirituality like their personal wish fulfillment service. I include myself in this critique. I found her pretentious, but also intelligent, like other semi-dangerous gals I have met who possess a certain charm but would incinerate you without blinking if they had heat vision. I didn't share much about my own spiritual experiences, and she was happy to talk about herself, so I listened and learned, interjecting occasionally.

As the summer sun descended, we relocated to an outdoor patio in a cute, low lit alley bar for drinks. It was a weeknight, with almost no one around but the waitresses. Danielle told me she had left her body multiple times, traveling and flying around rooms, something I've dreamt about for years, as many people do.

In my dreams I weave between telephone wires and big trees while floating down a street, and it's more a matter of levitation than an ability to fly, if that distinction makes a difference. I'm already potentially buoyant, and when I look at the ground and metaphorically toss off the sandbags holding down the hot air balloon that is me, I start to rise.

Danielle was certain she could leave her body again, but I said I thought she was too cavalier. How could she be sure

133

she had control? What if she left her body and couldn't get back inside? She admitted that, in one instance, she panicked because she wasn't sure how to get back. She saw her body below her, but didn't know what to do. Then somehow she got back inside.

(If I've painted her unflatteringly, one thing she said was spot on. When tempted to judge the seemingly poor life decisions of other people, she says to herself, "This has nothing to do with me." By withholding judgment she keeps her space free of negative energy. I do this more often since I met her. It's helpful.)

Spirits will almost certainly help you leave your body, and achieve other odd magical feats, but since you can never be completely sure who's assisting you and why, you can lose control of the situation as Danielle did. It reminded me of my mom's incident with the Native American animal guide and when I got obsessive about spiritual matters before the Night of Skulls.

I've never left my body, but have been close a few times. My brother Steve said it's happened to him without trying. He's observed himself from the top corner of a room, just the way you hear people describe it, as has my ex-girlfriend Jane, my first head bobbing eyewitness. My mom freaked when Steve told her. Though he wasn't afraid, he's since decided to no longer allow himself to leave his body for fear of a loss of control. Steve has dialed back most of his spiritual contact in the last few years because he found it overwhelming.

Since I'm human and stupid, despite cautioning Danielle about leaving her body, I was curious to see what more I could learn. A few days later I lay down to take a nap with my cat Gabe curled against my side. I pet his stomach, closed my eyes, asked if any spirits were passing by, and made a quick contact. I screened them quickly. I should have been more thorough, though I didn't sense ill intent.

I asked whether it would be possible to leave my body and float around the room, but I wasn't sure I'd go through with it. I felt the familiar, intense pressure of a presence in my Third Eye. As the stress increased, my head involuntarily tilted back into the pillow. It felt like my skull was being pushed down through the pillow and my body was passing into the bed, but I believe what actually happened was the opposite. It was the sensation of my essence being ripped upward, away from my body. I could feel my body below me simultaneously, held down while my soul rose up. I had my hand on Gabe the entire time to keep me grounded. I'd already decided if I could no longer feel him then I'd stop.

As the forehead pressure increased, my neck tilted back further and my spine arched. The pressure made my mouth open and curl, and the base of my skull tingled. I started to make an inadvertent moaning sound, an extended "ahhh" that was almost painful, somewhat pleasurable, intense, and fascinating. The force was now extreme. Gabe was scared by the moaning and jumped off the bed. With reliable connection to the material world broken, I'd pushed the experiment far enough. I broke off contact by opening my eyes and sitting up. The feeling dissipated.

I'd felt in control up until that point, but to let it proceed any further would've been foolish. Especially because, as I continue to harp, I couldn't fully understand the forces I was interacting with. I haven't attempted it again and won't. I've confirmed to my own satisfaction that it's possible to leave one's body, though we probably shouldn't. One of my brother's friendly visitors also strongly advised against astral projection and said it has nothing to do with faith.

TWENTY-SEVEN: COLLECTIVE ENERGY

Comedian Bill Hicks said, "All matter is merely energy condensed to a slow vibration, and we are all one consciousness experiencing itself subjectively. There is no such thing as death, life is only a dream, and we are the imagination of ourselves." I like that a lot. Is it true? I definitely believe our individual energies can interact and coalesce, to become a single more powerful energy under the right circumstances.

Think of the rush you feel at a large sporting event or rock concert. The excitement of the crowd is palpable. There's a feeling "in the air." This often-used choice of words is telling, much like "feeling someone's vibe." There literally *is* a feeling in the air, or more precisely, the energy of everyone's feelings all at once. In a hockey arena with 20,000 people that's a lot of juice.

As previously mentioned, every thought we have is released as energy, consuming calories for its creation. The resting brain burns about a tenth of a calorie per minute. The intensely active brain burns up to a calorie and a half. Our thoughts radiate outward whether we're paying attention or not. Perceptive individuals can pick them up. The sum of all thoughts and feelings in the air unconsciously affects everyone.

The crowd is a critical part of any sporting event and can affect the outcome. Fans are never separate from the players. If the home team is dominant, the crowd feels it and responds with loud support, initiating momentum. The arena starts rocking; the energy level builds and starts to cycle.

If the crowd brings anxiety and fear, it can hang heavy and adversely affect the home team as well, especially if things don't start well. When the visiting team senses that the crowd and home team aren't unified, the collective feeling of discomfort can be used to their advantage instead. Fear is a heavy feeling, but hope is more powerful. Hope and courage are inseparable, which is why players with strong "character" are the most dominant and valuable.

When a huge crowd cheers loudly the waves of sound resonate in your body and are absorbed by your cells. Positive vibrations help you get caught up in it. This is partly why professional sports are so popular. Each individual becomes aware of the greater shared feeling, and inhibitions diminish. (Beer also helps.) The energy can become collective and unified, and we may experience a harmonious, pleasurable unity of mind and purpose.

A large crowd can turn ugly if things aren't going well. Negative energy affects everyone differently. Some people barely notice or shrug it off, but to others it's like a pheromone floating in the air, triggering an aggressive response. The animal is awakened and, if someone is already inherently confrontational, or two sheets to the wind, then a collective bad feeling can incite him.

This is analogous to how we sometimes perceive "bad vibes" in a room of people the moment we walk into it. If an argument has taken place, we can feel the hostility in the air. The black energy of the arguers' anger collects in the space, hanging like a fart.

When any two people meet and shake hands, communication occurs even if no words are spoken. Their energies, auras, interact in the space between. Suspicion or hostility may be immediately perceived, and conversely, friendliness and openness. One becomes more perceptive when the ego is minimized. If you're wrapped in your own concerns, or are excessively self-consciousness, you're not open to what other people are putting out. You're trapped inside yourself.

I like when parties get loose and people are silly and playful. A few drinks into the evening, the social lubricant does its duty, and we let more of our true selves show. When laughter fills a room it's intoxicating. Joyful collective energies pack a lot of power. A room of people enjoying each other's companionship, celebrating the good fortune of another day on Earth, is a little slice of heaven, and a preview of the big joy to which we'll return. I like to think of the afterlife as a fun, unending carnival populated with everyone we've ever known, when all is forgiven, like the closing scene of Fellini's *8 1/2*.

Of course, if our spirits survive death, we'll presumably be disembodied. The priorities of our animal side will be dispatched. Part of me mourns the loss of the body, because sex and beer are great! However, my brother's visions imply there are different physical realms to explore, and my visit by Sex Ghost suggests sexuality somehow remains of interest to spirits, though I don't know why. Perhaps as pure essence we can choose different physical manifestations of ourselves, and otherwise exist as consciousness and intelligence. The best of both worlds.

TWENTY-EIGHT: GLOBAL CONSCIOUSNESS AND SYNCHRONICITY

I'm not a big fan of organized religion, but I've been intrigued to read about prayer experiments aimed at reducing gang violence in urban areas. This reminds me of the collective prayers of Buddhist monks for the proliferation of loving-kindness. Buddhists believe in vibrations too, and that when certain sounds and words, called mantras, are repeated they arouse good vibrations within a person that can open them up to a greater consciousness. Buddhist monks attempt to pool the sum of their individual prayers into more powerful collective prayers for peacefulness and empathy.

It seems that individual and collective positive energy can be focused upon an objective and affect change. What's unknown is just how far-reaching these efforts could be if hundreds or thousands of people decided to focus on simple, positive goals together. How much does our quantum reality bend towards good thoughts and prayers to make the world a better place? I'd like to believe quite a lot.

Scientists too have taken interest in the intentional and accidental coalescence of energies, applying statistical analysis to what was once thought to be an immeasurable, mystical realm. There have been some interesting experiments about the synchronization of human feelings and collective awareness. One of the first I became aware of is ongoing at Harvard University.

Harvard initiated the *Global Consciousness Project* in 1998. Academia would call it a parapsychology project. I don't speak academic, so I'll describe it as I understand it. It's an experiment to determine whether human consciousness can be detected and measured by inorganic "physical systems" like a computer. Sixty-five computers, called "Eggs," are positioned in labs around the world. The computers are programmed to act as random number generators. They spit out arbitrary data on a continual basis, independent of one another. Researchers discovered that when an event of global significance occurs, one that millions or billions of people are aware of at the same time, the random data being generated by the Eggs begins to take on a pattern, and that pattern is mirrored at each of the computer sites. Why would a bunch of independent computers generating random numbers suddenly begin to correlate unless the energies we radiate are measurable and affective?

The Eggs recorded a huge data spike when September 11 occurred. Researchers were intrigued that data correlation not only ramped up during and after the event, but for a few days *before* it happened, too. Great numbers of people seemed to sense or became aware of this impending disaster in advance, which means our understanding of time is incomplete, and also that precognition is possible. As I've said previously, I believe all of history has always existed. The past, present, and future are already written, but the only way to experience it as a mortal is sequentially, as separate moments. Psychics have been in demand for centuries because they can perceive a greater reality beyond the present, and predict future events of importance.

(One might argue that the reason the Egg data spiked in advance of September 11 is that the thoughts of those involved in planning and executing the attack were picked up by the Eggs, but even if hundreds or thousands of people - the population of a small town - knew the plan in advance, that's still very few people compared to the global population. My understanding is that the Eggs only register a spike when an event occurs that is known or experienced by millions, hundreds of millions, or even billions.)

Two days prior to September 11 I had a graphic dream about the destruction of an enormous expansion bridge in a major city that was not my hometown of Buffalo. I stood near the base of the bridge and, as I looked up, noticed that the tremendous stone gargoyles perched at the top were shaking. Pieces crumbled off, and I realized it wasn't just the gargoyles but the whole bridge that was beginning to fall. I was paralyzed with fear and everything happened in slow motion. I saw the pieces coming at me and everyone else around, but was unable to move. A massive cloud of white dust rose as the bridge pieces began crashing to the ground. Then I woke up.

I feel other aspects of synchronicity consistently. Some incidents are bigger than others. As previously mentioned, when a friend I haven't seen in a while comes to mind, an email, text, or phone call often follows within a few hours, as if I've either sensed the forthcoming communication in advance, or by thinking of them, they get a quantum message from me and decide to get in touch. We might consider this small potatoes, but the frequency of these experiences makes it harder to dismiss.

A few times a week I work out at the university pool. The youngsters blast by me, but I often get them on distance by swimming up to 90 minutes at a time. The swims were shorter until I bought an underwater mp3 player. I set the mp3 player to random play. Sometimes I know what song will play next a split second before it comes on. I feel the future, even though the interval of time is very small, a fraction of a second. I imagine that more evolved spiritual beings are able to see that much further ahead. Recently, when singer Josh Clayton-Felt came to mind, a few of his songs played in sequence even though the mp3 player is filled with 60 or 70 songs by various artists.

When my copy editor Kristy worked on this book, and was deep into the chapter about dark spiritual traffic, she said her stereo began to play unusual, discordant jazz song after song, even though it was set on random. I speculated that her exposure to, and thoughts about, some of these ideas kicked energies into the air that altered her space. Her stereo acted like one of the Harvard Eggs, playing songs in a more specific pattern instead of randomly. It synchronized with the energy of her thoughts, or some spirits wanted her to experience connectivity first-hand, to help her believe what she read, or to try to freak her out if they were mischievous.

When my musical group performed a few winters ago at the Hard Rock Café in Niagara Falls, we had an oddball occurrence of musical synchronicity. We'd just finished our one-hour set of songs, performing all original music, and another band was preparing to perform the final set of the evening. We shared equipment with them to make the transition between bands quicker.

The large bank of TVs behind the stage and around the restaurant played music videos when we first arrived, with audio pumped through the house sound system. When our set was over the staff turned the house TVs and music back on. The next two videos that played were "Band on the Run" by Paul McCartney and "Sir Duke" by Stevie Wonder. We were packing up our instruments while the next band brought theirs onstage. The singer from the next band told me that those exact songs by McCartney and Wonder were on their setlist to perform that evening. "Band on the Run" and "Sir Duke" also happened to be the only songs they'd perform that weren't written by their band. What are the chances of that? Again, far smaller than winning the lottery.

About a week later there was another synchronous music-related event. While editing music on my computer, I dug out an old demo for a song called "Shiver." With fresh ears it sounded good again, and I thought I might add it to my next CD. When I was done I shut down the computer and turned on the TV. I dialed through my half-dozen non-cable channels and found a music videos show. The band Coldplay performed a song called "Shiver," which I'd never heard before. The song title flashed on the screen at the end.

The next morning I wrote a note on my Facebook music page about the "Shiver" event, and also described the synchronous incident with the McCartney/Wonder songs at the Hard Rock show. (I also dreamt about the Beatles last night, by the way.) My cousin Mike, who performed with me at the Hard Rock show, replied in the form of lyrics from a song by The Police on the subject called "Synchronicity:" "Many miles away / something crawls from the slime / at the bottom of a dark Scottish lake."

That part of the lyric refers to the Loch Ness Monster, but the song is primarily about a middle-aged suburban man whose home life and work life are a mess. At the start of the song, something monstrous (the Loch Ness Monster) is stirring at the bottom of a lake, like the man's anger bubbling. Later, the creature surfaces. At the end of the song, a monster's "shadow" is on his door as the man nears home after a humiliating day at work. It's implied that he may do something terrible to his family.

Immediately after reading Mike's comment, I jumped to another website tab and saw a news article about someone supposedly capturing video footage of the Loch Ness Monster.

To summarize, a third synchronous event (seeing the article about the Loch Ness Monster, which is referenced in the song "Synchronicity," and was quoted by Mike) occurred immediately after I'd detailed two previous, related incidents *of* synchronicity, one of which involved Mike, leading him to mention a song *about* synchronicity, and all three synchronous events are related to music. Coincidence? No way.

143

This was mirrored in the summer of 2014 when my 1950s side band Wood Candy performed at Marinaro's Larkin Tavern in Buffalo's First Ward district. We did a three-set show from 8 to 11 p.m. The band was really cooking, each set a little hotter than the last. The crowd was supportive and very responsive, with lots of dancing, which always makes musicians feel good.

Our show consisted primarily of songs by Chuck Berry, Little Richard, Jerry Lee Lewis, Elvis, and Ray Charles, with a dash of Hank Williams, Johnny Cash, and Howlin' Wolf ("Back Door Man!"). People often ask for songs from other decades, but I don't know that many covers outside the ones I've learned for the group, and we try to stick to the format.

At the end of the show they applauded for encores. A gentleman of about 60 shouted for James Brown and said he'd buy the entire bar a drink if we did one. I love James Brown, but most of his hits are from the '60s. I wasn't even sure I could sing that high, but we jumped into "I Feel Good" anyway. And it felt pretty damned good! They loved it. (We might have to break the rules again for that one.) At the end of the song I told the guy to break out his credit card.

When Chris, one of the bar owners, turned the radio back on the next song that played was "I Feel Good." At first I thought maybe someone had picked it on the jukebox, wanting to hear it again after our performance, but Chris said the radio was tuned to an oldies station.

Two days later a friend and I went to the late show at a comedy club in the Cobblestone district. It was great. (Thanks, Pete Holmes.) After the show we stopped at a new bar with a bicycling theme (bar stools with ornate cast-iron foot pedals) a few blocks away on Swan Street. We ordered drinks. The next song that came on the sound system was "I Feel Good." A big grin broke out on my face.

A few weeks later I treated myself to a rare Monday evening out at a Belgian beer bar I love. The deejay was playing fun '70s and '80s R&B/pop, like Michael Jackson, Prince, (Buffalo's own) Rick James, Earth, Wind & Fire, Sheila E., and Bell Biv Devoe. His collection was entirely vinyl, mostly 45 RPM singles. I had two songs in mind to request: "She's a Bad Mama Jama," by Carl Carlton, and "Sensitivity," by Ralph Tresvant. I thought Tresvant might be too obscure, so I asked for Carlton. He played it a few minutes later; I flashed a friendly smile and peace sign from the bar. Two songs later he played the Tresvant song I'd been thinking of, but had decided not to ask for. He got my thought!

I was giddy and wanted to share what had just happened. I'm friendly with Lisa and Mike, two of the bartenders, so I told them. Then I told them about the James Brown song, and how it was just the tip of the synchronistic iceberg. Inevitably, Lisa told me that she and her brother are both somewhat clairvoyant. Earlier that day she'd received three phone calls from three different people immediately after discussing each of them with her co-workers and friends.

The energy of the room became noticeably more joyful. More people who knew Lisa arrived, hugs followed. It felt like a great private party with me as omniscient observer. Sitting at the bar I felt excited about the steadily increasing episodes of synchronicity. I hoped they were signs of something greater to come, like a joyful spiritual movement that spreads like wildfire and embodies hope. I want to see a love revolution of any size, but preferably huge!

So many synchronous moments have happened since 1997 that I almost take them for granted. I remind myself to be amazed. It's in tune with my new beliefs about reality.

A synonym of synchronicity is *harmony*. When we align with the vibrations of love and good will, we're in harmony with the universe. At minimum, synchronicity is proof of the possibilities for mysterious, deeper connectivity. The secret of life is that magic is real.

TWENTY-NINE: SUFFERING AND EMPATHY

Thankfully, I've never been in combat or had to kill someone to survive, but I know what being close to the bottom feels like. Millions or billions of people have been overwhelmed by life and contemplated suicide, and plenty have succeeded. Living through low times and coming out the other side smiling is like surviving a near-death experience and getting a second chance at life. I'm grateful. I hope to take advantage of it for a long time.

Most people who feel suicidal don't want to die. They feel powerless and don't want to be in pain anymore, and can't envision things ever getting better. The feeling can be so black it makes the future seem impossible. What often helps a person out of the hole is the passing of time and a change of perspective, plus counseling, medication, and/or family support. Some people manage to hang on long enough to outgrow the feeling of extreme despair. What follows may not be happiness exactly, but a safe harbor where you can catch your breath.

If you rest there long enough and the daily panic gradually subsides, you might imagine a day will come when you'll feel good. Then one comes. Even though you fear allowing yourself to feel hopeful, it's followed by another good day soon after. Then the better days start to rival the bad ones in frequency and you find yourself less focused on sadness. A change is gradually occurring that you may not notice until years later. Then you look back and realize how far you've come, and how much you've improved. You feel like a different person, and you literally are, right down to your cells.

Every cell in the body has a finite life span and is eventually replaced by a new one. With 75 trillion cells it takes 7 years for a person to become completely new biologically. There are many references to the number 7 in Christianity, from the Seven Days of Genesis to Seven Seals of Revelation. In Scripture 7 supposedly symbolizes completeness or perfection, though I'm reluctant to endorse any religious text. (At age 43 I guess I've started my 7th cycle of 7 years?)

It's no surprise that many veterans suffer from depression. Military suicides are way up because we've been in a near-constant state of war since the invasion of Afghanistan. (Don't even mention Iraq. As far as I'm concerned, George Bush and especially Dick Cheney are war criminals for starting a war under false pretenses and manufactured intelligence.) When you're trained to kill like an emotionless machine, the essence of your humanity is suppressed and compromised. Being rewarded for the successful destruction of other human beings is an enormous contradiction to overcome once you exit the service.

Recently I had the opportunity to help a young veteran get through an angry moment. It happened late on a Saturday "hip hop night" at a bar on Allen Street, half a block from my home. I've been going for years to booze and dance, though I'm one of the older people now.

I stood inside their small fenced-in patio, handing out postcards for a jazz-hip hop show I was promoting across town (the Robert Glasper Experiment, who later won a Grammy). I'd been at it an hour and a half and had a few drinks. Most of the young white kids going inside didn't give a shit about the show, but it's a percentages game. Give out a few thousand postcards and hope you get a 5 to 10 percent return, and don't take the 90 percent rejection personally. The more enthusiastic responses were from black patrons, who were also the happiest looking people.

By 1 a.m. the crowd was several drinks deep. A thin, muscular young woman of about 25, with straight brown hair in a tight ponytail, in jeans and a buttoned white shirt with little make-up, yelled over the patio railing at a tall, overweight young man with his back turned to her. The man's two female friends looked on helplessly. When I turned towards them one said to me, "She's nuts. She just came up and started yelling at him."

The young woman's name is Ginny. She stood outside the patio, leaning on the railing with a plastic cup in her hand. Water or vodka? Probably the later. Her eyes and gestures were wild. She's an Iraq War veteran. My inhibitions were low from the beers. From personal experience, I instantly recognize someone in great pain. I engaged her.

Ginny's combat experiences caused obvious damage. She was traumatized by all of the killing, and by the gruesome deaths of several of her colleagues. ("People have no idea what it's like to see your friend die with blood coming out of their eyes.") She admitted she harassed the overweight guy because she despised what she perceived as his softness and naivety. She was angry at nearly everyone there because she considered them clueless and shallow, and many probably were. While she was in Iraq getting shot at they were back here partying.

Ginny resented that they could not know what she did; that life can be brutal and things are so bad in some seemingly-cursed places that 9-year-olds are pushed into a cocaine habit to warp them into child soldiers who will shoot at enemy soldiers. American prosperity has insulated us from much suffering, another reason I don't always trust an entitled American perspective about the world, though I love my country.

I'll never comprehend Ginny's experiences, but I related to her resentment. In the not so distant past I used to get angry at nearly everyone around me for failing to acknowledge the fragility of life, and being unwilling to pursue a more enlightened existence, the way I felt I had. When I perceived pettiness it would set me off. But self-righteous anger is ultimately consuming, and it blinds you from seeing much of the goodness in people.

Ginny needed to vent. Her hurt appeared deep. At first she was foaming, but my mellowness seemed to calm her. Her face changed, from wild-eyed like a hurt animal, to softer and more in control as she understood I wasn't judging her and didn't consider her crazy.

I told her that it isn't satisfying, but that the dumb young people at the bar almost weren't to blame for their immaturity. They could have no idea why she'd become so angry, they would probably never know, and of course it was grossly unfair. Ginny said she was glad they'd been spared what she'd seen.

I suggested she probably chose the young man as a target because she perceived him as easy, like low-hanging fruit.

Even if he was an underachiever, Ginny was simply passing on her self-loathing. Maybe he had a rich inner world, and if we put ourselves in his shoes we'd see him differently. But, in that moment of anger, she found him disgusting. She said the military would never let him get or stay that fat. She'd become disciplined and tough, but intolerant. Her empathy was understandably diminished, like mine.

I said he probably wasn't happy to be fat. Ginny said that in the army a woman has only two options, to toughen up, or become a repeated rape victim. She had clearly decided to embrace her aggression and not be victimized. It felt parallel to my high school decision to fight my way through life without apology. We're both guilty of overcompensation. It's harder to dial back aggression once you've discovered its effectiveness, and if one's choices are to be savaged or to fight, fighting will win. You can lose touch with the better side of yourself though. We need tenderness too, and it can be hard to preserve without feeling like a sucker.

Ginny passed on her hurt, but she admitted it didn't make her feel better about herself. I understood why she felt that way, but it still wasn't okay. I said it wouldn't stop the cycle of anger, only perpetuate it. She agreed.

Fifteen minutes earlier I'd observed Ginny on the dance floor with two different women. I assume one was her girlfriend because she made a reference to her outside. Before we met, my impression was that she was forceful, possibly desperate. I noted the body language between her and the women. Ginny wanted to get more physical and was trying to initiate contact. (Forceful men try this all the time with women at clubs.) But each woman was uncommitted physically, turned slightly away from her.

I imagined other aspects of her life. She was having trouble with relationships since her return because she needed a lot of emotional support from other people, but was perhaps too aggressive in trying to get it, as I was. It easily causes miscommunication or discomfort. People shy away when they sense a combination of neediness and anger. There was no way many of the people in her life could see things as she does now.

Ginny was eventually discharged by the military when she broke her leg and literally could no longer walk. She would have served another tour of duty otherwise. I said that, although a broken leg is a serious injury, perhaps it was meant to happen so that she didn't have to return. She agreed.

I said it might take years to work through her anger, but that she would be okay in time. I sincerely believed it. I thought that a therapist could be helpful because they're not supposed to be your friend, they're paid to listen without judgment. She didn't think the V.A. would be much help. I said I didn't know, but if that was true she needed to find help outside the system. She needed to do whatever she had to to help herself, because no one else can.

We talked for about 15 minutes, then she said, "Let's go do a shot!" We walked inside together, energized by the emotional connection, and did a celebratory shot at the crowded bar. We hugged. I said I knew she'd be okay in time. She ran off to rejoin her friends.

Ginny helped me too. When I arrived I was feeling disconnected, but the conversation snapped me snap out of it. Funny how, when others need us, we're sometimes able to shelve or sort our own problems. The room seemed friendlier than before; I felt like I was glowing. I even began to feel flirtatious, and tried making eyes at a few women in the bar. I didn't feel any immediate connections, but then two African American women I've never met ran over and gave me random hugs, which made me smile. Is joyful energy that radiant and obvious that we want to run up and grasp it?

We recover from devastations. We don't need to suffer indefinitely and we won't. If we can ride out tough periods, even just treading water, in time we feel differently about our situation. Surviving the feelings at the bottom is all we need to do for the moment. Sometimes it's best to keep it simple and make your goal just getting through the day.

If I had the power I would probably try to fix anyone in pain. Suffering has troubled me since I was very young, partly, but not entirely, because of my brother's physical issues. My feelings were magnified as an alienated teen and adult. My mom's family experiences are mixed in, too.

But if you or I were able to prevent someone's suffering would it really be a favor, or might it rob them of critical experience? When we witness anguish on a large scale, as when countries are at war, we wonder what, if anything, we can do to help people halfway around the world we don't even know. Why won't someone make it stop? Why doesn't god intervene?

Unfortunately, there's practically no limit to the depth of suffering some must endure. But if suffering had built-in limitations imposed by god, then so too would powerful happiness be necessarily limited. Without some misery, we wouldn't know the difference between deep pain and joy, or have an opportunity to create ourselves by choosing between courage and cowardice.

Powerful, transforming bliss is available. It's waiting to wrap its arms around us, to transform the everyday into the extraordinary. The world is a dangerous place, but we can be brave enough to empathize and love.

Protecting the innocent and weak is one of the noblest instincts, even though it can place a courageous person in peril. When we do as much as we're able then we can live with our choices and maintain self-respect, even if we don't achieve our goals or fail to fully protect others from harm. We inch closer to heaven.

As I finished editing this chapter on my second-floor porch, a gospel band played out of sight, blocks away, their sound deep and celebratory in the early July evening air. The singer just let out a fantastic James Brown wail that mirrors the way I feel inside. Life can be sweet.

THIRTY: BLACK WAVES

My friend John saw black waves of evil in the air.

John's a full-time musician, living outside of New York City. He teaches private music lessons in Manhattan, going from one apartment complex to another. Like me, John's a "sensitive." He's always had an interest in, and awareness of, the supernatural.

In October 2012 John was teaching at the apartment building where Dominican-born nanny Yoselyn Ortega allegedly murdered two young children in her care. During the lesson he heard commotion and sirens outside, and went down to the lobby fearing a fire had started. When the door to the elevator opened, he experienced a chaotic scene, and a police cordon. He asked the doorman, who was noticeably shaking, "What happened?" The disturbed man said, "The nanny killed those kids." John heard a woman, the mother, screaming in agony. Her cries were the worst shrieks, nearly inhuman, that he's ever heard.

John had the sensation that time had broken down. People seemed to be moving in slow motion and everything felt "unreal," as if he was watching a movie. Psychologists call this a dissociative experience. The bodies of the children lay wrapped in white sheets on a yellow-framed stretcher. He could feel the darkness like a chill in the air and when he looked up he saw black waves swirling above the bodies of the children: spooky apparitions which soon departed. John thought he might be hallucinating, but whatever was occurring, he felt he was in the presence of pure evil, and I believe him.

John found himself standing only a few feet behind the traumatized mother. She moaned, holding her only living child tightly in her arms. She swayed back and forth uncontrollably and sometimes she would look up to the ceiling and utter something indecipherable to god. This seemed to last forever. Eventually, a calm, white-haired detective placed a large white handkerchief over mother and child and escorted them to an ambulance. Shortly after, John left the scene, amidst a media frenzy.

The incident left him deeply troubled. In the following months he had difficulty sleeping, suffered from nightmares, and experienced persistent, involuntary flashbacks of the scene while awake. He sought the help of a therapist who identified his emotional state as Post-Traumatic Stress Disorder.

A couple of months later, John woke up alarmed in the middle of the night. He felt like he was having a panic attack. In his mind he told himself, "It's coming back! The evil is coming back!" The next morning, the horrific shootings at Sandy Hook Elementary School in Newtown, CT took place. John had a premonition of the return of the same dark forces he had witnessed in Manhattan.

I suggested that the incident at the apartment complex had temporarily sensitized him to darkness. This is something that they love, for us to be aware of their power and afraid of them. Our courage and hope, and belief in the dominance of love, are our best weapons, especially when wielded calmly without anger or hatred.

John and I have a habit of getting into lengthy text message exchanges. A few months later he wrote me a message in several parts: "I saw a ghost of a woman sitting at my dining room table last night as I walked up the driveway. Thought it must be Amanda (his wife) but she was in bed. It was very late. Peaceful spirit though. I didn't mind. Every now and then I have spirit sightings. Well, like perhaps once every few years. We have a VERY OLD pre-United States cemetery near our home. 1st Continental Army camped out where my lawn is now back in the 1780s. I feel the presence of very old spirits sometimes in my village.

"Seriously, where I live could very easily be used as background for Halloween-themed movies. It is beautiful, not creepy, but about as old as America gets. Old colonial fences and homes built as far back as the 18th century. Mine is a new one built in 1900."

I wrote, "I have no trouble believing that. In my mind the spirit of anyone who's ever lived could pop in and out to say hello. My recent problem is making sure I stay connected to this physical world because I feel it would be very easy to trip out and disappear or fall somewhere between worlds if I contemplate it too deeply. I may be overly connected at present. Ironic that finding the 'truth' about reality and life after death means needing to be careful not to lose touch with this world & time."

John said, "Most spirits that wish to make their presence known are disgruntled. She was just praying peacefully. I knew when I entered into my home that she would leave. She is welcomed anytime. I think I am in HER space."

I wrote, "I've experienced many comforting spirits. They are definitely more subtle but they can be felt fairly often. Her prayers are for you and your family and your well-being. What a kind thing. You're being watched over perhaps because she knows you have experienced the underside recently. The knowledge of darkness is hard to reconcile. But beauty and innocence wins."

John: "We must always be careful but being over-connected should not be an overt worry because we are all one anyway... there is no disconnect. You might make me cry. You are right (about the woman coming to pray)."

Me: "(Smiley face.) Sleep well, pal. Hopefully we'll all be watched over and cared for. I feel that's how it will be indeed. Cheers!"

John: " 'Knowledge of darkness.' I like how you phrased that. Good word choice. I wish I had never been there, Rob."

Me: "I know. And I think of so many people who have faced great darkness with bravery. Love's about the only recourse available. There's a ton of positive energy in love. Try to focus on all the good stuff. That woman came to help you. Which is awesome."

John: "Thanks pal. I appreciate your keen insights. Indeed, love is the great mitigator. (Smiley face.)"

Me: "Happy to help! It helps remind me to focus on the good stuff too."

Two weeks passed. I heard from John again by text and we picked up the conversation at the same spot: "Never saw that spirit again. I wouldn't mind if she came back."

Me: "Just because she's unseen doesn't mean she's not around. (Smiley face.) But since you've invited her, maybe she'll appear."

John: "I wouldn't mind if she did. Her peacefulness was calming. She seemed pure and pious. Can these spirits ever talk? I would like to hear what her thoughts are. My dead grandfather once spoke to me."

Me: "My brother converses with them more regularly. So, the answer is yes. You could speak to her even without seeing her, I'd imagine. Then she may be able to get back to you."

John: "She is from sooo long ago. Must be easily 1700s... not sure what to ask. I suppose just be 'natural.' She will hopefully understand."

Me: "Yep, just speak naturally. It's like any conversation. Sincerity is key, as you know."

John: "You know on (Feb 17, 2013) when we were texting I asked if 'she' was here to communicate. I was out in my back porch room smoking a butt. A few moments later, the door to inside my main house opened. Yes, it could have been wind but it was a completely still night and I don't recall the door ever doing this. Almost sounds like something in a damn movie. It didn't scare me or creep me out though. It almost felt peaceful. I've always been so scared of ghosts. This one doesn't rattle me and almost feels comforting. It's new territory for me."

Me: "A lot of people seem scared of ghosts. I've been fortunate - my big events have all been peaceful and joyful. Not frightening. Fear attracts fear. And peacefulness attracts peace. If you feel good vibes and stay positive then you should be good."

John: "The strongest ghost encounter I had was with a man who had been murdered at point blank range and it was an awful, frightful experience. I still shudder to recall it in my mind. This spirit was sooo angry. I realized that I had attracted this spirit because I was not mindful in my approach to the spirit realm."

Me: "Yep, gotta respect it. Anyone can get hung up on thinking of it as a fun thing to dabble in, like a hobby. But the stakes are real and they will definitely let us know it if we get flippant. Fortunately the darkest visitor I ever had - I treaded carefully to collect information on how they think. Their goal is to expand suffering. But joy is wayyy more powerful. Right down to our DNA unfurling and reaching out."

It's great that John and his family have someone peaceful watching them. The calmness he experienced in her presence reminds me of the powerfully positive experiences I've had. It's hard to explain to someone who's not yet experienced it that, in the presence of a pure spirit, there's no fear whatsoever, only clarity and deep joy. It's an incomparable feeling.

Good spirits want to help us. We might think of it as a prayer, but really it's just asking for the involvement of greater goodness. It's asking god to come closer to help you, and the world. Perhaps someday I'll be a spirit who helps others, too. You can ask good spirits to help guide you with something specific or general, but you might not always get an immediate or obvious answer. They want to help, but sometimes they have other priorities. You might not get exactly what you want, though there's always a bigger plan. If a good spirit assists you, don't forget to say thanks. I imagine even spirits like to feel appreciated.

THIRTY-ONE: DOES GOD CHEAT?

I've had lots of fun, odd musical adventures. I sang with a Buffalo punk band in high school and created obscene cassettes with friends in various joke groups like Chainsaw Barmitzvah, Hacksaw Synagogue, Rectal Thermometer, and AYDS (named after the short-lived, unfortunately-monikered diet supplement). My brother and I recorded as Vik and Vinnie Maverik when I was 16 and he was 10. I made him sing ridiculous songs, like "Your Grandma is One Hot Mama" and "Poop." When I was 18 I taught myself how to do sloppy Eddie Van Halen-style guitar riffs for a punk parody band called Train Wreck, whose hits were "Metal Babe" and "New Kids on the Chopping Block." In college I played guitar in a Sundays-style group called Franklin, with my friend Karen on vocals. In my twenties I was in a group called Plaster Sandals, whose 15 seconds of fame was to be named one of the first prize winners in the 1996 Conan O'Brien College Band Search, missing the grand prize of appearing on the show. In my thirties I sang Sinatra tunes with an 18-piece big band, and accidentally founded a Hank Williams Sr. tribute group that's lasted 10 years. The constant, my true passion, through these side projects has been writing and recording my own songs for

25 years. I recently released my eighth CD, and have started on number nine. Me, me, me, me, me, me, me.

My bearded bassist buddy Jim has been in the All Hank Band almost from the beginning. He and the other guys have about 10 years on me. It's nice to play with seasoned musicians, and cuts down on drama. They've been nice enough to carry me through a few gigs when I Hanked it up in excess. Hank Williams liked to stash small liquor bottles in his cowboy boots to sneak a nip, but my standard poison is beer. On one gig that I don't remember so well Jim told me I still sounded good but that the tempos got reallly slowwww. My friend Noa liked it, for she too had been drinking. Jim eventually had to halt our last marathon set after two hours because his back was bugging him and he needed to sit down. I was on quite a roll, apparently.

One Friday morning last spring we four Hanks drove to a restaurant in Arcade, NY, to do a live-to-air performance on WXRL, a vintage country station in the Buffalo area. Nellie's is a classic rural diner with a nice staff and good chow. (It's fun to call it chow.) The room was filled with regulars plus many older musicians who gather for the monthly radio broadcast, including several pedal steel guitar players. That doesn't happen often because there aren't that many of them; it's a specialty instrument that gives classic country its twang.

After the gig an 83-year-old man named Bernie introduced himself. He had been a country singer in the 1940s somewhere in rural Pennsylvania. A local car dealership owner decided to promote country music shows in a large park, and Bernie helped book the headliners, while opening some of the shows. In 1948, when Hank Williams was just coming up, they hired him for $1,500. (That's worth about $15,000 now.)

I asked Bernie what he thought of Hank at the time. He shrugged his shoulders and said, "He was okay." That made me laugh; I appreciated his honesty. Bernie said that Hank seemed much like any of the other emerging guys of the day, not exceptional. Bernie said his chest was caved in, he was skinny as a rail, and either drunk or on drugs backstage, rambling away in conversation. He talked more on stage than he sang. I said, "He was pretty tall though, right?" Not so much, according to Bernie.

I give Hank a lot of leeway, possibly too much, because I feel like I understand him, and his songs move me, especially the sad ones. Same with Sinatra. They were both extreme, manic-depressives with neurotic artistic sensibilities. Each tended to overcompensate for being slight of body, though Sinatra filled out later and imitated the bullies who'd plagued him. Hank's life was complicated by poor health and spina bifida, and I imagine the roads of the mid-1900s were unkind to his back when traveling to gigs. Coincidentally or not, I have an exaggerated lumbar curve that's always made running unpleasant, which is why I swim. Hank died age 29 in 1953, but looked more than 40.

On the drive home from Nellie's Jim asked how my book was coming and said he might have a story for me. Jim has been a full-time musician for more than 35 years. His father died while Jim was doing a New Year's Eve gig in 1978. He said he knew the moment when his dad passed, he could feel it. Jim's sister's watch stopped at 1 a.m. that morning, the time their dad died. This made me think of my mom's visit from her mother at precisely 4 p.m. on Christmas Eve, and when George the comic shop owner felt his mom's passing in the night.

Jim's mom Millie is 84 and was diagnosed with lung cancer in July 2012 after a couple months of coughing. Having watched friends of hers go through surgery and chemotherapy only to live another six months in pain, and given her age, she decided to ride it out naturally.

Millie's lived in Mesa, AZ for 35 years, with the rest of Jim's family nearby. Last winter her condition worsened. In addition to cancer she developed a severe lung infection with lots of fluid. A drain was installed; she was pumped out every other day. On Christmas Eve she went to the emergency room. They gave her the strongest antibiotics available but there was no improvement. Her health was slipping fast and she enrolled in hospice care. Jim prepared to fly to Mesa to be with her and his siblings.

The morning of January 2nd Millie was about to take a shower when she received a phone call from her sister-in-law informing her that her brother had died that morning from pancreatic cancer. He'd been diagnosed only three months earlier himself. Millie had phone calls to make but decided to bathe first. As she stepped into the shower a scorpion dropped from the ceiling and stung her at the base of her neck, into the spine. In her three decades in Mesa, she'd never seen one in her house.

The sting was quite painful. Her body went numb and her vision blurred. Jim's niece was there at the time and called poison control, but they said there was nothing they could do; she'd have to ride it out. Millie couldn't believe this had happened to her on top of everything else. For the next three days she was in great pain and essentially blind.

Unexpectedly, as the pain from the sting receded so did the fluid in her lungs. Within a few more days her lung infection completely cleared. There were no remaining traces. The scorpion's sting may have inadvertently saved her life by wiping out the lung infection. She was discharged from hospice care and got back to her normal routine, including driving her car, which she hadn't done since the previous summer before her cancer diagnosis. She turned 84 in April 2013. Jim sent her a silver scorpion pendant for her birthday.

Studies support the use of epidural drug delivery for acute pain, especially to prevent chest infections. If Millie hadn't been stung in the upper body, specifically the spine, the scorpion's venom may not have been as effective. I read online that Cubans have been treating cancer patients with a mixture of blue scorpion venom and water for more than 20 years. Some have seen their tumors shrink and disappear. Thousands have attested to pain relief, increased strength, and renewed energy while on the medicine, and Cuba's state pharmaceutical company has begun producing a homeopathic version for distribution.

Did some helpful spirits, or Millie's recently deceased brother, manipulate a scorpion into helping her? Is this a form of cheating? If I were god, I would absolutely intervene. Why not? God made the rules of reality, so who better to break them? Why should god and the angels "play fair" when the devil's entire enterprise is based on deception? Perhaps angels should cheat more often, though if they did then people might always expect miraculous solutions to their problems. I often wonder if a larger plan is always in play. Does god manipulate the chess board towards the end game? (Yes.) But does the game ever actually end?

THIRTY-TWO: "HEAVEN IS A PLACE WHERE NOTHING EVER HAPPENS"

Those are lyrics from the Talking Heads song "Heaven." I've considered the meaning for years, but as with most clever, poetic turns of phrase, an exact interpretation is elusive. Still, it kick-starts fun, unanswerable questions, like: does time exist in heaven? If there's no time, does anything happen there? Can spirits choose to take physical form? What do they do with their (non) time, if anything? Does one's essence maintain independence, or do we merge with the original source from which we came? Would heaven's presumably endless peace eventually become boring? Is having a finite physical body essential to understanding the necessity of both ambition and empathy? Do spirits have aspirations like people, or is one "detached," with nothing (left) to achieve? Is life as spirit pure joy? Are we reincarnated over and over again until we learn all a soul needs to know? Do spirits make whoopee? Am I very far up my own bum?

Perhaps in the afterlife we exist as eternal, intelligent energy, but can choose to continue to interact with this universe. Maybe some spirits use their freedom to traverse time and space like a tourist, to visit places and people they loved in the physical world or to experience vistas they never knew, but from an omniscient point of view.

My mom doesn't ponder the afterlife like me. Most people don't, which is probably smart. (I'll do it for ya!) Her attitude is that there's no way to know anyway. It'll be whatever it is. Obviously true, but I enjoy speculating even though I know I don't know. Mom said she thinks when we die we just exist as atoms, floating outside time, not really thinking at all, just *being*. Sometimes we're called by those we cared about back on Earth, like a quantum phone call ringing in shared atoms, and we momentarily return.

She doesn't believe that spirits have any power to assist us. They can only provide a comforting presence in times of need. I feel like spirits do help, though I'd concede that god's will is the final word. In a network of compassionate spirits they might act as proxies for Jebus. Not necessarily to engineer a final result, but to favorably tweak some of the variables, slightly bending reality. As mentioned, I believe our altruistic hopes influence existence, as if the universe is a single, gigantic being which responds to the needs of its individual organs. We receive answers to our prayers and wishes, though we may not always recognize or like the answers at first.

Perhaps mom resists the thought of spirits having an ongoing "mission" in the afterlife because her life as a caregiver has been challenging and essentially unending since Steve and I were born. The idea of duties after death is unappealing, because it's just more work! I'd think that all projects in the afterlife would be optional. Different strokes for different soul folks. For some, perhaps the afterlife is a period of rest from the challenges of the physical universe. Maybe some spirits go into hibernation, an extended dream state of rejuvenation, and emerge ready for another spin on the flesh carousel.

It concerns me that mom still worries about the future. I'd hoped, with our amazing experiences, she'd trust fate more. I fear that obsessive energy adversely affects her health, her pets, and my brother Steve. I can't seem to help her let it go, even in retirement. The only option is to pray that god makes her eventually see things my way. Ha ha.

(Having not experienced the responsibilities and burdens of parenthood, maybe my opinion is void. My friend Bob once said that he didn't feel afraid a day in his life until his first child was born. I didn't tell him that fear has been a constant companion since age 13, and that only over the last dozen years have I grown to feel *nearly* fearless.

My brother experiences consistent public discomfort. Life in a wheelchair means you never blend into a crowd. It's probably why he sometimes prefers being alone, or with friends at his apartment, as I would. Even without physical handicap I sometimes retreat, preferring the uncomplicated company of cats to the messy, seemingly unending neediness of people. That's judgment creeping in again, unfortunately. Sorry!)

Let's return to afterlife speculation and consider time. Given that psychics, including my brother, can accurately see future events in the physical world, and there's scientific evidence of collective precognition (remember Harvard's *Global Consciousness Project* and the "Eggs?") then the future must already exist. If the future exists, then the past almost certainly continues to exist after we pass through it, too. Therefore, all events always exist, and some quantum advocates would say all possible versions of all events exist, in infinite number. Our fate is already written in this reality, but we've yet to make the choices that take us where we're headed. This is strange and contradictory, and not intuitive to us as humans, but existence is paradoxical and absurd.

The only way to experience individual moments is through the variable of time. It's the agent of evolution physically, mentally, and spiritually. Time allows us to experience growth, to see life from many different perspectives as we age and change, and in turn, hopefully, to help soften our judgment of imperfect others as we acknowledge our own imperfections. The mission is to love despite abundant challenges. Finally, we impart knowledge to the next generation, and then we move onto the next stage of our spiritual journey.

If we exist solely as energy in the afterlife, without a body and its accompanying needs, we will obviously be very different. Reconciling the trinity of mind, body, and soul on the physical plane is one of the great challenges of being human. Each has different needs, and sometimes they're in conflict. At minimum, as animals, physical existence requires us to acquire basic assets (food, water, clothing, shelter, etc.) to survive. Over the long course of history, conflicts between individuals and civilizations are nearly unavoidable in the competition for resources, especially as global population and geographic density grow.

Primitive life must have been stressful on the simplest organisms and mammals, not that it's easy now. Aggression must be a natural evolutionary trait given that even the simplest life form requires some instinct to hunt for food, compete for a mate (and pass itself forward via procreation), and defend against other predators.

Aggression can lead to violence, but violence and aggression aren't the same. Aggression is a cousin of competition. Without it we'd be docile, and wouldn't survive as a species. There'd be no such thing as ambition, and fewer unique, intriguing differences between people. (Thanks, testosterone.)

Since some aggression is needed, the counterbalance of empathy is vital to mute potential excesses. Empathy is a form of love. Without it, aggression is a runaway train that destroys everything in its path, including itself.
Most people are many potential beings in one package. Almost anyone's capable of violence under the wrong circumstances. When and where you were born contribute to which potential version of yourself you become, which is why good people can go bad, and the rotten are *never* beyond repair. If you were born in a war-torn, impoverished country like Afghanistan or North Korea you'd be very different.

People with a more liberal ideology embrace the idea that, in a society, we don't fully exist without other people, however imperfect we find them. This goes against almost all my own personal instincts, which steer me towards the fewest number of dependent associations. Yet intellectually, in the most idealistic sense, I know that we all belong to each other.

Conservatism advocates self-reliance and personal responsibility, which is undisputed. Yet life provides no guarantees. A person may believe he's prepared for every contingency, but fate may deal bad cards. We may unexpectedly find ourselves dependent on someone at a critical time, and, to our credit as a species, often a person we barely know answers the call, helping us overcome an overwhelming threat. Someone you least expect might one day save your life. Altruism speaks to our common vulnerability.

I have trouble understanding people who lack empathy for the less affluent and disadvantaged. Yes, some people will always game the system and take advantage of government assistance. Waste and fraud are inevitable in any social system, but the poor are rarely living large even when they collect a government check. Looting by the elite is on a grander scale, and has a greater impact on the health and future of the country and world. Their games can be more treacherous, because they're highly intelligent and competitive. The recent bank and Wall Street bailout scams offended me much more than someone perhaps buying beer with food stamps.

There may come a day, though hopefully not, when one of us might need the social safety net. That's what it's for, and part of belonging to each other. If we never personally need it, and we pay more into it than we ever get out, we should consider ourselves fortunate to have never been in a situation that threatened our survival.

What conservatives believe that liberals won't always concede is the violence of existence, the realpolitik versus the ideal. History has proven that not every conflict can be peacefully resolved. In the modern nation-state, and a world of 8 billion people, the need for a strong military and an accompanying (though hopefully appropriately humble) nationalism can't be escaped because, as idealistic as we might like to be, permanent world peace isn't realistic, so we strive for as much peace as possible.

War is partly a consequence of our competitive nature. Ambition and the desire to improve and grow, the qualities that help people achieve great things, sit on the flip side of aggression, our best and worst qualities rolled into one. Without ambition there's no achievement or survival.

Some communities have grown very hardened and accustomed to conflict. In inner-city neighborhoods, and countries torn apart by generations of war, nerves are worn. Daily life can be a matter of survival, and the empathy they were born with has been greatly compromised. The more sensitive the child, the greater the potential damage because he'll find it more difficult to keep strong negative feelings out. When a traumatized individual or community feels threatened, he may respond angrily and violently reflexive, like a wounded animal in pain.

Unfortunately, conservative politicians sometimes exacerbate sensitive global conflicts by provocation and by seeing *all* human interactions as warfare. They seek and create the violence they fear, as in the march to the second Iraq War, a perverse redirection of the strong feelings of sadness and anger elicited by the World Trade Center attack.

The United States had little choice but to go to Afghanistan to pursue Osama Bin Laden and Al-Qaeda, but Iraq was optional, and based on faulty intelligence about weapons of mass destruction gleaned from torture, an affront to god. In our name, the U.S. military (and private security contractors like Blackwater) killed perhaps tens of thousands of Iraqi civilians. A minority of soldiers tortured prisoners. We plunged Iraq into extended instability, poverty, and misery. One can't just break a country, say "I'm sorry," and expect it all to be forgotten.

One quiet summer evening, lying on my couch enjoying the sunshine and safety of the neighborhood, I wondered what it's like to be a child in tribal northern Pakistan, where the sound of American drones hidden among the clouds creates a constant hum, worrying that a targeting mistake may destroy my family in its sleep. What's our responsibility to these distant strangers? If we're indifferent to, or unaware of, what our government does on our behalf, do we condemn the politically-weak to a life of constant fear? Are the insurgents our military kills, among the civilian losses, so threatening to our survival that we're entitled to make an entire region fear random death from above?

The extent to which military forces serve the interests of powerful American corporations and individuals is an open question, as is whether it's historically inevitable in every wealthy nation-state. Capitalism and representative democracy, despite obvious flaws, work better than communism and socialism, which subjugate individual liberty and creativity, and institutionalize corruption. But, since Reagan and deregulation, abundant corporate takeovers and consolidation have created powerful companies we're simultaneously loyal to, dependent upon, and afraid of.

The very wealthy are peers of the politically powerful. The two behave in a somewhat insular, self-reflexive fashion, even when their decisions have a great impact on millions outside their circles. Especially today, in the unipolar world of a single superpower, politicians necessarily jockey for leverage among the rich and powerful, and this commingling can be treacherous.

Despite daily news horrors, the United States is a more peaceful, integrated country than 50 years ago. The divide between the many racial groups that make us an eclectic nation has narrowed, and there are more rights for the LGBT community. To our credit, multi-culturalism and tolerance have become part of the national character, though more in some regions than others. We have a historical legacy of addressing and rectifying our national mistakes, though many individuals are victimized in the meantime. It's important in order to preserve a just society, and it matters in a moral universe.

Ah, but ideological debates will probably be moot in the afterlife. A non-physical existence is presumably stress-free. We'll also see that no single viewpoint is ever the whole truth. On Earth, when operating from the most generous version of oneself, we make choices which better benefit the majority. We see others as our brothers and sisters because they are, even when we don't understand or like some of them.

One thing's for sure. If you die, go to heaven, and come back to Earth, you'll *never* have a life like this one again. In every micro-moment that passes you change ever so slightly, and the world changes too, plus the galaxy and universe, such that each version of you is a singular, fleeting phenomenon in time, never to be repeated or precisely duplicated. We don't see how we've changed with the world until we look back. Finite, linear life is all change. It's nice to treasure moments of perfect joy, slow time, hold them up to the light.

THIRTY-THREE: WE WILL BE CYBORGS (THE POST-HUMAN FUTURE)

If you want to get a glimpse of what the near future may be like, I recommend futurist Ray Kurzweil's book *The Age of Spiritual Machines*. His website is regularly updated with news about technological developments and thoughts about how new technology will affect mankind. (I have no affiliation with Kurzweil.) *Spiritual Machines* altered my thinking, even if his predictions don't all come true. It's probably good to anticipate the future so you don't one day get caught like a deer in the headlights of progress.

Kurzweil invented the first reading machine for the blind; Stevie Wonder bought the first model. At Wonder's prompting, he then created the Kurzweil keyboard, which emulates orchestral instruments. Kurzweil considers himself a "trans-humanist" and hopes to live long enough to achieve immortality, by either merging with forthcoming technology, and/or having his consciousness copied and uploaded into a non-biological body. (There have been successful human face transplants, and some doctors believe a full head transplant may be possible. We may end up in a *Futurama* world with decapitated human heads mounted on new bodies, either human or machine.)

Our brains process information at approximately 100 million instructions per second, pretty good for knuckle draggers. Kurzweil estimates that the exponential growth of computing power and processing will match and then greatly exceed that of humans around 2030. He predicts that artificial intelligence, once just a sci-fi concept, will become reality. Machines will become sentient.

All technological progress has an obvious upside and downside, nuclear energy being a great example. Future technology will solve many problems, while creating new ones. People will have the opportunity to "upgrade" themselves by incorporating technology into their bodies to improve senses, memory, brainpower, and strength. Eyesight has already been partly restored in blind lab rats with implants, and many people have benefitted from in-ear cochlear devices, which will only improve in quality.

The benefits of enhancement will be obvious, though some will be justifiably apprehensive or afraid at first, including me. But history is full of tipping points, where the unthinkably strange eventually becomes the new normal once enough people embrace it. (Eugene Ionesco's absurdist play *Rhinoceros* comes to mind. The inhabitants of a small town start randomly and inexplicably changing into rhinos. There's great alarm about it until enough people transform, then there's a tipping point where nearly everyone *wants* to be a rhino.)

A day may come when you install some form of "data port" on your body to make it possible for you to interact directly with technology, instead of having to hold it in your hand. Technology is insidious like that. Many people practically have their cell phone embedded in their face already.

The integration of technology into people will begin innocently enough with medical applications. Nanotechnology may transform medicine. Nanobots are microscopic computers programmed to perform simple functions. Kurzweil believes that advanced nanobots (with built-in cameras) will be injected to administer drugs and help fight diseases in the body. They could be programmed to blast cancer cells, boost white blood cell production, and other corrective functions.

Nanobots are small enough to travel every pathway of the body, and will be able to send back digital information about how we're constructed, a concept called "reverse engineering." Once we can map the brain, we'll be close to replicating it digitally on a computer. We'll likely diagram it in full, as we mapped the human genome, before we fully understand everything the brain can and does do. In 2013 President Barack Obama announced an initiative to further this research.

The integration of technology will lead to a heated moral, philosophical, and religious debate about the potential end of biological humanity as we've known it for thousands of years. However, history proves that technology always advances, and never retreats, unless a civilization comes to an end before it reaches a technological tipping point, by nuclear disaster or an asteroid that wipes out intelligent life.

(There is an inevitable forward march towards an unknowable end, and it must be the same for civilizations throughout the universe. Given an estimated 60 billion planets in the habitable zone of Milky Way stars, we are surely not the only intelligent life. Perhaps fortunately, even the nearest star is too far away for practical communication or visitation, which prevents us from preparing for potential war with another populated planet. Maybe that was an inherently clever part of god's design, with each solar system nearly isolated, leaving deep space exploration to intelligent, evolved machines.)

174

Kurzweil speculates that people will make digital backups of their brains as a way to "live forever." He hopes to live long enough to be copied. I'd note that the digital copy of a person would diverge so greatly in its development from the moment of its creation forward that, in a short time, it would have little in common with the human intelligence from which it was derived. Would the human identity from which the machine intelligence evolved be retained? Will our intelligent machines embrace values derived from humans, since we fragile biological beings will have been their creators, and essentially their parents?

Will the technology we incorporate into our bodies allow us to explore more of our intellectual potential? Will we really still be human if we're 10 times as smart and half-machine like the Borg?

There have already been experiments to connect artificial replacement limbs to the brains of amputees, and one American test subject has regained limited use of his right hand after being rewired following an accident that left him paralyzed. He was able to move his own fingers again. This technology will also improve. The military is experimenting with exoskeletons for soldiers, to enhance their strength to superhuman levels. American military interest and funding will drive much of the technology forward, as it has for a hundred years.

It won't happen overnight, but, by definition, many humans may become cyborgs (a living combination of organic and inorganic material) like in the sci-fi flicks I enjoy. At least initially, however, we'll still look human because the technology will be microscopic and/or internal, and therefore less perceptible. Younger generations will more willingly incorporate new technology. They'll think it's cool and their fear threshold will be lower, and they'll be less attached to the idea of being purely biological. Previous generations, perhaps including my own, will be more "biased" against cyborgs, or at least more skeptical about the trade-off.

The growing popularity of super-humans in movies and on TV *(The X-Men, Man of Steel, The Avengers, True Blood, etc.)* seems to anticipate the arrival of enhanced humans. The decline in popularity of the typical action hero like Sylvester Stallone implies it's not good enough to be human anymore, or we're becoming bored by the physical limitations of even exceptional mortals. In a way, it's a compliment to human imagination that we're beginning to accept the possibility of much stranger existences, but we may also be celebrating the beginning of the end of mankind.

At \$13.3 billion, the revenues of the sex industry are bigger than the NFL, NBA, and Major League Baseball combined, making sex robots a near-inevitability. Once they look and act as convincing as humans do, we might have relationships with machines like on *Battlestar Galactica.* (That show was brilliant, and dealt with the cyclical relationship between humanity, its advanced technology, and the virtually immortal mechanical beings that arise from human intelligence.)

You may find these ideas troubling. Some days I do, and others I don't. If I have the opportunity to become "enhanced" I don't know if I'll go along with it as Kurzweil hopes to. It's fascinating to see it coming, though. Every week there seems to be another news article that confirms some technological development Kurzweil has predicted. I believe it's the ironic fate of mankind to see its digital creations become the real intergalactic explorers. We already have a glimpse of this with the 2012 Mars rover. Organic people simply aren't built to withstand space travel, but an intelligent, inorganic computer will have no need for water, air, or food, just energy to run, easily obtained from the abundant interstellar cosmic radiation that would kill humans.

Technology marries greater computing power with miniaturization, so our popular depiction of UFOs is probably wrong. Huge, flying-saucer type spacecraft carrying biological humanoids are unlikely. We should expect space explorers to be microscopic and imperceptible. (There will likely be sentient machines from Earth wandering the cosmos in due time, too.)

This raises the possibility that Earth has already been visited by miniature machine life forms from other solar systems that evolved before us, though of what interest we might to them be is hard to fathom. Unless, having obtained the equivalent of immortality, intelligent machines long to know what it's like to be mortal. Aren't we always fascinated by whatever it is that we're not?

I've also considered that what I've described as frequent visits by spirits could have been visits by microscopic machine life-forms instead. Civilizations that have already reached *The Singularity* and explored other galaxies would have the technology to hide their presence from less evolved life forms like us, unless they intentionally chose to make themselves known. If they wanted to interact with us, they could easily enter our bodies and zip around our brains, sending messages along our neural pathways which we might interpret as spirit messages, instead. If people can believe in a savior via a virgin birth, this isn't any less weird a concept. My current belief is that my family and I have interacted with spirits, but I would reconsider if new discoveries and experiences challenged that idea.

We might presume that becoming nearly immortal by merging with technology is superior to fragile human mortality, but I'm not convinced. The most we can say is that it would be completely *different*. If we have immortal souls, or if we're players in a virtual reality game running on God the Computer, we'll find out anyway, regardless of advancing technology.

The search for new knowledge is what drives intelligence. Our immortal interstellar progeny will seek to accumulate more information and experience, but all the time in the universe might not be the gift it seems once they run out of things to discover and learn. Would an immortal being eventually crave mortality so its life would be more focused and urgent? Mortality forces a certain set of brackets on our lives. How will we make best use of our time before we're dust? There's a sad beauty and poignancy in knowing everyone we love will eventually cease to exist, at least in this form. It's easy to get caught up in trivialities and forget to be amazed that we exist at all. It seems we're often afraid to embrace and celebrate life, and this makes me feel more alone than I'd like. It's another reason my family is so important, because they understand impermanence.

A lot of different variations seem possible in terms of future life forms on Earth, and beyond. All of the following are possible: civilizations which are completely synthetic "copies" of biological beings; completely biological, but genetically-engineered humanoids who do not effectively age; cyborgs (a mixture of biological and mechanical components); and artificial machine intelligences that do not have any past existence or experience as organic beings. There are more possibilities, I'm sure.

Since you're reading these words, our universe has not been destroyed by a highly advanced, immortal, post-*Singularity* civilization from another galaxy. From this I conclude that a certain amount of rationality prevails in technological civilizations as well, and literally universally. No sane being wants to bring about the end of everything.

Maybe intelligent, nearly-immortal machines will create new universes (and maybe they already have, including this one), or figure out how to leap into other overlapping universes, if they exist. Perhaps some will decide that their immortality has reached a logical conclusion and the only thing left to do is to cease to exist.

(Speaking of the death of everything, a current theory about how the universe may end is the "Big Freeze." Given the gravitational attraction of the existing observable matter in the universe, its expansion should be slowing. For reasons that are not understood, the universe is still expanding, and at a higher rate of speed. As galaxies continue to spread farther apart from one another, eventually there'll be so much distance between them that no other stars will be visible in the night sky of any planet.

In one hundred trillion years, when the last stars burn out, the remnants will be too far from each other to coalesce and form new ones. Our universe could end up as a big, dark, empty nothing without light or heat. Maybe super-intelligent microscopic machines have figured out how to prevent the "Big Freeze" from occurring, and the universe is already filled with their intelligence, accounting for the imperceptible dark matter that scientists have been trying to find for decades.)

The march to a future technological bizarro world is also called *The Singularity* because it's like the event horizon of a black hole that one can't see past, or fully imagine or comprehend. It appears that our future will be *unrecognizable*, and beyond our current imagination. We'll have to try to steer things forward without destroying ourselves, while debating what it means for our survival as a species.

THIRTY-FOUR: 200 YEARS OF THE MODERN INDUSTRIALIZED MAN

The Industrial Revolution began a little more than 100 years ago. Fifty to 100 years from now we're likely to reach *The Singularity* and move into the post-human era. Assuming other biological civilizations similar to humanity have existed and will exist in the future, the era of the Modern Industrialized Man (MIM) might turn out to be only 200 years from start to finish before we either merge with technology, are replaced by it, or cohabitate with it, but are physically and intellectually "inferior."

In other words, the MIM only gets about 200 years as the dominant life form before he is toast, marginalized, or irrelevant, and we're living through the middle of it. Meanwhile, the pre-industrialized man lived without advanced technology, or even electricity and indoor plumbing, for tens of thousands of years without much change, and our post-industrial creations (cyborgs or fully digital creatures evolved from human intelligence) will dominate for the next tens of thousands of years while changing more rapidly than we can conceive of or accurately project. We stand at the crossroads between life nearly free of technology and life where technology is everything.

It struck me as profound to exist in this very small window of time, a mere wink historically. You and I are the rarest of the rare in the history of this planet, and this will be true even after we're long gone and Earth is post-human. Yep, we're *special*. How will we be regarded once we're gone? Are we just an evolutionary stepping stone?

As the sci-fi future gains speed, here's another thing to ponder. Mind-reading technology is progressing. Your thoughts are electrical impulses that can be measured by external hardware. I previously described how, in a quantum universe, our thoughts travel outwards to their object. In the future this ability might be amplified technologically. We'll also need to develop ways to shield our minds from others (tin-foil hat?) so our deepest thoughts aren't constantly, involuntarily mined. Online problem-solving hive minds are likely to develop, with participants able to plug and unplug themselves as desired.

Mind-reading technology will almost certainly be used on our enemies, foreign and domestic, and by autocratic governments. Once we implant technology into our brains, the government and other entities may be able to download our thoughts in real time, the way Facebook and Google scoop (somehow legally!) all our data and email content for targeted advertising.

(The government already has a sophisticated email data mining program, and they're storing everything they can long-term. I've come to no longer expect total privacy in the Patriot Act era, which is different than approval. My feelings are mixed and evolving.)

The sovereignty of the human mind will be challenged and may come to an end with the MIM. Please take a few moments to appreciate the sanctity of your currently un-monitored, private thoughts.

Under the circumstances, at this odd juncture, I have great reservations about procreation! In the past people had some reasonable, though maybe naïve, expectations about what the future would be like for their children, but now it seems anything is possible. A dystopian nightmare; techno-paradise; division in mankind between high-end cyborgs and lowly organic servants (us); computers deciding we're living completely wrong and forcing new social structures on the world; digital people leaving Earth behind for the stars. Who knows!

THIRTY-FIVE: SIMPLICITY AND COMPLEXITY

Sometimes I wonder if the universe is literally a big binary computer, a number-crunching mechanism. A *New York Times* article I read a few years ago suggested we may live in a virtual reality, and that god is the machine on which it runs. Assuming that god is an unfathomably large computer, wouldn't that mean that all life and existing matter in the universe can ultimately be expressed mathematically? That means your real name is: 011010101010101010010101011110101010101010101001001 010100100101010101001001011101010101010101100000000 000101010101111111111110101010101011111111111010101 0010101010101001010. Not really, that's too short. Your name might be an infinite, irrational number like pi.

There's great complexity to life, but all complexity arises from utter simplicity - a sequence of yes/no decisions or individual pieces that, once accumulated and assembled, may appear complex as a finished product, whether that's a physical object, a set of thoughts, or a work of art. The amount of complexity which one perceives is based in part on your ability to imagine the simple individual steps that constitute its creation, even if there are hundreds, thousands, or millions of them. Once you realize that all complexity arises from simplicity, the basic computing of one yes/no after another, it becomes possible to replicate the results.

Since I know a lot about music, when attending a concert, my brain can focus on small, individual aspects, like a performer's technique, or the harmonic layers and arrangement of the composition, the quality of the soundsystem and the sound engineer's approach to the mix, the acoustics of the room, or how the lighting enhances the emotional content of a certain song. There are many variables. Perhaps there's a simple beauty to the composition which is elevated by the collective skill and chemistry of the particular musicians. The person sitting next to me will have a totally different experience of the same performance, and may perceive more complexity than me because their brain doesn't break it down into its component parts.

Conversely, if a mechanic were to lift the hood of a car and start talking to me about the specifications of a particular component or system, my brain would just see an impenetrable and overwhelming metal and plastic sculpture. My lack of knowledge about how an engine works makes it seem more complicated than it is, and it's more likely I'll get ripped off, but to the mechanic it's a bunch of small components that relate in a logical way.

To say that something is simple is not an insult. Sometimes something that was once simple is over-engineered and becomes unnecessarily complex, to its detriment. Simplicity can be as valuable and dazzling as complexity, and complexity can come full circle back to simplicity again. The simple zeroes and ones that are the foundation of binary computing. The egg and sperm, which ironically happen to resemble zeroes and ones. The early universe, which contained only two elements: hydrogen and helium, and which, by gravitational clumping over millions of years and the explosive death of the earliest stars, was able to spread heavier and more varied elements throughout the universe. The magnetic spin of quantum particles, towards either a positive or negative orientation. Endless strings of compiled thoughts like a mathematical equation, growing in apparent complication, but still based on individual choices between One and The Other.

I like a fair amount of emotional and compositional complexity in art, especially music. I prefer the content to be not too spoon-fed, and I love surprises. However, sometimes utter simplicity is perfect. John Lennon, a complex man, composed two of the most powerful and joyfully simple songs (lyrically and melodically) about love ever written: "Imagine" and "All You Need Is Love." The songs have been played to death over the years, perhaps diminishing their emotional impact, but not negating the original, innate beauty. When I hear either one I still get goose bumps sometimes, and feel a spiritual connection. "There's nothing you can do that can't be done. There's nothing you can say that can't be sung." Poetic and hopeful. Three chords and the truth. A reminder that many of the best things are essentially simple. Kindness, loyalty, and generosity. Unconditional love. All uncomplicated.

Consider the digitization of music and movies over the last 10 years. A digital file constituting a song is really just a long numeric in binary code – a series of ones and zeroes. Does that mean, once the physical body of a human being is digitally mapped by nanobots and copied to a computer, that what constitutes a person or any physical object is an enormously long binary numeral? Can every experience a person has ever had - each moment, thought, and feeling – also be expressed as a set of numbers accounting for every variable at play at any given moment in time? Would that number be finite or infinite? (If it's infinite, we're in the magical realm of paradox once again.) Once technology has advanced further, will we be able to answer this question, or will it remain unknowable? Is consciousness derived from the matter that makes us up, or from somewhere outside of us? When computers eventually claim to have souls, will it be true? Does the Pope shit in the woods?

The problem I run into when I think about this stuff is I'm not smart enough to take it further! (Perhaps I should be thankful.) I don't have a handle on the numeric language that dominates the deepest scientific ideas about the nature of reality, so eventually my mind goes off the tracks. I become fascinated by complex systems that make my head spin, and I like for the systems to break down in my brain so I can still appreciate the simple beauty of a July sunset, or the colorful fragility of a ladybug.

THIRTY-SIX: THE CIRCLE WIDENS

I've worked with a terrific drummer from Buffalo named Ray Hangen since 2008. We perform together about a half-dozen times a year, and he played on my last CD. A few weeks ago Ray came over to record parts for some new songs. There's a modest home studio in the small front room of my apartment, off the living room, where I've spent hundreds of hours writing and editing music like a mad scientist. It has abundant natural light, and a screen door leading to the second floor porch, overlooking the block. Our neighborhood has much greenery among the large, historic homes. I prefer to keep the blinds open to feel the energy of the street while I'm working.

From 2005 to 2007 Ray toured extensively with a talented blues guitarist from Atlanta named Sean Costello. At 16, Costello released his first of five critically-beloved records until his unexpected death at 28 in April 2008. (I knew none of this when we started working together months later that summer.) Like many artists who've walked an emotional tightrope, including myself, Sean struggled with anxiety and depression.

About five years before she met, and eventually married, popular blues guitarist Derek Trucks, singer Susan Tedeschi and Sean lived together. He met her when he was 17 and she was 26. Apparently it was a barnburner relationship. Tedeschi recruited members of Sean's band and Sean for her recording projects and touring. Sean was a contemporary of rising young blues guitarists Kenny Wayne Shepherd and Jonny Lang. Both Sean and Lang toured as the opening acts for B.B. King, and his notoriety was growing.

Ray is in high demand for freelance gigs in Buffalo. He also gets work in Atlanta and Memphis, where he's taken part in fundraisers for the Sean Costello Memorial Fund, the charity established after Sean's death to help others struggling with bipolar disorder. Like many of the talented people I've been fortunate to meet, Ray is humble and disinclined to self-promotion. The universe looks out for people like him. They might not get rich off their talent, but they'll never lack what they need. Somehow spirit will provide.

I like to break out the high octane beers during recording sessions at my place. Ray shares my love of fine Belgian and German brews and told me some funny stories about his two European tours with Sean. The Belgians really know how to pound their homemade concoctions, where they're cheap and plentiful on draft. (As imports to the States, they're expensive, but worth it.) Ray said the band's Belgian driver drank three or four strong beers every day during lunch, then whisked them off to the next gig. Ray stuffed his suitcase with bottles for the flight home.

We had a few German wheat beers (Aventinus and its delicious cousin Eisbock) and got loose. I don't know why I brought it up, and didn't know what he'd think, but I told Ray I was almost done writing a book about spirits. He said he'd had experiences, too. I was pleasantly unsurprised.

The first story occurred when Ray was 28 and his Aunt Fran died of colon cancer. Fran was one of nine kids. Ray's mom Barbara, who also died of colon cancer years later, was the second youngest child. Ray felt crushed at Fran's wake when she suddenly appeared to him. He wondered if his eyes were deceiving him. Was this really happening? Fran was transparent and shadowy, like smoke. Only Ray could see her, not his wife Gabrielle. It felt as if time was moving very slowly, almost at a standstill. The interaction seemed like it was five minutes long, but Ray knew it was probably only a few seconds. He was aware that the moment was special and might never be repeated.

Fran said, "You gotta let go, Raymond." Her voice was unmistakable; that's when he was certain it was real. As soon as she spoke, Ray's sadness and fear instantly evaporated, as if she lifted it from him when she rose up slowly through the ceiling. Calmness washed over him. He felt certain Fran was fine, and all would be well. This is common for those who've interacted with peaceful spirits. The experience leaves no doubt as to its divinity; nothing is comparable. If everyone had a spiritual experience it would be a different world. Once it happens you can't continue as if life is meaningless or that your actions, and everyone else's, don't matter. It's impossible to think like that anymore.

Ray comes from a religious family, and has believed in god since he was a kid, but, like me, he doesn't claim to know what happens after this life. He said he was intuitive as a child, with good instincts and good luck. He always wondered where it came from. Perhaps some of the thoughts we have that seem to come from nowhere are good spirits whispering in our ear.

When we took a break to sip our beers on the porch in the early June heat, Ray said he had a clairvoyant experience when he met his wife Gabrielle. When they first spoke he had a vision of their wedded life together. He saw her in the backyard of their suburban house, with three kids and a dog. It wasn't a hopeful fantasy so much as something he was suddenly certain would happen, a clear picture of the future, like the sun rising tomorrow. Still, he was puzzled by it, so he asked her, "Do you have kids?" "No!" she exclaimed. But it all came to pass.

Ray told me this only minutes before I introduced him to the next song he'd play drums on, called "When I See You," which is about meeting someone and instantly knowing you're meant to be together, just like his vision. The chorus of the song is: "I'll know you when I see you / I'll feel it in my soul / I'll know you when I see you / When you enter my life I'll know."

A soul mate isn't something I gave much thought or credence to years ago. For most of my sarcastic life I've considered the idea a romantic cliché, but now I believe it's not only possible, but that there may be someone you're destined to meet and the plan was in motion, prearranged, before you were born. (This doesn't mean that life will be perfect if/when a soul mate is found!) I also believe, as Ray described in his vision, that there are moments in life when, with the assistance of spirit, you *know* exactly what is going to happen. You receive a personalized, unambiguously certain message from the cosmos.

Ray had another customized connection in January 2010 when he travelled to Memphis with some other musicians from Buffalo to perform at the annual International Blues Challenge (IBC). Ray and his bandmate Ian were walking down Beale Street and about to call it a night, when Ray felt compelled to walk back towards a bar they'd just passed. Then Ray recognized the sound of an obscure, traditional song which he used to perform with Sean Costello, and which Sean learned from folk musician Levon Helm, called "The Battle is Over (But the War Goes On)." Fans of Sean's had uploaded him performing the song live online, but Sean and Ray never recorded it in a studio. (Sean's live version was officially released in late 2011 on a CD called *At His Best.*)

Ray couldn't tell if the song was playing on a radio inside the bar or if it was a live band performing it, so he and Ian went inside. A guitarist from New York City named Greg Gumpel was onstage singing the song with his band. After his set, Ian introduced himself to Greg, and told him that Ray used to tour with Sean. When Greg realized who Ray was, he became excited: "Holy shit, you're Ray Hangen!" To Greg, who was a big fan of Sean's, Ray was famous. Greg and Ray became quick friends and kept in touch over the next two years.

In 2012 Ray returned to the IBC to perform with the same group of musicians from Buffalo. He planned to get together with Greg while he was there, even though they wouldn't be performing together. The night before Ray flew to Memphis, Greg had a dream about Sean, which he shared with Ray upon his arrival. Greg said he was in a park and saw Sean sitting on a bench. He said to him, "It's great

to meet you. I was such a huge fan of yours. Ray's coming to visit." "I know," said Sean. "He really misses you," said Greg. "Yeah, I know, I really miss him, too."
Ray has had a few very real dreams about Sean. He found himself emotionally drained when he woke up. Sean's presence in the dreams was very strong. We believe these are quite possibly visits.

In the spring of 2014 Ray invited Greg to Buffalo to perform with his band at the Hamburg, NY Music Festival. As is often the case, Ray had double duty. He performed with my band at a bar from 5 p.m. to 8 p.m., then ran over to Memorial Park to play with his own all-star group from 8:45 to 10.

After packing my equipment and collecting our pay, I went to the park to catch the last 20 minutes of their set. They sounded great. Greg and Ray were synchronous. They performed in a large band shell with a high wooden ceiling and a large PA system. An abundance of shrubs and flowers were in front of the stage.

I noticed that the sound engineer placed two microphones high above Ray's drum set to capture his sound, instead of closer to the individual drums. This, plus the acoustics, made the drums seem dramatically reverberant, and far away. It was as if they were piped in from another time, like the birth of rock and roll. It was pleasantly spooky. When Ray introduced Greg to me earlier, his low-key demeanor hid his hot guitar skills and strong vocals. Three young women were dancing in a tipsy trance next to me, calling for encores. Maybe Sean was there too, enjoying the show from a park bench in the back.

Perhaps the most significant spiritual event in Ray's life came after the birth of his youngest child. Grace was born prematurely with complications from spina bifida, a defect of the spine in which part of the spinal cord is exposed through a gap in the backbone. It can cause paralysis of the lower limbs and developmental disabilities. A high-risk surgery was unavoidable and the doctors insisted she would need a shunt afterward to drain excess fluid, for the rest of her life. Ray and his wife Gabrielle were a wreck.

At this exact time, Ray's sister Barb had an appointment with a psychic. During Barb's reading the psychic asked her, "Did your brother just have a baby?" Barb said, "Actually, both my brothers just had babies. (Ray's brother's son was born nine days before Grace.) The psychic said, "One of the babies is sick. I see a lot of prayers around the baby and a woman with dark hair (Gabrielle) who is crying. There's a neurologist taking care of the baby. Don't worry, she won't need a shunt." Barb delivered the message to Ray and Gabrielle. Sure enough, their daughter's surgery was successful. No shunt was needed. Grace has grown into a healthy young woman with minimal complications. Good spirits at work? (Angels?) Absolutely!

THIRTY-SEVEN: BACK TO THE FARM

The Barking Spider Tavern is my favorite live music venue in Cleveland. The bar name is a fart joke. When you pass gas in mixed company, but don't want to own up, you blame it on the "barking spider" in the corner. Their logo is of a fat, bearded guy in a fisherman's cap and vest, smoking a pipe, leaning back on a chair to let one rip.

The intimate pub was built into an old coach house on the Case Western University campus; the walls and ceiling are finished hardwood. The lights are kept low; a candle warms each table. A wood-burning stove keeps it toasty in winter, and in summer its rows of large bay doors open on opposing sides, leading to two small patios with picnic tables under shady trees. Framed portraits and paintings fill the wall behind the bar. Singer-songwriters have been a staple since it opened in 1986, plus an eclectic mix of jazz, folk, blues, country, and spoken-word. It's meant as a listening room in a world that seems to keep getting louder.

Like Buffalo music club Nietzsche's, which it reminds me of, there's a bohemian vibe that defies any strict time period. Both venues host live music seven nights a week. The crowd is eclectic, drawing a mix of college students, artists and musicians, academics, retirees, and professionals of varying backgrounds and ages.

From Buffalo, Cleveland is a straight southwestern run along Lake Erie on Interstate 90, passing through Pennsylvania. It takes three hours to drive there. I go two or three times a year.

The Spider is a challenging venue because the tables are just a few feet from the stage and there's little reverberation with the hardwood. Your performance is virtually naked. I usually appear as a soloist, so I'm under the magnifying glass. Sometimes it feels like survival! Or like I'm a magician with only so many tricks up his sleeves.

When my head's on straight, and I've had a few beers to relax, I seem to know what songs to string together to maintain interest for the 90-minute first set, and my repartee flows. It's easy to lose the room if I'm a bit off. Audiences tune out quickly when things aren't quite right, and I don't blame them. You earn every house you keep.

Buffalo and Cleveland are cousins in professional sports frustration and enthusiastic beer consumption, where downtown, urban liberalism co-exists with a conservative suburban ring. Neither has won a sports championship in the modern era, and each seems to have suffered from long-term Rust-Belt poor self-esteem, which manifests as defeatist humility. Both cities are charming to me.

- - -

Jenna Juredine has run the Barking Spider since her dad Martin died of throat cancer in early 2011. Jenna and Martin have the same attractive, symmetrical face and smile. When I first met her, I tried not to stare. She looked so much like him. I didn't really know Martin beyond calling him for bookings, and our brief conversations between my sets, but I liked him. He seemed like a holdover from another, more fluid American era, when you could wander a few adult years after school without fearing permanent unemployment. A time before the corporatization of most of our cherished cultural institutions and popular performers, though perhaps I'm nostalgic for an era I didn't see. Martin grew up in Cleveland Heights, but one of his favorite places was his uncle's farm outside of Columbus, Ohio. Their family bred boxers. Martin visited most summers and holidays as a child and young man. It matched his mellow, rootsy vibe.

Jenna says Martin was a traveler and philosopher. He loved to talk, debate, and meet people from other places. When he finished high school he wanted to see the world, but his father convinced him to get a college education first. After graduation, Martin's dad gave him some money to travel for a year. His favorite destinations were Greece, Morocco, Afghanistan, and Paraguay, which he returned to over the years. He made friends in Morocco who eventually moved to Cleveland. He knew how to rough it abroad, enduring hunger, illness, and bed bugs in humble accommodations, in exchange for mind-expanding experiences.

When Martin returned to Cleveland, his nomadic tales mesmerized Jenna's mom Nancy and they globetrotted together for months after. Jenna's sister Shisha was conceived while they were in India. Four years later Jenna was conceived in Morocco. After Jenna's birth the family settled in Cleveland and their travels halted for a while. Martin and Nancy divorced when Jenna was four.

Martin's buddy Bruce, a real estate whiz, bought the Spider in 1986, and their lifetime arrangement was for Martin to run it. As a teen and young woman, Jenna ran errands for Martin and learned the ropes. Sadly, with Martin gone, she has no one to help her in the same role, which makes it tough to take time away.

Jenna says the bar is family to her, for better and worse. When people are disrespectful in her dad's place, she struggles not to take it personally. Dealing with loud, sloppy drunks must be a challenge. Jenna is the flame to Martin's coolness, which is probably necessary for a young, attractive bar owner on her own. She's strong but also sweet.

But you want to hear about ghost stuff, so let's go. When Jenna was a freshman in high school, she and her mom lived on the third floor of a house on Overlook Road, in Cleveland Heights. Jenna's mom Nancy's bedroom was at the end of a long hallway, off the kitchenette, and adjacent to a large, unfinished part of the attic which could have been made into another room. Often the French doors and windows in Nancy's room would rattle inexplicably, making it difficult for them to sleep.

Nancy habitually placed spare change on her bedroom dresser. Sometimes when they were in the living room or kitchen they would hear coins sliding across its top and onto the hardwood floor. Clink! Clink! Clink! She'd walk in to find a pile on pennies on the floor. "The Penny Ghost is at it again!" they said.

Jenna decided to move into the unfinished area of the apartment because it was a larger space, but soon discovered this was where the energy was most concentrated. One evening she came home to find an old seven inch fileting knife in an odd leather sheath on her bed! It didn't belong to them. Up until that point they'd felt that the presence was more an annoyance than a threat, but the knife crossed a line. Jenna immediately moved out of the unfinished space and they moved away the next month. Years later she ended up at a party on the second floor of the same house, and the current tenants also had strange stories and sensed bad energy.

Jenna went away to college at the University of Delaware, in Newark, DE. The city used to be named New Ark, and was changed at some point to a single word, but is still pronounced "new ark." Mispronounciation of Newark as if it is the city in New Jersey perpetually pisses off the locals.

Jenna and three other young women lived in a Civil War-era house, at the corner of Amstel Avenue and Elkton Road, which used to house soldiers. Elkton Road leads into Elkton, Maryland, at the edge of the Mason-Dixon Line. From her window, Jenna witnessed her first and only Ku Klux Klan rally down the street. (Happily, it was poorly attended.)

Given its age, the whole house was on one electrical circuit. If they ran two appliances at once it would blow out. Jenna said the home was so old she always felt a breeze through the cracks in the window seams, and, as a college squat, it wasn't well maintained by the landlord.

The house had two bedrooms on each floor. Jenna lived downstairs and shared a connected bathroom with Mary Ann. Jenna was student teaching in the morning and bartending at night, doing lesson plans after work at 1 a.m. before getting up at 6 for school. She often got only three hours of sleep and would pass out on her bed. Then she started waking up in weird places around the apartment. One morning she found herself on the living room couch with her legs over its side and her head almost on the floor, not a position in which one would normally, or comfortably, fall asleep. As she sometimes sleepwalked when stressed and sleep-deprived, Jenna thought that might be how she got there, but on a different morning she woke up on a different couch in a similar position.

Jenna's bedroom light often flickered crazily, and when she slept she sometimes felt a presence leaning over her bed, as did Mary Ann. Jenna woke up many times from a sound sleep as if someone was staring curiously at her face. Jenna saw the presence as a thin shadow, and she could almost see the whiteness of his eyes. When she'd awake startled the shadow would get spooked and dart into a corner, then shyly shrink down and disappear. Mary Ann wasn't remotely comfortably with the presence and woke up screaming in middle of the night when he'd get close to her face.

After waking up splayed on the couches a few times, Jenna conducted an experiment. She began to lock her bedroom door and the adjoining bathroom door before bed. (Sleepwalkers are less likely to unlock doors, especially deadbolts.) A few days into the experiment she woke up in the middle of the night with someone promenading her in circles around her bedroom, like at a country dance. Her head had been down until she woke up on her feet. Her elbow was pointed out like someone was looped in, and she felt like she was having a conversation. "I prefer this stroll to being upside-down on the couch," she thought. She found the presence more curious than creepy. Her sense was that he was a Southern gentleman in his mid-twenties, a Civil War soldier, just a few years older than her. Eventually, as she was leaning on the ghost, he couldn't carry her anymore. She flopped to the floor.

She didn't feel the soldier was perverted, just curious about her and Mary Ann. Maybe he'd lost a love or died too young to have one. He seemed to crave companionship. Other than the promenade, all he did was stare at their faces, watching pretty girls sleep. She said he was a very present presence. Very felt.

Jenna and the girls lived in the house for a year. Some fraternity guys moved in after they left. Jenna didn't tell them about the ghost, but one night they visited her while she was bartending. "Jenna, did you ever notice anything in the bedroom? The light kind of flickers like crazy. Sometimes I feel like somebody's in there with me and he hangs out in the corner of the room." This seemed like confirmation of her experiences by an outside party.

Eight years ago, after the death of her grandfather, Jenna and her mom visited her grandmother in Necedah, Wisconsin. (Jenna's grandmother has also since passed.) Jenna's grandmother was very religious. She had a plethora of angel figurines and Jesus portraits in her home, plus a 10 foot cross with Jesus on it in her front yard. One afternoon Jenna took a nap in her grandfather's room, which is where he preferred to nap. She felt that her sister was sleeping next to her, though no one was there. The presence woke her. She felt compelled to check on her grandmother, and found that she was having a massive asthma attack. Jenna gave her some coffee to help calm her. Jenna and her mom were sure it had been her grandfather, prompting her to wake and aid his wife. Jenna's mom had also previously felt her dad's presence in the room, and she believes in an afterlife based partly on physics: energy can't die, it can only change form.

When Jenna's father Martin was at the end of his life, he went into hospice. Given his globetrotting, on the first day Martin was there, he immediately picked up on the accent of a preacher who visited him. "Kenya?" he asked. The preacher was pleasantly surprised, and they established a quick rapport.

The last days of Martin's life were difficult for him and the family. His eyes were limp, and he was barely conscious, but just before he died they popped open. He had a huge smile on his face and his eyes lit up. He was seemingly looking through the ceiling. He exclaimed, "Oh wow, the farm!" It was the farm he'd grown up on outside Columbus. That's where they were waiting for him. His happy place is where he was received. Then he passed and all the light in him went out, instantly, leaving the gray, empty shell of his body. When Jenna told her uncle about the farm he got tears in eyes.

(My drummer friend Ray said that his dad described the passing of Ray's mom just like Jenna described Martin's death. She was illuminated until the moment she died, and then, in the space of a finger snap, the light exited her body. This implies our souls may be pure light, slivers of god, like the sun. As light is hope, we spark in the darkness.)

(Sci-fi bonus thought: what if the sun is a massive collection of souls, nurturing all life here for billions of years, or the repository from which we came? Can we hang out there once we cross over? What would it feel like to be enveloped by hundreds of billions or trillions of pure loving essences?)

Before Martin's illness, when he was having an especially good time at the Spider, he liked to grab his camera and take photos of everything and everyone. On evenings when there's a happy energy in the bar, and her smartphone is sitting behind the bar, Jenna will walk by to discover it's been turned on and shifted to the photo or video mode. If she turns the phone off it turns itself back on in that position. This has happened with multiple phones she's owned. Dad saying hello.

Jenna doesn't feel Martin's presence all of the time. She figures he hangs out in other places he loved, like the traveler he was. This matches my understanding of spirit life. Sometimes we call for them, but they're otherwise engaged. Again, praying and talking to spirits is not a wish fulfillment service, and the results aren't always instantaneous. Jenna says that the Barking Spider is not a huge money maker, but it's self-sustaining. She feels she's not allowed to be greedy, but when she really needs something it always comes through.

For example, six or seven years ago, when she said aloud, "I really need a new dresser," her modest, nearly inadvertent wish was heard. The next day another bartender at the Spider spontaneously offered one because she was moving. The universe delivered the message, or maybe just one helpful spirit.

We discussed this idea further. I said that many of my prayers or hopes are thought, but not verbalized, believing there's no significant distinction in terms of result. Jenna feels you have to say what you need out loud to get help. I don't know whether a sound wave is stronger than the energy of a thought, but the last few days I've been testing her verbal method. We'll see what happens.

During one of my gigs at the Spider last year, when I only knew the outline of Jenna's experiences, I spontaneously asked the audience if anyone had ever had an experience with spirits. The room dropped to an immediate hush. It took me off guard, but I found it interesting. I didn't know if the silence reflected fear, reverence, curiosity, or a mix? Maybe the audience was surprised that I spoke casually about something that many people think of as private and intimate. It seems the more openly I discuss it, the more comfortable and certain I become. It doesn't embarrass me. I also discover that more people in my circle of friends and acquaintances have had experiences than I ever expected.

No one in the audience raised a hand or voice to acknowledge a supernatural experience, but everyone listened carefully as I briefly explained that I'd had many inspiring encounters, anybody could have one, I was writing a book about it, and I was convinced there's more than this life. I mentioned that Jenna had had experiences too, without getting specific. She smiled and waved from the bar. The energy of the performance was different after that. More dialed in. I haven't mentioned the book again in subsequent performances, so as not to turn it into a cheap gimmick, but I'll surely have copies of the book with me the next time I'm there this fall.

THIRTY-EIGHT: GHOST TOUR

Somehow I nearly forgot to mention that there are ghost tours on my street every summer, in the Allentown district of Buffalo. I'm gonna have to look up the guy who gives them because he regularly discusses three houses on my block, all within 50 feet of my home. I was working on the final edits for the book on my laptop when he came by with a tour group of 20 young Asian tourists or students. I eavesdropped with ease; he wore a little headset microphone that amplified his voice up to my second floor porch.

Here's a summary of what I learned: House Number One is a few doors down from me, across the street. The tour guide said there was an unfriendly presence in the second floor apartment. An unnamed woman who previously lived there felt "oppressed" in the flat. Her dog often barked at seemingly empty space. (Animals are perceptive in ways we probably can't even imagine, like Oscar the therapy cat at the Steere House nursing complex in Providence, RI. I read about him online in 2010. Oscar paces the halls, only stopping to visit patients who have hours to live. The cat has "predicted" at least 50 deaths and is so reliable that doctors will notify family members when the cat jumps on the bed to comfort an occupant.) The night that she moved out her electric clock kept spinning in rapid circles. The tour guide didn't say whether this presence is still felt by the current tenants. They must have been thrilled if they overheard him.

House Number Two is a few doors down from me on the same side of the street. The tour guide said it used to be a bra factory in the early 1900s, and, when it caught fire, many young girls burned to death because they were chained to their desks to sew the bras. (Never underestimate man's capacity for inhumanity towards his fellow man.) The rebuilt house became a bike club. Now it's a residence. It looked like the tour guide was pointing at the home my uncle and aunt (dad's sister) used to own, but I couldn't see clearly enough through the trees to be certain. As I child, I played games in the vaulted attic with my cousins. I never experienced anything odd there. I should ask my cousins if they did.

House Number Three was nearest to mine. He said three old women lived in it. One used a cane which made a familiar tapping sound that residents in the other apartment often heard. When she died the new residents still heard her cane, and they found a secret compartment in her bedroom. It housed a small box of odd items, including tree slices dressed as people, with pin cushions sticking out of them. "Apparently the old ladies were into the juju," the tour guide said laughingly.

I listened and briefly considered yelling, "Hey, if you think that's good, I've got spirits over here all the time, and I'm writing a book about it that will blow your mind!" But that would have probably been rude.

The tour guide also discussed a rectangular plot of cement, about twice the size of a coffin, in the middle of the street, fairly equidistant among the three houses. It keeps sinking into the ground, as if something bad is associated with the spot, though this story was short on details. Was it a makeshift grave? He said when city workers used normal paving materials on the street this plot always sank within a short period of time, forcing frequent patching. Eventually the workers took to using heavier grade sidewalk cement instead, so that it lasts longer.

I was intrigued when the tour guide said that he thinks there are centers of spiritual energy that seem to be related to geography. As I said, the three houses on the tour are all within 50 feet of my own house which he described as a typical focal radius. And sadly, there was a murder in another cute cottage house across the street when my grandparents still owned and inhabited my house. The tour guide didn't mention this, and I've heard nothing about any bad spirit presences there. A terrible event in a space doesn't necessarily condemn it to haunting.

(The part of me that resists associations, self-aggrandizing, or seeing mystical connections in *every* minor daily event hesitates to mention the tour at all, yet it seems relevant. It's easy to overestimate one's connectivity, or the importance of one's role in the bigger plan.)

After both of my grandparents died, my father and his sisters inherited their house. A real estate agent told dad that he wouldn't get more than $30,000 for it. He found this unacceptable. As he'd recently retired, he decided to rehab it with a few hired hands. He rented the two apartments out until I purchased it several years later, and he helped with additional renovations, as did mom. After more than a decade of facelifts and the opening of numerous new businesses down the block, the value of houses in my neighborhood has increased tenfold.

I either just ruined the tour guide's business by telling you everything I overheard, or helped with his future bookings. I don't know how I'd feel about my house being lumped in as a tour stop with the others, especially if I'm on my porch at the time. This house isn't haunted. There are no questionable presences of any kind. The truth is that spirits are EVERYWHERE. They travel freely and pop in to visit where they like, though it does appear that certain spirits are very attached to places they inhabited while living, and some do haunt them when they can't let go.

After purchasing the house in summer 2006 and just before I moved in, I had a bad dream in which ghosts taunted me and said they would haunt me here. It scared me a little, but I knew much less about spirits than now. I don't believe unfriendlies can physically inhabit spaces that have abundant positive energy, or where no negative energy has accumulated. They can't find a nook to hide in or infect. Nevertheless, mom got some holy water in a small brown bottle from a local church, and we spritzed the apartment for the heck of it. Couldn't hurt, right? I've never had any problems here, though I'm (mostly!) cautious about the spirits with whom I communicate. The bottle of holy water is in the pantry, but there hasn't been a reason to use it again.

Just for the record, and in case this book somehow gets read by more than six people, if you're enchanted by these spirit accounts, you are absolutely *not allowed* to treat my block and/or home as a weird mecca/destination for spiritual energy! My neighbors and I are entitled to privacy. If you are insufficiently respectful I will break out the juju on you!

THIRTY-NINE: GLADJ

As you know, my younger brother Steve has had many friendly visits from our brother Justin, mom's second child. Justin's the member of our little gang who, perhaps, volunteered to stay behind to help orchestrate this dream composition from a higher vibration, plucking cosmic strings. For no particular reason, at some point we started referring to him more often as "J." At the midway point of writing, I realized the acronym for my book is *GLADJ*, as in "GLAD Justin." It made us smile.

In our email correspondence Steve, mom and I often add smiley face emoticons, typed as :-), to the end of a note. For the last few years, when they received an email, a capital letter "J" inexplicably appeared in place of each smiley face I'd typed.

I only became aware of the odd substitution when they wrote back. I'd read their note and then scroll down to re-read my original message to find Js instead of smileys. I chalked it up as a software quirk, though no other characters were consistently, similarly altered. As mom had no way of knowing that smiley faces were missing in the first place, she eventually asked why I kept including Js. I explained how I'd deduced the substitutions, but that I didn't know why they were occurring.

Mom felt these were instances of Justin playfully reminding us of his presence, and to think of him. I wondered whether to write about it in the book. Was it too much of a reach, a case of interpreting every coincidence as a cosmic sign?

Then one hot weekend afternoon this summer, mom, Steve and I went to Forest Lawn Cemetery for a stroll. In just a few minutes our team humor kicked in. We twisted the last names on various headstones into silly puns and made other dumb jokes, like when mom asked if I needed any ketchup after we passed a "Heintz" stone. I practically slapped my forehead.

"I smell dead people," I said, inappropriately echoing the boy from *The Sixth Sense*. There were more goofy comments which I can't recall. We amused ourselves. We decided it's okay if people make fun of our names after we're dead, too. We'll be gone, it won't matter.

If you've never heard of it or visited, Forest Lawn is an amazing, sprawling campus. There are more than 150,000 graves on its 269 acres. Established in 1849 in downtown Buffalo, the abundance of ornate monuments, mausoleums, statues, and sculptures makes it clear that Buffalo's wealthy historical families are well represented.

We pondered who some of them might have been, especially when inspecting the large marble and stone vanity pieces, as their financiers likely hoped we would. Why else would someone require a 30 foot obelisk announcing his departure from Earth, if not to signify status even in death? We couldn't envision ourselves lodged in something as flashy as a mausoleum, as beautiful as many of them are. Besides, what if purchasing a big, expensive funeral monument in advance somehow makes you die sooner because the universe knows you're even materialistic about death, the supposed great equalizer?

(Note that the grave of Dorothy Goetz, a singer born in Buffalo and the first wife of celebrated songwriter Irving Berlin, is quite modest. She died of typhoid in 1921 only six months after their wedding, at 20 years of age. Berlin wrote his first ballad "When I Lost You" for her, supposedly the only song he admitted came directly from personal experience. The Sinatra version is appropriately restrained and mournful.)

A black rectangular marble sculpture standing about 6 feet tall and 3 feet wide held dozens of drawers of ashes from various families. Although mom, Steve and I each think we'd like to be cremated, it seemed like a good time (for a smart ass) to mention that the big problem is that 95 percent of the person goes up the smoke stack. (A lot of it is water.) Mom put her hands in the air and wiggled her whole little munchkin body like a wave. She said, "Look up at me and I'll do a little dance while I'm going up." She would, too!

I said the real ceremony should probably be outside the crematorium when the person is incinerated. When the smoke hits the air is truly the last goodbye. The 5 percent of ashes one receives afterward seems like an inadequate remnant. There might be no better option, except perhaps an open air funeral pyre, the body wrapped lovingly in shrouds!

We stopped to cool off on a marble bench beneath a small tree. It was less shade than we wanted, but we had to get off our feet after a few hours. I asked mom and Steve if the smiley face emoticons turning into Js was significant enough to include in the book. We didn't come to a conclusive answer and were soon making jokes again.

Afterward mom suggested we go for a snack at the new Coffee Culture shop on Elmwood Avenue near my place. On the way over I sang "Coffee Culture" to the tune of Culture Club's "Karma Chameleon": "Coffee, coffee, coffee, coffee – coffee cul-uhh-turrre." It didn't match up at all syllabically, which helped make it stupid and funny. The lyrics got progressively more inappropriate as we neared our destination. I clutched Steve's knee in the passenger seat for dramatic effect. He said he would always think of my song when passing a Coffee Culture. (Two days later Culture Club announced their first reunion tour in 15 years.) These truly are the moments we cherish later in life.

Inside the air-conditioned shop we ordered sandwiches and coffee. Steve got a Coke, which the friendly cashier grabbed from a cooler behind the counter. When we got to a table Steve showed us the side of the plastic bottle. It said, "Share a Coke with *Justin*." Justin's name was in the same font as the Coke logo, with the familiar white wave below it. We thought it was a sign from J that the smiley face conversions were indeed his work.

I took a picture of Steve grinning with the bottle in the foreground. (Mom later blew it up and framed it for his apartment. She also made one for her desk. I asked for one for my wall. Mom filled Justin's empty Coke with small stones. It sits on a shelf with other souvenirs above Steve's TV.)

I pulled back the only unoccupied chair at our table, moved the open bottle in front of it and invited Justin to have a seat and sip. Mom and Steve laughed. I mimed the soda pop going up through an invisible plastic straw. I so wished the liquid would float upward, or bubble a little.

Our curiosity piqued, I looked up "Coke names promotion" on my smartphone, and found info on the British Coke website, which appeared first in the search results. It said the promotional campaign used more than 1,000 different names. Coke encouraged people to take photographs with their bottles and upload them to their website. It's a clever, obviously effective concept as they've received a lot of free press here. (I want royalties, you high fructose sugar pimps. You helped make America fat.)

With more than 1,000 different names in circulation, the statistical chance of Steve receiving a bottle with Justin on it is less than 1/10th of 1 percent.

Unfortunately, the smiley faces theory popped the next day, after I'd started writing the chapter. A web search uncovered several online articles about the "J" email substitution phenomenon. It turned out to be a common issue with a specific email program. One personal computing website explained it this way:

If you've ever received an email with a mysterious "J" in the body of the message, you may have been perplexed by its meaning. Some messages have a single J, while others have several. Most J's appear at the end of sentences, but they can appear anywhere in the message. So what does this enigmatic character mean and why does it show up in email messages?

The J is actually supposed to be a smiley face.

This is because the letter J represents a smiley face icon in the Wingdings font. Microsoft Outlook, a popular e-mail client, automatically converts the :) and :-) text emoticons into smiley face icons using Wingdings. Therefore, when Microsoft Outlook users type smiley faces in an email message, they are sent as visual smiley face icons (but appear as J's to recipients who don't have the Wingdings font installed).

Even though the mystery of the Js was solved and our fun theory debunked, I still think it's cool that smiley faces have turned into Js in thousands, millions, or perhaps billions of messages. Maybe Justin's plan all along was not just to pepper *us* with Js (which are equivalent to smiley faces), *but the whole world*! He is *GLADJ* after all! He's just sharing the love. (Why J anyway? Why not Z, Q, F, B, or K? But no, it's J.)

Yes, the lesson is that one may err when trying to make every seemingly synchronous square peg fit a round cosmic hole. Yet we still felt Justin near when Steve showed us the Coke. And in a brief moment of seriousness during our conversation at the table mom said, "Justin died on Earth without sin." I felt my eyes moisten at the realization, the truth of it in my heart. He had only lived for a few hours. His innocence was preserved.

We were pleasantly reminded of J even if it was only by coincidence this time. Previous events have been so unmistakably clear that one instance which doesn't line up neatly doesn't shake our faith or joy. J ☺ J ☺!

FORTY: HEY, GUESS WHAT, LOVE IS THE ANSWER AFTER ALL

Brace for abundant sincerity. Love is the only thing that can save a human being. It's that simple, though love has many forms. My family's the greatest source of comfort, with music right behind. Ideally your family is your gang and refuge, the ones who prop you up on your journey through the great dirty world (thanks, Larry Gowan). I wish everyone's was as supportive.

Speaking of sanctuaries, my bro Steve is working on his metaphorical "Cave," where we plan to eventually retreat from the insanity of humanity, if necessary. We joke about it whenever things get shitty or people shock us once again with powerful stupidity and selfishness. "Well, time to pack up and move to The Cave." "I'm stocking up The Cave with canned foods and chocolate. Can't wait to go!" The Cave has cable TV; we still need to watch pro hockey, and my mom likes *True Blood*. (She says Eric is her boyfriend, as is comic book movie hero Thor.)

Many people who didn't get love from their family struggle to overcome it. Some eventually experience it in a romantic relationship, or they're passionate about something like painting, sports, hot rods, chess, knitting, or whatever. Fortunately, we live in a more interconnected world of diverse interests, and people with shared activities can more easily find each other, if only in cyberspace.

Anything that brings pleasure, that you can give yourself to wholly, is an expression of love. Perhaps, like my mom, your dream is to be a caregiver who nurtures a family of conscientious humans, or you give stray animals a home. Mom has rescued a few dogs, and sometimes volunteers at the S.P.C.A., feeding birds with an eye dropper of moistened food.

(By the way, the night before her last volunteer shift, mom dreamt she had mealworms in her bed! She had no idea why, other than that they regularly feed mealworms to the

210

birds there. She told her co-volunteer Dawn about it, and Dawn said that she'd accidentally infested her own bed with mealworms earlier in the year. Dawn took some home in her purse, but they got out of the container, and transferred to her bath towel, which she eventually set on the bed. So there you go. Mom dreamt Dawn's experience!)

Have you noticed the near-glowing aura of compellingly alive people? They're the ones who've figured all this stuff out, how to enjoy life by finding someone or something to love. Their skin shimmers as if the joy and light inside of them is radiating off their body, and maybe it is. You want to be near and feel the warmth. You can't get that kind of skin by rubbing in all the cream in the world. Your face helps tell the story of your life. Live well and you will be more beautiful at all levels, including the cellular and sub-atomic.

Your DNA sits on tiny twisted ropes of molecules called chromosomes. At the end of each chromosome is a match-tip shaped piece of DNA called a telomere. Telomeres help cells to divide, but each time a cell divides the telomere gets shorter. When it gets too short, the cell can't divide anymore and becomes inactive; it dies. As your cells die you age. Tightness, worry, and stress are damaging to cells, especially the telomeres. You can help slow telomere shedding by taking care of yourself physically, emotionally, and especially spiritually.

Happiness is literally good for every cell in your body. The vibrations from laughter and pleasure permeate you, aiding longevity. When you're stressed and unhappy your DNA coils in tightly upon itself. Every cell shrivels up like testicles in a cold swimming pool. When you're happy and open your DNA stretches out, unfurling like a happy cat lying in a sunbeam.

Sure, living vibrantly isn't always possible. There are endless tragedies in the news. What's a tiny person supposed to do with it all? The Buddhists probably have it right, that practicing loving compassion towards others is the best answer. Less judgment, more understanding; or at least suspension of judgment for as long as is possible.

If you feel overwhelmed by the world, the goal is to change your mindset so that what's going on outside of you has little effect on the core. You're safe and calm in the hurricane eye, nearly unaffected while chaos swirls around. This helps you to make good decisions at critical, stressful moments. If you can be brave in the face of darkness you will learn what love is really about, and what you're made of.

I love Martin Luther King Jr.'s quote, "The moral arc of the universe is long, but it bends towards justice." We will likely witness many injustices in life, but in the long run doing the right thing ennobles us. It's to love honesty, clarity, and truth. You don't necessarily know how your daily contributions help others, but the universe keeps track. Your selflessness gets added to the bank account of your soul. The energy of each generous act is released from your core, traveling outward, reverberating in the universe. Doesn't it seem like when you're open that the world responds more openly in return?

I'm beginning to believe that the universe may be constructed, at the quantum level, for us to create reality as a mirror of ourselves. Yes, high intelligence, a genetic quirk, leads to problems because the mind entertains unlimited contradictory possibilities, and the universe and god are a paradox. Absurdity is truth and reality, and, therefore, some madness is normal, not the other way around. But life in a quantum state paradox means the "rules" aren't fixed. They're bendable, and reality can be influenced by the energy of our thoughts, intentions, and actions. In quantum mechanics the observer forces an electron into position. The electron is everywhere and nowhere at once until an intelligence helps it land. Everything is neutral energy and possibilities until the possibility drops into position. We can aim our intent towards the results we want, and when we're generous it gets returned to us somewhere.

Martin Luther King wasn't a saint, and I'm sure not. His extramarital affairs were well-documented and publicized by the F.B.I. under Hoover, which sent him anonymous letters suggesting he kill himself. His flaws are part of the point. Think of how much courage he must have had, as a contradictory person like you and I, to maintain his crucial message for racial equality. History has made him mythical, but he was just a man with hopes, dreams, and problems.

Jesus and Muhammad, too, may have simply been messengers, posthumously anointed to prophets (the same thing really, just a fancier title implying divinity), and made superhuman. Which means any of us can do as they did. (Though If Jesus, Muhammad or others truly performed miracles, that's a new conversation. We won't likely learn the truth of this while human. However, as existence is paradoxical, we're already in the realm of the impossible and supernatural. Reality might be malleable to any being operating exclusively from the high vibration of love.)

It took longer than MLK's lifetime, but the dream of a more integrated, harmonious society has been largely successful, and the rights of homosexuals are finally being addressed, too. The seeds bear fruit 50 years on. What would the country be like if he hadn't been courageous and loving? Think of the impact he made as *just one man*. If we too are brave we can help heal the broken world, one person at a time, beginning with ourselves. Light is always more powerful than darkness, no matter how it sometimes seems.

FORTY-ONE: RELATIONSHIP KARMA

Childhood and adolescence is the early encoding of a human being. Your programming is hard to overcome if it has been negative for a prolonged period of time and you have no early working examples of affection and love. If you don't have at least one ally in your family who loves you unconditionally, it affects your concept of life. People overcome their upbringing, but it adds another barrier. The women I've dated who lacked real family support were more conflicted, unstable, and unpredictable. The most inclined to run.

Affection and love may be rare because it takes courage to express these feelings, and some people treat basic survival as their first and only priority, to the subjugation of their emotions, when of course they're never separate. It's not okay for parents to neglect children by emotional omission, but this must happen a lot because I've met many who feel unloved. Even when they don't say it, their actions give them away.

I wondered for years why daring, damaged women can be so attractive. Part of the answer is that we attract what we are. Romance isn't always logical. I'm drawn to people who do their own thing, so women with an intentional disregard for caution and conventional boundaries have been hard to resist. Some of the least inhibited women also had the worst self-esteem. There's a likely link between promiscuity and depression, and it's a not-well-kept secret among men that "crazy" women can be great in bed.

214

It goes both ways. There are many semi-to-seriously-dangerous bad boys, too. Women know they're trouble but still toss themselves with abandon, then get mad when it goes to hell, and commit emotional energy to the drama. (Remember how popular, hypnotic, and truthful that song by the Eurythmics was: "Some of them want to use you / Some of them want to get used by you / Some of them want to abuse you / Some of them want to be abused.") Some wild women sleep with bad boys, then later marry a kind provider and have a family, tucking the memory of their hot romps in a secure brain corner their husbands will never find. Some people outgrow a hedonistic phase and find true love.

Is the problem that a lot of nice people are a bit boring, or repressed and unaware, while many of the exciting people are vain, selfish, and narcissistic, but realized and perceptive? Lust for life is a turn on. If everyone is holding out for the "perfect" person who happens to be respectful and responsible most of the time, yet a wild animal in the sack, what are the chances?

Perhaps semi-dangerous people appear to be, or actually are, liberated, detached, and cool; in touch with, or unwilling to deny, their primal side. One day a switch flips. They indulge the animal, which is part of the truth of being human. Some are so deluded and self-absorbed that they disregard danger because they can't conceive of failure, and it inadvertently helps them succeed, or for a time. They consider it their right to take without reciprocating.

They seem confident and powerful, which makes them attractive, but they're perpetually riding a knife's edge. They don't want their mask to fall. They provide exciting company in short bursts, but are difficult or impossible in a long-term relationship. There are strange secrets at the heart of existence, which might include an unconscious death wish we don't really understand.

Some people gleefully transgress against convention, risking the wrath of polite society. I think most of us want to taste some freedom. Staying always inside the lines gets dull, and women who are too passive and agreeable haven't always interested me, which made me feel guilty for years. I'm changing though. Age and experience have conspired to alter my perceptions and preferences. I'm trying to reconcile the trinity of soul, body, and mind, but keep the spark. I wrote a new song: "I wanna laugh my head off every day with a kick ass girl / And have it be me and her against the world." I don't know if this will happen or not, but I think that's actually my ideal now. We'll see!

I've gone out of my way to show contradictions in my relationships and music. We all have them. It seemed like this was the only way to be an honest person and artist, though not everyone I dated reciprocated, or acknowledged their own inconsistencies. I revealed too much sometimes. I'm empathetic, curious, fun-loving, and honest, and value this in others. I've also been hedonistic, intense, and selfish. Some women love a whiff of danger and will break their rules for you. The discovery taught me a contradictory lesson.

(Artists autobiographically mine themselves for content, to get closer to the heart of things. Some artists see truth as the golden standard, even when it's partly ugly - Bukowski comes to mind, alienated and angry from his disfiguring acne - and put their messy glory on full display. Some are exhibitionists who wish to both titillate and provoke, as expressions of power and/or to ignite social change, like Madonna. It's very easy for any artist, including me, to cross

216

the line between interesting revelations that help us better understand ourselves and *Too Much Information*.)

The moth cliché is true. You can pursue total pleasure straight into a flame. You can flirt with danger and think you know how close to get without burning up, then get absolutely torched, by accident or in a moment of carelessness, as in a drunken stupor when you have overestimated your self-control. Some people have a strong attraction to the fire by nature. They seek the edges of human experience so that they know what it feels like to flirt with death but live to tell, though not all survive. It's true there's thrills to be found chasing a flame.

What is a death wish? Is it a longing for rebirth, and a chance at a completely new and different existence, by wiping the slate of life clean? Is reincarnation certain, and somehow tied into the eventual death, and repeated or eternal rebirths, of the universe? Are we drawn to imitate the billions and billions of stars being born and dying, and reborn and dying again and again? Does the part of us which craves obliteration know that death leads to renewal? Atomized and returned to the smallest bits of matter is about as connected to the entirety of creation as one could hope to be, though I'd like to take my time getting there.

(Dinosaurs ruled the Earth for 160 million years (!) until an asteroid impact wiped them out 65 million years ago. Humans have only dominated for a few hundred thousand years, and it's unlikely we would have thrived without their disappearance. The death rock that killed the dinosaurs was traveling at 40,000 miles per hour when it hit with the force of 3,000 atomic bombs. The heat at impact destroyed every living creature above ground for 1,000 miles, kicking up 20,000 tons of organic matter into and through the atmosphere that fell back to Earth, around the entire globe, as tens of thousands of burning meteors, setting every forest on the planet on fire. The ash kicked into the atmosphere blocked out all sunlight for another six weeks. Temperatures plummeted. When the ash dispersed it returned to Earth as acid rain, killing the few survivors, and a period of great global temperature increases followed. The Earth was scorched clean. Sterilized. The death of the dinosaurs allowed mammals to eventually rise from the oceans and evolve into us. The asteroid set a whole new cycle of life in motion after the complete destruction of the dominant species.)

I don't watch much TV but the most popular programs seem to focus on gruesome murder forensics (presented in intricate, graphic detail), the omniscient authority of the police and C.I.A. (spreading gunfire like spermatozoa), dramatic sexual relationships, and millionaire lifestyles. We're morbidly fascinated by the body and its functions, as well as its mutilation. No one would pause at a highway car wreck otherwise. As mentioned, there's more money in the sex industry than Hollywood. (And since the dawn of AIDS, sex with the wrong person can kill you. That's harsh, and charges relations with additional danger.) We're captivated by death, power, sex, money, and destruction.

In the sober light of day I know I don't want to get killed in a gruesome car accident, by an asteroid, or in my bedroom. I want to enjoy life. I'm afraid to do drugs because I don't want to break my brain and end up in a ditch. But under cover of dark, with glasses of booze tinkling, smiles all around, and perfume and possibility in the air, logic is impaired and some of us walk the line (thanks, Johnny Cash), over and over again, courting the possibility of destruction, risking rejoining the universe, and partly craving it.

I've had two really accurate tarot card readings while visiting New York City; one from 10 years ago floored me. The psychic told me a past relationship that ended badly was still messing with my karma, impeding the way forward. The psychic mentioned the woman by her first name, Leia. It was like being smacked in the head. I had perfect clarity of the situation, as if a thin veil had been lifted. I had to patch it as best I could. I wasn't fully to blame, but it didn't matter, because I was partly to blame.

The psychic told me that Leia "was in pain too" when we crashed. Sometimes two people are attracted to one another, yet both so insecure, that they unconsciously engage in war. They use built-up resentments to try to best one another. Things can get strange and messy quickly when we mix the longing for deep affection, acceptance, and understanding with our desires, insecurities, and need for control. (Pure love seeks no advantage.) A person who has been hurt a lot or felt powerless, as I have, and some of the women I've dated have, may develop too big a chip on his/her shoulder. We overcompensate and come to see all human interaction as combat, and try to "win" in every arena.

Some women who feel powerless in everyday life, like Leia, discover they have a lot of sexual power over others. Some women grant access as an expression of that power. Some trade sex like a commodity, an exchange for social status or dominance in a group of people. Some hope it leads to love. Power dynamics can be prevalent and unconscious. There are also free-spirited people who just like to do it without strings, but I've come to believe there's no such thing as sex without an emotional component, even if it's a strange numbness.

I thought Leia was too pretty for me. Tons of guys were chasing her. Maybe she thought I had a social advantage because I'm a musician, though she never said, or she felt attractive enough to not need to say. In trying to prove something to ourselves and each other about strength, we both lost, proving our weakness instead.

I was vulnerable and angry. I found the world unsatisfactory in its incuriosity and negligent cruelty, and tried hard (I'm still trying) to believe in love, light, and goodness in people. I found too much suffering for many years, or it found me by attraction, and sadness weighed often, creeping into my bones. I internalized the perceived unhappiness of others, whole countries of less fortunate people suffering grave injustices, as if it also belonged to me. I made art to explore my feelings about it, mixing darkness and light, seeking truth. I wanted to change the world and myself, but often felt like I was swimming in mud. I still want to find an unlikely way to make the world better, though I don't know how. Idealism persists.

Shortly after the New York reading, I followed the psychic's advice. I sent Leia a message wishing her well. I said I was sorry if I'd hurt her, that it was never my intention to cause the resentment she felt, and I'd gladly talk about it any time.

She didn't respond initially, but I'd done what I could, to own my role and make amends, and from there I'd need to let it go and hope for the best.

The weight lifted, and my life opened up. If she'd already moved on and didn't want to be in touch with me that was her right. I accepted it. Finally, a year later, I heard from her. She didn't mention the note, but expressed interest in meeting up.

As the psychic revealed, it's possible that something from your past has a cloud over you, which you can't outrun. Energy and action aren't always easy, and decency's a lifelong effort, but helps free the soul from weight and regret.

FORTY-TWO: MARIE

Among the special people I've been fated to meet was a sweet, troubled woman named Marie. We corresponded through an online dating site in 2002. She had a teenage son and lived in a cute, little house in the canal city of Welland, Ontario.

Marie had a quick mind, sharp tongue, and could see through bullshit instantly, calling others on it. She was empathetic, honest, and laughed often. I loved her expressive, cartoonish paintings. It made her mad that her self-portraits were perceived as adorable when she meant them to be serious expressions of her mental state. She had a tiny, quarter-sized tattoo of a mermaid on her ankle. Like her, it was subtle and tasteful. She organized environmental events in the city and tried to live small, contributing a minimum of waste. She was an idealist in the best sense, and her own person.

Marie was divorced and having trouble making ends meet, with low-paying, part-time jobs that involved little creativity, a sad fact of life for so many. She was the first woman I'd dated who had a child; it was another signpost for getting a bit older. I'd recently turned 30.

Her situation made me think of my mom, and the challenges and burdens, but also great joys, of raising kids alone. Marie was close to her son, too. Visitation rights for a father aren't remotely equivalent to the deep relationship one develops with a divorced parent living together day-to-day. I think my dad sometimes feels that he missed out on our upbringing, and he did to an extent. Mom took on the full responsibility of raising us, as if she had a choice, and ended up with more of the joy and closeness, too.

Marie struggled with depression, but it wasn't the same as with previous girlfriends. She was sexually communicative and liberated, reserved in public, but not in private. She expressed what she liked and didn't like, though it also caused guilt because she considered sex addictive. Her clarity was different from other women. We loved to make each other feel good, often making dumb jokes in bed.

Marie had reservations about oral sex because parting her legs made her feel vulnerable. It was the first time I'd thought of it that way. I don't know how many men (savages mostly, sometimes including me) appreciate what it means to a woman. We eased our way into it, going slowly with everything. My perspective widened.

The connection with Marie cleared away much of the past. The healthy, open expression of physical and emotional love helped me let go of conflicted relationships, including Leia.

I would have gladly continued seeing her, but she decided that dealing with depression, her job and financial situation, and raising her son had to become a full-time endeavor. She felt that her strong libido and resultant relationships were sidetracking her from her personal goals and getting her life straight. She said she had to be by herself to sort her feelings.

Tears snuck down my cheeks as I drove back to the border on long, sparsely-lit back roads, in quiet winter darkness.

Despite the sadness, I felt awake and alive. We parted without resentment, only affection and gratitude. She helped me see how a positive relationship could work in the future. I loved her for it and said so. When she said she loved me too, I knew there would always be a part of her with me, and me with her. We kept in touch over the next five or six years, whenever either of us needed a trusted friend.

I did right by Marie, but there are a few women I wish things had worked out with somehow. I wish I'd been a better man at the time, but it's turned out as it had to. I'll attract the right person when my heart and soul are ready. The universe will know.

Amazingly, in 2012, 10 years after dating Marie, I met her across-the-street neighbor Nina online. She knows Marie only in passing. Out of all the women in Canada, or just the province of Ontario, I've dated two who live directly across the street from each other. God is winking at me.

FORTY-THREE: MORE MEDIUMS AND MESSAGES

My most recent tarot card reading was in summer 2012, across the Peace Bridge in Fort Erie, Ontario. It was during the Friendship Festival celebrating the long, sexy relationship between Canada and the United States. Nina suggested we meet there for our first date. There were carnival rides, games, and live music. The weather that weekend was amazing, as was the whole summer. As we strolled along the street of vendors offering fried food and trinkets, we found a friendly psychic. Her name was Gina.

Nina went into her tent first, for 20 minutes. I sat on a curb across the cordoned street, watching people go by and occasionally checking Nina's expression for signs it was going well. Nina liked her reading, so I went ahead. During her introduction Gina said I could ask her about three different topics she'd address at the end. I wanted to know about the longevity of my family, whether my brother Steve should do anything specific with his medium abilities, and what I could expect to happen, if anything, with my music. Then I picked out tarot cards.

I don't recall all the specifics, but Gina said she saw a mixture of colors in my aura, some bright and some dark. I wasn't entirely surprised, though a bit disappointed. She said that once I understood what I wanted out of relationships then that part of my life would resolve.

Gina said my health looked good long-term. I thought, "That's good," because I've been swimming my nuts off for 13 years. She didn't address the health of anyone else in my family as I'd hoped. Regarding Steve, she said that he was where he needed to be with spiritual endeavors for the moment, a bit removed from mediumship.

I told Gina that in 2011 Steve had begun to feel overwhelmed by the volume of spirit visitors he constantly received. He would literally be in bed trying to sleep, going to the bathroom, or brushing his teeth, and visitors would pop in to try to converse with him. This is because mediums are in demand by spirits. They're the only ones who can carry messages from the other side to this one, and many spirits try to get word back to their living relatives.

Gina totally understood this feeling. When she first discovered her psychic abilities she too felt overwhelmed by the volume. It was as if there was a full-time crowd of spirits around trying to get her attention. This let me know my brother's experiences were common to mediums. Over time Gina said she began to see how she could help people and earn a living, too.

Regarding music, Gina said she could see success in the future, but she believed it would be significantly tied in with writing somehow. Not music writing, but some other kind. I realized that the shell of this book had been sitting dormant for a few months. I asked if that was it, and she said perhaps so. I resumed writing for the rest of the summer. I needed to finish it in the sunshine, and spent many beautiful evenings on the porch with my new, cheap laptop, the cats, and fine Belgian beer. The first draft was an indulgent, bitter manifesto that unsuccessfully mixed in a spiritual element, but as I grew over the three years I worked on it the tone became more hopeful. More than 50,000 unnecessary words were dropped and I added new chapters about recent inspiring events.

Gina said I would definitely know when it was time to transition to the next stage of life. It would be unambiguous. I hope that's true. I'm tired of my day job, though it's way more pleasant than many people's, so I shouldn't complain.

No wonder so many people have a mid-life crisis though. You've worked 20 to 25 years and you look ahead and see another 20 or more and think, "How the hell am I going to put up with this shit? I'm not getting any younger. I'll only get more tired and jaded the longer I'm here!" That must be why so many people play the lottery, though I found it sad when I was younger. Now I get it. It would be great to have an artistic breakthrough. I imagine the fun new creative endeavors I'd cook up with more time and freedom.

When mom saw a spiritualist in late 2010 she took notes about things related to me. The psychic said that two gentlemen came in. She asked mom if I sang because she was seeing a lot of musical notes. Mom said yes. The reader acknowledged that as the connection and said that my Grandpa Falgiano (Samuel) watches over me. Grandpa Falg showed her he knew me "growing up." My Grandpa Bella (Angelo), mom's dad, also arrived. He showed the psychic he knew me "very young," because he died when I was 2.

Grandpa Falgiano did most of the talking. The psychic described him as a big man with big hands. He was 6 foot 4 and owned a tire shop downtown for many years. My father said, as a child, the only time he ever saw his own father cry was after a huge truck tire burst at the shop. Grandpa Falgiano took the blast in the chest, and if he'd been a smaller man he would surely have been killed. He had heart problems for the rest of his life until a triple bypass. Ironically, when he died, his powerful heart held out the longest. I visited him a few days before he passed, his long body now strangely thin, turned and folded on his side to fit the hospital bed. I held his hand and listened to his shallow breathing.

By contrast, Grandpa Bella was about 5 foot 2. In the psychic's vision he showed her his muscles, meaning he was strong. He worked with his hands. Grandpa Bella arrived at Ellis Island, by himself, when he was 13. He spoke no English and earned his living working on the railroad. The reader said they both have a vested interest in me, which is humbling.

She asked mom if I played an instrument like guitar and wrote music. "Does he have a song on the radio?" (A song I wrote in college was in regular rotation on a Buffalo alternative music station for a few years.) She told mom to encourage my music; she saw it going somewhere. She said that there would be an opportunity to join a band, but that I should stay away from it. I should "be on my own" and "find my own voice." The grandfathers were adamant about this. As flattering as that is, I don't put total stock into a life-altering breakthrough occurring. I'd be glad to just continue being creative.

The reader asked if I was single. She saw me as married and split, and asked if I was divorced. Mom said no, but that she thought I'd had a heartbreak. (Who hasn't?) The reader said yes, it didn't work and it put me off, and I chose to focus on artistic work instead, which is true. At this point my Grandma Bella came in waving a rolling pin and said, "It's about time (to settle down)!" I can see this perfectly. She was probably wearing her waitress uniform.

FORTY-FOUR: I LOVE MUSIC

German philosopher Friedrich Nietzsche wrote, "Without music, life would be a mistake." During high school mom ordered a literary T-shirt for me with that aphorism on it in black type on white. I'll add a Ben Franklin twist by stating, "Great music is proof that God exists, and he wants us to be happy."

My adjusted Franklin quote would probably irritate Nietzsche, who claimed god was dead. However, if there's an afterlife, then Nietzsche knows he was wrong and is probably resolved to it by now. Maybe he and god get together for a beer at a James Brown – Michael Jackson cloud concert to talk it over.

I love sound, and am opinionated about music, but not elitist. I consume great music with joyful lust. I've blown out my favorite recordings on repeat listens, and, as my understanding of music deepens, what impresses inevitably narrows. Standards rise as awareness and knowledge grow.

Great music is inherently spiritual, irrespective of the lyrical meaning. I feel there's honesty in sound itself, the vibrations of the voice and instruments. My favorite music and art risks everything without guarantee of reward. When performers defile music solely for money or fame, it's like they're pimping my religion. Don't treat music like your whore!

Intelligent, exploratory sonic madness is fun, but I also appreciate artists who figure out how to communicate with a large audience, while maintaining a high artistic standard. The greats know or learn how. Michael Jackson's *Off The Wall* from 1979 is brilliant. It's disco-infused pop, but with top-notch songwriting, musicianship, and arrangements by Quincy Jones. The grooves and melodic hooks are huge. Jackson's vocal performances are joyful, and it sounds like it was a blast to make. That's nearly impossible to fake.

Off The Wall was recorded quickly. Jackson did two or three songs worth of vocals per day, and songwriter Rod Temperton wrote several of the hits over a weekend prior to the start of recording. Nowadays, weeks might be spent trying to perfect the vocals on one song, and the performance might still get heavily edited and pitch-corrected by an army of studio engineers. Some of Jackson's later albums took years and thousands of studio hours to complete, but are inferior to his earlier, quicker, less self-conscious work.

One might argue that *Off The Wall* and his huge follow-up *Thriller* are disposable pop, but that ignores the truth that Jackson brought a ton of joy to millions of people. Sadly, he got weird over the years, disappearing into the cult of himself. He seems to have been a deeply troubled soul who never had a real childhood, yearned for an impossible return, and wanted to live in that artificial bubble forever (like many artists), but at his height he was magic.

You need some ego to write music and think anybody wants to hear it. You need enough belief to put yourself out and get anything done in the world. Hopefully your ego doesn't eat you if people don't respond to your heartfelt sentiments the way you'd hoped. Conversely, hopefully your head doesn't explode if you have a huge breakthrough, because, once you lose touch with reality and regular people, future work will suffer from detachment, delusion, and self-importance.

In 25 years of songwriting the process remains mysterious and I wonder where another idea could possibly come from. I used to believe that the change in awareness represented crossing a boundary between my conscious and unconscious mind. Now I wonder if extended creative periods are like wading into the deeper hidden stream, connecting to the underlying creative force responsible for the universe.

Hours pass quickly and I feel very alive and realized. Many songwriters become addicted to this high. All other daily activities get structured to allow for that potentially brief window of creativity to happen, sometimes at the expense of important, but mundane, things like doing the laundry! I have to pace my energy to leave room for it.

The high from performing is similar. A great musician can cram a lifetime of emotion into a two-hour show, inadvertently masking the years or decades of writing, recording, rehearsal, and sacrifice that precede it. Tolstoy said that "art is a lie that enables us to see the truth." A great performance isn't really life. It's a heavily concentrated, idealized, refined, and perfected version.

But it's a beautiful lie that liberates us when it's truthful. A great performance rejoins us with the creative spirit. We feel kinship with the people around us because we've been united in a big feeling. The everyday barriers we build to protect ourselves fall away and we remember how nice it is to feel uninhibited and childlike again. Great art reconnects us to the best parts of ourselves, though the feeling can be scary for some because it's so intimate.

There's a post-show glow, an energetic bubble, which lasts a while after a great show. Connected individuals can live there for extended periods, access it more readily, and use it to make more art. When I'm creatively engaged I ride the wave for days, though I have to remember to come back to "real life." There's a danger in falling so in love with esoteric, dreamy thoughts that one loses touch with the real world.

Inevitable dry spells make me feel unplugged, and I'm susceptible to depression. Many artists are moody, but it's not okay to act like a tortured, misunderstood soul, because everyone is misunderstood to some extent and has hard times. A non-artist's depth of feeling is just as important, whether they're able to articulate it or not. Creative people are often self-centered, but great ones explore the ways in which we unite. They invite you into the way they feel life, and you leave your inner world to stroll around theirs for a while.

Humans are driven to create, whether it's making art or making babies. The passion is built into our DNA; it's part of our survival instinct. It's also partly an attempt to achieve immortality by pushing critical aspects of ourselves into the future, either genetically or intellectually, past our natural lives. I once explained to a friend that the reason many musicians become obsessive about the smallest of details is because the art we make is our only opportunity at perfection in life. There are so many things that I can't control, but if I can write and record a perfect song it's like being a small god.

My writing generally starts with a vision, but once I'm working it's more fun and satisfying to leave room for discoveries. Happy accidents, improvisation, and serendipity are welcome. It's steering without steering, and the result is more authentic. The universe will contribute.

I don't tend to hear or think of music in rigidly defined genres. I realize that we have a natural tendency to categorize things as a way of trying to understand them, so that we can articulate what we like and don't like by saying that one thing is *this*, while another is *that*. But I get more excited by subtle (or not so subtle) mash-ups and reinventions of styles. The same song can be arranged a million different ways. There's no reason that most every song on the radio needs to sound similar, but that's usually how it works in mainstream pop because anything that's too different stands out too much. It breaks the flow of music as sonic wallpaper, and, as a result, music has lost much of its importance in the culture. Pop artists and record producers who want to get radio play deliberately imitate what's already being played.

I admire musicians who ignore the supposed divisions between genres because it usually means they're consciously swimming upstream in trying to build an audience. They've made it harder for people to describe or compare them to established artists and styles they already know and are comfortable with. But bending the rules is the only way to advance music forward. Every style that we've learned to love, whether it's early rock and roll, funk, jazz, rap, blues, bossa nova, metal, industrial, alternative, etc. began as a bastard child that people resisted because it violated their expectations and what they'd been exposed to up until that time. Creative people don't want to get stuck in a box just repeating themselves endlessly. That's artistic death.

I'm always digging to find new music to listen to (even if it's old music, but new to me). When something new excites me I often attempt to write a song in that style to help better understand it from inside, while putting my own spin on it, pulling it towards my own melodic and stylistic preferences. I love music writing as exploration!

I've pondered whether I should be more overt about my evolving beliefs in music. There was a spiritual aspect to many of my songs, even before I believed. A songwriter should draw on life as he experiences it, like a reporter, right? In 2010 I recorded a song about my tickler and other spirit visitors called "All My Life," but have been cautious otherwise. ("Will we be together when this life's through? / Is there anything that I can do? / I had a visitor I felt but could not see / And I don't know what it means / But it must mean something.")

About five years ago I wrote an unrecorded song called "Angels," based on my friend Sonya's experiences, mixed with my own. On vacation in Japan, while lighting candles at a temple, she felt teasing, energetic spirits dancing above her head. She said there was a foreign, completely Other, ancient presence. I wrote: "The giddy joy of angels circling above / You invite the angels in, it's love."

Being tuned into the energy of the people in a room, and how I'm feeling in the moment, has provided some of my best performances. The songs pick up colors from the day instead of forcing them into a pre-fab shape. The same lyric can take on a slightly different meaning depending on how

232

it's felt and delivered. Memories can be triggered, old feelings accessed and re-contextualized. The performer discovers as much about himself/herself as the audience does. We well up with feeling when musicians get deep.

The first time the Rob Falgiano Band performed was in the summer of 2008, opening for Jakob Dylan (Bob Dylan's son). It was at an outdoor concert downtown of about 5,000 people. Circumstances aligned. The weather was great and we were in good spirits. We had a good rehearsal, a good meal, laughs, and a few beers. I didn't feel very nervous, though I'm always at least a little.

We came out like a sports team jacked up for a big game. Often the opening group for a national act is minimally tolerated, but I felt like it was our day. The audience was dialed in, not talking or checking their phones. Ray, our drummer, was killing it, driving the songs like a locomotive. I turned to him mid-song to yell, "You're a monster!" He laughed and kept slamming away. We were alive in the moment, and electric.

A friend of mine in the audience said he overheard two guys standing in front of him say, "Next time these guys are here they'll be the headliner." It was nice to hear, though untrue.

When Dylan hit the stage the crowd became chatty and distracted. He strummed somewhat detachedly behind dark sunglasses. The newspaper review said the same. I felt we'd stolen a bit of his thunder even if few people remembered my difficult-to-spell last name.

I managed to sell a few thousand CDs in the '90s, but I can't quit my day job. I sometimes think of Kurt Vonnegut's alter-ego Kilgore Trout, the bitter, failed science-fiction writer he felt he was before (and even after) his success with *Slaughterhouse-Five*. It would be hard for me to be bitter, having enjoyed so many unique experiences. My appreciation for what I have has greatly grown. When I read Vonnegut I feel his humanity, empathy, and internal conflict. I hope Kurt is doing great in heaven, because he never believed in it.

My goal is to always feel excited about writing and performing music, or to stop if the joy fades. People will hopefully remain interested. I hope my enthusiasm and curiosity remain childlike, and that my songs reflect the best parts of me, indefinitely!

FORTY-FIVE: WEIRD DREAMS

I love the abstraction and weirdness of dream logic. You never know how your brain will combine elements from life with (supposedly) impossible scenarios outside of hard reality. I've had more dreams than I'll ever recall about the vast, enigmatic universe, often in the style of science-fiction movies. I've visited planets populated by exotic, sentient non-human beings, watched distant stars and planets explode in the sky and entire galaxies whirl past Earth as if my eyes are telescopic.

Apocalyptic dreams have been constant since I was young. In high school I dreamt of strange geometric shapes filling the sky, entering from another dimension through slices in the universe. Columns of solid destructive energy, like cartoonishly thick lightning bolts, slid horizontally through the slits, then changed direction at perfect right angles, pulverizing the ground below.

I dreamt I was a microscopically small particle falling through the clouds. No arms, legs, brain, heart, or body. Nothing except an awareness of my own existence. Just a twinkling bit of matter. (Straight up Descartes.) The clouds parted as I descended through layers of puffy white and grey to daylight, overlooking the ground.

I've been on spaceships and experienced alien invasions and hostile biological takeovers wherein my entire DNA was converted from the inside out by an intelligent invading organism, like The Borg on *Star Trek*, but a transmogrification to something much less humanoid. I've seen rogue planets ejected from solar systems enter our own on a collision course with Earth, like in the movie *Melancholia*.

I sat on the moon watching sunlight move across Earth, similar to how we observe moon stages from here, but within minutes, not days. The Earth seemed so close I could touch it, and it filled almost my entire field of vision. It appeared to be projected onto a large screen. And either I was very, very large, or the moon was very small, because it was like sitting on top of a 20-foot rocky gray ball.

I had a dream about being on an airplane, except it went into deep space. There were windows on the floor to see out and below. I gazed at abundant stars and darkness. I saw little geometric shapes that looked like sharp, angled bundles of wire. I said to the guy standing next to me, "What are those?" He said, "Those are time." I felt dizzy and went back to my seat. People were walking around and partying. The aisles and seats were wide and far apart like a club. I may have been standing on my seat at some point singing. I felt connected to the Bigger Thing, transported and happy.

I had a dream about a person who comes back to Earth as a "being of light." He was a disembodied intelligence who tried to manifest a human body from the awareness of his own existence, but he failed. After a couple attempts concluded with a poorly formed body collapsing (as if it was made out of thin loops of clay, like a human "Mr. Bill," or my mom's bendable leg in Rose's vision), the being tried to draw attention with light. Pulling energy from the night air, it formed tube-shaped lights (like 5-foot-long neons) at various angles.

The tubes popped in and out of the air, with gradually more in play as the being learned how to express itself. It attracted people's attention. The patterns became more intricate, the lights no longer just straight lines, but circles and other shapes and lengths. The scope and scale increased, too. The lights filled a whole field, swooping from sky to ground, passing over and through the assembled crowd. All kinds of colors; the changes were rapid and complex. It became a destination, with people regularly expecting to see the lights, which communicated faithfully each evening.

There was playful exuberance to the display. The being was excited to have found a way to communicate, and the crowd was filled with wonder watching it perform. (I sometimes envision good spirits as little beings of light. My friend Cathy was recently told by a psychic that the sparkles of light she sometimes sees when she thinks of her deceased father are indeed his energy, as she intuited.)

My recording studio friend Mike Rorick speculated that my constant dreams of strange life forms on other planets are actually memories of previous lives in exotic places, as different alien beings! He suggested that reincarnation, if possible, may not be confined to Earth, and could happen anywhere in the universe.

Presuming each of us has an immortal soul that experiences cycles of birth, death, a return to the immortal ether, and back again, why would previous and future incarnations of us always return here? There are one hundred billion stars in the galaxy, and at least one hundred billion galaxies in the known universe, and we're not sure this is the only universe. (There are also one hundred billion neurons in the brain.) Ours may sit at the intersection of an infinite multiverse of connected realities.

Maybe I was once a 20 foot purple slug lady on distant planet Flabia, or a liquid methane intelligence floating in a sub-zero degree lake a million light years away, a million years ago. Perhaps the methane me existed so long ago that the light from that planet's star is only now reaching Earth. In anticipation, maybe I sent a telepathic message to my future self on Earth a million years ago from the methane planet, and, travelling at the speed of light, it's just now reaching me on Earth. Two mes communicating in real time, even though one is a million years dead. (If any sci-fi writer steals this idea, I want some cash.)

Mike also told me that he and his girlfriend had the exact same dream about her mother on the same night! They interpreted it the same way, too, that it represented his girlfriend's difficult relationship because her mom's always been unable or unwilling to enjoy life. What are the chances of having the same dream as someone on the same night, or ever? More evidence.

I collected comic books as a kid, and I don't mind if every big movie in the next 20 years is based on one, because I had to wait a long time for the technology that's brought my favorite childhood heroes to life, especially Batman and Wolverine. When I was 5 or 6 I had a bad flu and dreamt the Green Goblin was terrorizing me on his Goblin-chopper. The dream was so realistic it felt like he was floating over my bed, against the green diamonds wallpaper.

This Goblin was from the trippy 1960s *Spider-Man* cartoon, specifically the opening scene of *The Witching Hour* in which the Goblin has broken into a magician's library to steal a book about casting incantations to conjure spirits for his sinister bidding. (The ghosts eventually turn on him.) Given my experiences, it figures that the image would have come from that episode.

Another feverish childhood dream was of walking through an endless series of doors and hallways, but never arriving at a destination. That's fairly existential for a 6-year-old. I kept bobbing in and out of consciousness, so the dream kept starting and stopping, which was annoying because every time it restarted it was the same. In the real world mom was talking to a friend of hers in the kitchen, and I went downstairs in a daze to try to explain about the endless hallways, but I was aware I wasn't making any sense. I think I was wearing my favorite blue Batman pajamas, rubbing sleep from my eyes.

In another teenage nightmare I had recently died and was on my way to the next world. Two nebulous, hooded figures awaited me on a cloud. As in lots of fables, one was cloaked in heavenly white while the other wore the red robes we associate with badness. I couldn't see their faces under the hoods. I thought I was headed for heaven but red robe reached out to grab me. I yelped and woke up. The next morning I went downstairs to hang out in my corner for a little while before school and the three-digit counter on my stereo cassette deck was locked on "6-6-6." Nice! I immediately pressed reset to flip the counter back to "0-0-0." I didn't believe in anything at the time, so I filed it under "weird coincidence" and nothing more, though it stayed with me. Now I see it as a prank by sneaky spirits.

A few summers ago I dreamt that a group of people, distressed by all of the suffering, prayed to bring about the end of the world. They mounted a coordinated prayer campaign to try to summon Jesus back to Earth and end things. A decade ago, in a moment of existential despair upon reading about the apparent abuse of a teenage prisoner at Guantanamo Bay, I prayed for god to end creation. I won't ask again. (I felt compelled to write a mournful song about torture called "Two Feet in the Sea.")

Some naughty spirits tried to kill me in my sleep a few years ago. My then-girlfriend Vanessa was staying over and I had a dream I was being physically attacked by someone. It ended when I tried to sidekick my assailant, but the action in the dream carried into reality. My hard kick sent the sheets and cats flying off the bed, startling Vanessa. The momentum flipped me out of bed and I hit my head on the corner of the dresser. "They're trying to kill me in my sleep!" I exclaimed. Fortunately, their aim is crappy and I was only grazed. You'll have to do better than that to take me out, ghost jerks!

I have a recurring dream in which I wake up in a different body than my own, like on the TV show *Quantum Leap*. One scene is always the same: I look at myself in the bathroom mirror of the house I grew up in, and have a completely different face. Sometimes I have long, luxurious hair, or rotten teeth. I've been both male and female, taller and smaller, younger and older, though never by much. I've been both more attractive and less attractive. Each time I swap faces I wonder how long it will last as I'm not sure I'm going to be able to get back into my own body, and I don't know if someone else is occupying my body or what they're doing with it. In the most recent version of this dream I was a young woman with a flowing pink Mohawk and tattoos. The makeup on my face was elaborate and I wondered how

I'd ever be able to reproduce it if I was in her body for more than a few days.

I dreamt I was at an arcade. Nearly every game was related to Wolverine and the X-Men. The next day, without my knowledge, mom took Steve and his friend Jim to play arcade games at the local laser tag. So I dreamt his activity a night in advance.

I dreamt I sang a duet with Frank Sinatra, taking the harmony part. There was also a vivid dream about being an emcee for Johnny Carson. In this scenario he was still alive, though long retired from *The Tonight Show*. His demeanor was the same as we remember. He was friendly, almost shy, dignified without conceit. I was somehow involved in convincing him to do a one-time *Tonight Show* reunion nearby, in a large, green field with bleachers, not dissimilar from the one in my light show dream. His trademark desk was there, and maybe some lighting instruments or a studio camera, plus a simple pipe and drape backdrop.

From the wings of the bleachers I riled up the packed audience with his trademark introduction, including an extended "Here's Johnny!" (Ed McMahon's is superior.) People were so excited. Carson took a microphone up into the audience and we sang an old school American pop standard together. (I wish I could remember the song.) I realized how great he was as an entertainer, how much he wanted to please the audience and the satisfaction it brought him. It occurred to me that I should try to be more like him.

His show was supposed to be 60 minutes long, but Johnny and the audience were having a great time. I looked at a big clock (floating in space near his desk?) as the hour neared. I encouraged him to do a full 90 minutes, for old time's sake, as they did when he first took over from Jack Paar. Everyone was happy. It was so real.

I've worked in the arts for 20 years and have developed a strong appreciation for professional dance. The amount of discipline, training, strength, and coordination involved is equivalent to any elite athlete. I had an intimate dream about a dance collective. I was on some kind of retreat; my hosts were generous patrons of the arts. One warm summer evening on the front lawn of their home, a small group of about three dozen people sat on the grass to watch several groups of young dancers perform their original work.

The last group, dressed in white, broke the fourth wall separating performers from audience, wandering into the crowd to interact. The leader of the group, a small, friendly young woman with short blonde hair approached me. She had the mysterious quality one might associate with a muse, or an otherworldly manifestation of creativity. There was nothing lewd about her movement, but she was crouched above me in an intimate way. She pressed her forehead against mine and ran her fingers through my thinning hair. We didn't kiss, but it was sensual, like she was loving and nurturing my spirit while our faces touched. I felt connected to the mystical infinite I adore, the place where beautiful art originates. I felt a strong bond with everyone there. Though we were new friends, we would always be connected. It was love.

FORTY-SIX: STILL DREAMING

I often dream about animals. In one there was a small room at a shelter with some regular-sized cats, but also a small bucket filled with thumb-sized cats. There was a mini-duck in there too, which probably got into my head from a Federico Fellini film I'd watched a few days prior. (In

Variety Lights, the flaky magician carries a duck around in a basket for the whole movie, though it's normal-sized.)

I posted a note about my thumb-sized cats dream on that social networking website. My friend Shelly wrote, "I am interested in obtaining a bucket full of thumb sized cats. I checked craiglist (sic). I didn't see any there." I replied, "Perhaps if you invent a machine that converts ideas in dreams into reality then we can just grab a bucket from my head." My former West Utica neighbor Carolyn chimed in, "A bucket of thumb-sized cats? I don't understand any of this. I feel like a surreal failure... :(I want to go back in the machine that converts reality back into dreams."

I replied, "I don't understand it either :-) But I'm amused by it. I like absurdity. It makes me laugh. Isn't life absurd? The absence of life would also be absurd. My dreams are often surreal. Eventually you will go back into the machine that converts you to dream." (Note: I don't do drugs, but I just had a Belgian beer.) Shelley got in the last word. "I think you're on to something with the dream machine. We could be hundredaires."

Here's what I posted on the same popular Internet social networking website which began-to-make-me-feel-depressed-and-obsessive-and-which-I-eventually-quit about another animal dream. "My cat somehow either got cloned or there were multiple versions of him from overlapping universes. I found myself having to try to collect all four versions of him so that there wouldn't be strays. It seemed like a lot of cats to take care of but he's awesome so I decided to suck it up."

My friend RoJo chimed in, "If I may attempt an interpretation... that dream says much about your ability to embrace the full scope of those you love. More than willing, you actively seek out an understanding of the complexity of others where in (sic) many become confused or frightened by what they cannot perceive, encumber or control. You are a rare character Rob. Your cat(s) is (are) quite lucky to have you!"

I said, "I like your interpretation RoJo! And thank you for the compliments. I have always sensed your soulfulness and complexity. I'm fascinated by a certain level of complexity and then I love it when it all breaks down again to simple, simple things, like a one and a zero. What is and what's not. A sperm and an egg. Openness is simple. Honesty is simple. Truth is direct. Stack stack stack to complexity then push over, start again. Hahahaahhaa I'm going to be an old zen weirdo. Can't wait."

RoJo had a good take on one of my other dreams. I had posted, "Would anyone like to explain why I had a dream about a talking monkey? You can't make this stuff up folks. He was my pet btw. I have no interest in a monkey pet."

RoJo said, "If it talked dirty, it was your id. The significance of your talking monkey will be found in its spoken words. You can assume that the message is primal in nature, has core implications and may not be accessible via the level of language/consciousness. More details?"

I confessed. "Stupid talking dirty monkey. Now I get it. It's my own fucking internal monkey man talking back at me. I'm a fucking monkey! That's annoyingly literal."

RoJo: "Yes. It is. Say hello to your ID Rob."

Me: "Hello Id."

RoJo: "Id: When you gonna get laid you freakin' monkey butt."

Me: "If you'd seen my company on Wed you'd have had that dream too. You monkeys. Hahahahah. Shock the fucking monkey."

RoJo: "Before you shock ID the chimp, consider there are potentially deeper interpretations, such as, 'You're stifling intellect, evolution or social status,' but you've not conveyed the specifics of the verbal exchange. So who knows. Sans more disclosures Occam's Razor (simplest answer is THE answer) deems that you are working on things at the animal, mid-brain level. That would suggest food, fear or fucking. Have a wild libidinous weekend, monkey boy."

Me: "No, it's just sex. Straight up. I rarely squish my intellect or evolution and I clearly couldn't give a good monkey shit about my social status, though I probably should. Thanks for your couch Dr. RoJo. Now somebody bring me some bitches. What a life!!!!"

RoJo: "Hahahaha… no charge. Now JUST DO IT!"

Here's another animal dream. I was attending a special performance or gathering of great creative, artistic minds, but only as an audience member. They met at my grandparents' house, where I now live. Two rooms were being used, one upstairs, plus the basement. Some of the stars arrived late. Most were laid back but a few were surly. The combination of people didn't entirely reflect my tastes. Paul Simon and Steve Martin were there, both of whom I was interested in meeting, plus Larry David, Bruce Dern (love him), George Lopez, and others. I don't know why there weren't any women because there are plenty I consider great artists. There were about 10 creatives altogether, and a small audience of 20, sitting comfortably in recliners.

For no good reason, once everyone had arrived and settled in, they became dogs. It wasn't that they transformed, it's more like they had always been dogs but didn't appear that way before. I too was now a dog. I tried to talk to Paul Simon dog first. Steve Martin was nearby, plus two others. I told Simon that I admired his songwriting. He was friendlier than I expected him to be.

As we chatted, a famous, shaggy writer dog who may have been wearing circular glasses, slithered nearby, more snakelike than canine. He was tidy and tight, and looked a little like Teddy Roosevelt. I didn't know who he was. He may have been an older, deceased writer, like Faulkner, or someone of that generation. I asked the entire group, "Don't you think all great artists start off as individualists? Don't you have to be willing to be your own person before you can develop your own style?" No one had a chance to answer before writer dog slid in front of the others and brushed against me, seemingly trying to intimidate me. I knew something was a little off with him, but I played dumb and didn't offer resistance.

Writer dog came in close and whispered something like, "If you use any of my ideas, I will find out." He seemed to think I might mine the conversation for my own artistic purposes. He worked himself on top of me with his snout in my face. I think his pelvis was moving and I got the feeling he might try to sexually assault me. I looked back over my shoulder. Someone who I knew would provide support was also there and I wanted to establish eye contact in case things got weirder. Writer dog gnawed lightly on my hand (now an actual hand, not a paw), to let me know his teeth were sharp. He said, "If I don't like your questions I will come back around to you."

I felt his darkness and intelligence. I didn't believe that his real concern was my stealing his ideas, or anyone else's. He had a personal issue with me, of undetermined nature, and wanted to deliver a warning from a position of power. I was neither afraid, nor intimidated, for he'd played a card revealing his weakness. I continued to play at non-threatening and docile, and planned to resume talking to the others once he left. Then the dream ended.

In a more recent animal dream I owned a beautiful, gentle, loving giraffe named Maisie. She would curl up with me on the living room rug. She ducked her long neck down to fit into, and fill up, the entire back seat of a compact car to go for a ride. The morning after the dream I vaguely recalled that she was spotted and purple so I typed "Maisie the Giraffe" into an Internet search engine and the first result that came up was a small clothing company in the UK called Purple Giraffe Clothing, run by a woman named Maisie. Her logo is a spotted purple giraffe. When I started my shower minutes later I turned on the radio, which was set to NPR. The topic of conversation was the American circus. They didn't mention a purple giraffe though.

Another recent animal dream had a synchronistic aspect. I dreamt about an unidentifiable animal about the size of a pig, but a little longer and more sausage-shaped. It was some kind of fish, but it had a short-haired, rough hide like a mammal. Its legs were short and stubby, and it only walked an inch or two above the ground.

The animal was meant to be in water but it was flailing about, somewhat joyfully, on concrete. But with every flop on the pavement bits of its body flaked off, and it began to bleed. The animal was dying in the process of its excitement, and that was the intention of the people watching it flail. I'm not sure if they planned to cut it up and cook it for dinner, but I found its unintentional suicide painful to witness. I grabbed a blanket and wrapped the animal into it. I told the people that if they planned to eat it they'd have to put it down in a less cruel way.

Later the same night I dreamt I was in an old apartment similar to my first Buffalo pad (where I adopted my cats Gene and Gabe). I've dreamt of this apartment variation many times. Unlike the winding staircase of my real apartment, this one headed straight from the street to the second floor. But, like my real apartment, the dream apartment was long and narrow with many bedrooms and a bathroom on the way to the rear.

The dream apartment merged with another in the back. Other tenants had access to my rear bedrooms, and I to theirs. Even though my apartment was locked from the outside, these unknown occupants could access my place any time from the inside and rob me blind if they wanted, though they never do. I often hear them back there and expect to see them, but don't.

My apartment was a little more run-down than in my previous apartment dream. There was fake wood paneling in the bedrooms and holes in the walls. Some of the paneling was damaged and jutting out, and I could see bees flying in and out of holes and gaps between the paneling and drywall, presumably building hives.

In real life the next evening my friend Leslie and I went to see a comedy show at a new downtown club. Before the show started I told her about my fish-mammal dream. She said her friend Kim had just put up a new profile picture on

247

Facebook, which she'd commented on. It was a picture of an odd Photoshopped shark-horse combination. It had a shark's mouth and fin, but the body was essentially that of a horse, as was its rough hide. The main difference from my dream was that the shark-horse had long horse legs, but otherwise the torso was almost the same as my fish mammal. *Ding!*

During the show the featured comic made a joke about the new unknown affliction that's killing swarms of bees, a reference to my second dream. *Ding, ding.*

Here's another dream I shared online. "Last night I dreamt I was on a manned moon mission, except when we landed there was a problem with the ship, so we were figuring out how much oxygen and food we'd have to last us while they tried to think of a rescue plan. The ship had living quarters and common areas for hanging out. Me and about a dozen people went out to walk on the moon, but it was like a frozen ball. I remember looking up at the sky and it was loaded with stars and phenomena and I was in awe." My mom replied, "Sometimes I truly believe dreams are actual journeys we take." I wrote, "Sure feels like it. I'm game for believing."

I dreamt I was on a small futuristic jet, on a cross country flight with seven stops and seven passengers. I can't remember where I'd vacationed, but I was headed home and had souvenirs I was excited to unpack. This futuristic airline, which may have been owned by Exxon (?), was completed automated. No pilots, no flight attendants. The route was preset. Illogically, some of our course was at super low altitudes, basically street level. We were maneuvering down city blocks, barely up and over trees and buildings at ridiculous inclines. When we passed through Detroit, it was in civil unrest, with people rioting on the streets. At our low altitude someone was able to hurl something that hit and exploded on the left wing, but the futuristic plane fabricated a new one, though it was more skeletal than the original.

At our last layover they switched planes on us. Inexplicably, our new "plane" was barely more than a transparent shell with tight seating. I'm not even sure there were wings. It was more like a floating, flying bullet. Due to the slim design, there was no baggage storage. Our luggage was magnetized to the top of the plane, floating slightly above the hull. But as we continued to fly through city streets the bags were sheared off by wires, signs, and stoplights, one by one. I was bummed to lose my goodies.

Things got worse when more of the already-small plane was chipped away. Then we found ourselves off the plane for some reason, standing on a city block. Again, this is nonsensical, but in order to rejoin it we had to fly outside the plane, hanging by wires with little hooks. (Why no one simply called the whole thing off, and took a bus home is anyone's guess.) We looked each other in the eye and fastened our individual hooklines to a metal ring, waiting for the plane to yank us through the clouds for the final leg. I yelled out, with false bravado, "If I survive this I'm going to dedicate the rest of my life to tearing down Exxon Airlines!"

It was frightening to be pulled up into the dark, wet sky. I couldn't see anything, so there was no point in opening my eyes. I could feel the weight of the seven of us, so I immediately knew when one person lost grip and fell away, because the overall load lessened. Apparently it was actor Gabriel Byrne. Sorry Gabe, you should have held on tighter. I don't know why he was there as I can't say he's ever consciously been on my mind. (I looked him up online the day after the dream, and the third result was an interview in a British newspaper with the headline, "Religion didn't do me any good." Ironic, yes? Byrne critiqued the Catholic Church in Ireland during his upbringing. Byrne described them as monstrous and in sympathy with the Nazis during World War II. He seems to like them even less than me for good reason.)

The rest of us held on tight, hoping the wires and hooks would hold. When we landed safely there was a crowd of journalists waiting in an airline hanger. I didn't feel like talking and tried to avoid them. I exchanged hugs with my remaining co-passengers. A crew of workmen handed us each a bundle of scraps of our damaged belongings somehow collected from the ground. There was nothing recognizable or salvageable. It was almost a joke, but the guys were so sincere about trying to make us feel better than I was grateful anyway.

Recently I dreamt that human life on Earth was going to end because the sun had unexpectedly grown in size. This will actually happen in another billion years, so get ready. Illogically and impossibly, it was common knowledge that the sun would be just enough larger the next morning to kill everyone. We all knew we only had one more day to live. I was with my family, trying to find some comfort. I stared up at the sky and felt the enormity of the sun bearing down on us.

I had a dream I owned a talking cat who turned out to be the Roman emperor Nero, or a reincarnation. He didn't reveal this at first. When he first spoke I said to him, "I always knew you could talk. I was kind of waiting for it." We had a friendly conversation for awhile, but then he seemed more ominous. I laid back in bed and Nero Cat leapt back and forth over me at a rapidly increasing pace, which began to near an inhuman blur. He maniacally, but darkly and calmly, said, "Rome... is... burn... ing," with each syllable falling upon another leap over me.

Prior to the dream, I was vaguely familiar with the legends about Nero, so I did some web research. Supposedly he was so demented and ruthless that he purposefully torched sections of Rome, killing his own subjects, in order to make new construction possible and pave the way for "progress." My sense of Nero Cat was of a strong and insane appetite for chaos and mindless destruction.

On a lighter note, a cosmic dream I had a few years ago was the inspiration for a song on my second last CD called "Weightless:" "I had a dream I was weightless / In a gym on a ship, heading 'round the sun / I wore goggles and this vinyl suit / Like some parachuter astronaut / I floated 'round doing somersaults / Bouncing from soft wall to wall / Got turned around so many times / That I wasn't sure which was the floor."

This dream is brand new. It's 4:30 a.m. and I've just woken. It was in the house I grew up in. My mother and brother were there. For some reason we knew that we were all going to die on the same day: today! The information had been imparted to us by spirit friends on the other side. We stood at the staircase to our upstairs bedrooms talking about the logistics. We were each given a slightly different time of natural death, but within a few hours of one another. (You'll recall, in real life, my grandmother and her brother died within a few hours of one another.)

I was made aware I would die in the early afternoon, and as we stood discussing it, we realized that my mom and brother had already passed away that morning! We'd missed it without even noticing they were dead. This made us laugh because the big event had already been set in motion and we were just catching up. Even though my mother and brother were both dead and I was still alive, we could see and hear each other plain as day. In the dream I interpreted this to mean there was no real barrier between the world of the living and that of the dead. They didn't look like ghostly apparitions; they appeared as flesh and blood. I loved that we were laughing about it because it's in keeping with the lightness we often feel when we're together in real life. Nothing's off-limits for a good joke, not even death.

(An aside: my brother and I have a sick running joke about being very old and lying side by side in hospital beds, with a hand on each other's respirator machine cable, ready to pull the plug like a couple of cowboys at a shootout. It's a morbid comical showdown to see who can kill the other faster. We laugh our balls off.)

I decided I wanted to leave a note on the kitchen counter explaining to whoever would find us, and to the world, that we didn't kill ourselves in some weird family ritual, and that we knew we were going to die together on the same day because some spirits told us so, and it was okay. I tried to explain the whole nature of spirits to the entire world on a piece of scrap paper from the drawer (that already had writing on the other side – a grocery list I think!). It was a severely inadequate effort. I tried to simplify the message and language and make it quick because I was getting tired. In fact, I was already falling into my death sleep. It wasn't painful; I was just drowsy. My mom said, "Don't even worry about it. It doesn't really matter anyway," about writing the note to mankind. I realized she was right. It didn't matter what the world thought of our synchronous deaths. But a part of me still wanted to share it, to once again try to help people realize how mystical existence is.

We may have been waiting for someone else to arrive. From the living room I told my mom I wanted to lie down. She called back from the kitchen, "If you do, then you'll go." Then she said, "Well okay, go ahead and lie down if you want. It'll be fine." Don't ask me why, but I think we were waiting for Superman, who was apparently an acquaintance of ours. Maybe I wanted him to be present or something, to make sure everything went okay. He felt like a random dream detail, unless maybe Superman is a comic fan's version of Jesus.

I gathered my blankets and pillow to lie on my favorite old couch in the living room. (I took this couch with me to my first and second apartments. It was eventually infested by fleas, and discarded, when I adopted my cat Gabe.) I looked down at it and thought about how great it was going to be to rest. I was a little nervous about falling asleep and crossing over, but mostly I felt happy and resolved and was ready to go. A few minutes prior to this I went to the bathroom to play with my hair so that it was in some semblance on my head. That way they wouldn't have to do something weird to it that would make me look like a jerk in the casket, even though my wish is to be cremated.

I had at least one of my favorite afghan blankets there. In reality we've had these since I was a kid; they were knitted by Grandma Falgiano. One is a combination of brown, red, orange, and black Charlie Brown-style zig zags, and the other is red, white, and blue. The brown one is slightly longer than the red, and fully covers me when lying down. I still have the blankets, and both covered me last night while I dreamt. They're on me now as I write.

I lay down and felt very sleepy, so I knew it wouldn't be long until I croaked. I thought I might have a little more time to organize my things in the house or call a few people and let them know I was checking out, but it was setting in fast. Then I realized there was no one I needed to get in touch with, as the most important people in my life were already in the house with me. It would be fine for everyone else to find out soon enough after.

Sleep came quickly, like an anesthetic before surgery when you're surprised at how fast it puts you down. I felt myself going under and, at the moment I fell asleep in the dream, woke up in reality. It was clear and fresh in my mind so I fired up the computer. That was 20 minutes ago.

FORTY-SEVEN: NO SOUL LEFT BEHIND

Human beings often have it hard. You get pulled into the world and you don't know anything. Everyone's a lifelong student of life. We travel towards a final destination we can never possibly arrive at. Our work and lives go unfinished, but others take up where left off, into the seemingly infinite future. Maybe that's not entirely true. Perhaps at some point we narrow our goals to the things and people who are truly important to us and it becomes enough to live for and feel satisfied.

I think this is how my mom feels. Raising Steve and I wasn't easy, but she was destined to do it. Almost certainly from the childhood moment she saw an angelic disabled girl at that wedding reception and asked for a life of mixed blessings. I don't believe in coincidence anymore. To ignore the evidence of my family's experiences would be a denial of reality.

If some doubt lingers as to the existence of more than this life, I'd ask you to leave a tiny door ajar somewhere in your mind. Keep it open to incredible possibilities which you haven't yet conceived, but might discover and explore in the future. That small sliver is all you need for new good things to potentially come through. My family's journey wasn't reserved only for us. It must be available to anyone who seeks a deeper understanding with an open heart and mind.

I'm reminded of the Dalai Lama's speech at the University at Buffalo a few years ago. He said that empathy for all living beings is the key to life, including those we perceive as our enemies. He acknowledged the difficulty of trying to live this way at all times. His ease in relating his philosophy was inviting and kind.

The Dalai Lama ended by saying that, if those who'd listened had found it valuable, he was happy. If others felt it did not apply and was to be dismissed entirely, that was fine. I thought that was perfect. Similarly, if you find my ideas useful, I'm glad. If not, that's okay. The teenage atheist version of me would have been highly skeptical and dismissive, and maybe that's the way it should be. If this were a movie, the present version of me would go back in time and wrestle with my teenage self to save the future. If I make it to my seventies or eighties I wonder what that guy will say about the man I am now.

I think it's worth repeating, and I often say to myself: it's never too late to change. You can always take a different course, and become a better person. Life on the outside sharpened my edges, and, as much as I try to be empathetic when I encounter willful ignorance, some anger remains. I've told myself for many years that I need an edge for self-defense and survival. That's how it always felt, but at times I've been too harsh. I work to stay peaceful in my mind, to let stupidity slide off like slime, to smile at the challenge and gift of life.

One of the things I loved about writing this, which simultaneously drove me nuts, was to discover that no matter how eloquently or clumsily I may have stated my thoughts on a subject, inside my brain the strength of my position was usually still challengeable from some angle. As if the more I wrote, and the closer I thought I might be getting to a truth, then the more fixed my position became. Once you fix your position then you have eliminated and closed yourself off from many other possibilities. Well, all of them.

On a quantum level scientists believe they've discovered that the universe is *all* possibilities, which may be why, when we think we've reached a destination, we still experience uncertainty, as if the act of slotting into place is unsatisfying. Which also implies that, no matter how much we think we know, it's always good to rethink our bedrock ideas. No single perspective is truth. Many ways of living work for as many different types of people who exist.

Perhaps there's a perverse beauty to building our supposedly core beliefs and identity, only to realize it can all be stripped from us by a natural disaster, unexpected illness, asteroid, bloody political conflict, or by aging. How much of identity is rooted in the luck of circumstances, and how much is one's unwavering soul? Some of us find out when things get rough.

All time is borrowed time. No promises exist. It likely caused your parents or guardians great pain when they first realized that no matter what they did while raising you, there were no guarantees they could forever protect you from harm. Hope becomes that much more critical.

My mom was the last born of five sisters, and nearly neglected. Her parents were probably all worn out by then,

256

or her mother was severe because she lost hope in the future, while her father was permissive because he didn't want to be the heavy. My mom told me that, even as a child, though she felt largely unloved and unsupported, she always knew she'd be okay, that she would survive. This amazes me. She has core strength and was always self-assured, even when nothing external should have given her this idea as a child. Perhaps this is what it is to be blessed, and looked after by angels.

Without her and my brother's support I'm not sure how I would have gotten by. I'd likely be a wreck, which explains why there are so many screwed up people all over, badly messing things up. Those poor, unloved bastards. (But hey, we've got problems too!) I guess we should empathize and pity them to the extent we're able, and then we should push them down a flight of stairs. (Not really.)

You can't predict the future (unless you're clairvoyant), nor can you control it. But you can *influence* it. From there it's about not just enjoying the mysterious ride, but loving it. For most people, life leads somewhere unexpected. A state of mind and place you never could have envisioned. You didn't know it existed until you arrived. Then you looked around and thought, "This is pretty good."

There are great challenges ahead for humanity. Global income inequality, climate change, explosive population growth, repressive religious and autocratic governments, corruption of democratic institutions, and the diminishing utility of people due to advancing technology will test the world. We'll have to be brave, and we'll need each other to solve these problems, even people who are very different from us.

Lately my quickie prayer is, "god, please be with the world and also me." That way no soul's left out. We're all one anyway, fragments seeking a return to wholeness. Everybody's a small slice of the universe.

EPILOGUE: THE BEST VISITOR

The first wordy draft of this book was complete by fall 2012 when my mom told Steve and I she was about to have surgery for early-stage breast cancer. But Steve already knew she was having the procedure. Three days prior he'd been visited by a friendly spirit who told him about it and assured him everything would go well and mom would be fine. It put him more at ease. He told me about his visitor after mom informed us of her situation, and that her surgery would be in just a few weeks.

The night I found out about the surgery I had a dream about people forced to participate in dangerous life or death games of amusement, in a sadistic future television show. I was a contestant and so was mom. I don't recall the precise task, but I accomplished it and "advanced" forward. An older couple followed me. They had to arrange objects on a large field in some particular manner like a jigsaw puzzle, but they were almost too senile to compete. They failed badly. The platform on which they had been working was rigged and flipped upside down, ejecting them ten stories below where they were crushed by a mountain of girders, bricks, and debris. The deaths of the older couple made me realize more concretely that these games were not just some joke.

Mom was the next contestant. She stood before an enormous grid of glass sheets, about the size of a football field. Many of the sheets were perfectly rectangular, the size, weight, and thickness of shop windows. Her task was to find the large, deadly-sharp broken and fragmented plates of glass and eject them from the field.

I watched my 5-foot-nothing mother run into the grid and start lifting large, person-sized fragments, tossing them aside as she advanced. But as I looked at her face, she was smiling. What should have been a life-threatening situation that would frighten some people into paralysis, like the elderly couple, was instead a challenge that she knew she had to rise to in order to survive. That's when the dream ended.

I prayed often in the weeks leading up to her surgery, and to my deceased cousin Georgine (Gigi), and to my Aunt Joni, Gigi's mother. Aunt Joni had been depressed a long time before she died. She was addicted to painkillers for years and her emotional issues adversely affected her relationships with her five adult children and also her four sisters, including my mom. But I remember happy holidays at her home too, Aunt Joni cooking and laughing, and my older cousins around me at the long kitchen table. I liked the affectionate way she said my name ("Robbie"). I hear her voice and see her smile.

My mom felt extremely angry at Joni because, when Gigi was very sick and in the hospital, Aunt Joni and my Uncle Joe told mom that she, Steve, and I were not to continue to visit her, and that Gigi didn't want to see us. Mom felt it was a lie, because visiting with Gigi was a great joy. But she angrily honored her sister's instructions, as did I, and Gigi died not long after.

Aunt Joni died a few years after Gigi. My mother refused to attend her funeral. I asked her to reconsider more than once, to consider forgiveness even though Joni had been unfair, but she felt strongly betrayed. I prayed to Gigi and

Aunt Joni to look after my mom, to help protect her. It may not have been appropriate, but I told Aunt Joni she "owed" it to my mom to help see her through. That's how it felt.

Mom's surgery lasted three and a half hours but her recovery took almost as long because she had a bad reaction to the anesthetic. She'd come in at 5:30 that morning, but didn't make it back to her room until 3:30 p.m.

Earlier that afternoon, while my mom's second husband John and I were waiting at the hospital, I ran into two people I didn't expect to see. The first was my friend Sonya, who I vacationed with in Key West nine years ago. You may recall Sonya is the one who felt the presence of ancient spirits in a Japanese temple. I hadn't seen her in a while; we'd lost touch. I didn't know she'd been working at the hospital for several years. When I stepped out of the waiting room we nearly walked into each other. If it had been 10 seconds earlier or later I'd have missed her entirely. She was surprised to see me. I was surprised, but not surprised. You know me and good old synchronicity.

Sonya grew up an only child in a religious household in Kentucky, and felt her parents' fundamentalism badly stunted their relationship. She went home when her dad was dying, but she didn't feel connected to him during their last visit. Her father tried to reach out to her in a way he hadn't her entire life, but she couldn't feel it. It was too late.

Sonya spent many years trying to deprogram from Christian brainwashing whereas I've gradually come to embrace the idea of a creator, though, as I've harped, *god is non-denominational.* She's not sure if she believes in heaven while I'm convinced there's more to come.

An hour later John and I were informed we could go to the floor my mom would stay on. On our way up I ran into Ron, the drummer I'd performed with for nearly 10 years, the same guy who rolled over with me in the truck in Oswego. Like Sonya, he was amazed to see me. He was there with his own mom. She was scheduled for the next cancer surgery with the same kind female surgeon my mom had had that morning.

He said, "What are the chances of running into you here?"
"None at all. I no longer believe in coincidence."

John and I visited with mom for an hour. She was still groggy, but coherent. After awhile I told her how we'd run into Sonya, and Ron with his mom. She was astonished.

John went home to take out their dogs, Nellie and Mike. I helped mom order dinner from the hospital room service menu. Grilled cheese, red beans and rice, vegetable soup, a banana, and carrot cake with vanilla ice cream. She was starving.

I told her about my dream of her running through the field of broken glass. I said how moved I was by her apparent joy in the face of the deadly, dangerous task. She said, "Oh my god, that's LIFE."

Yes, the dangerous game is life. To face it bravely, with joy in the face of tough odds, with one's life literally hanging in the balance, is the lesson. How we cope, how we live, who we decide to be when challenged is the entire test of a human being. To be loving and courageous, even when life is littered with broken glass.

Nearly two years later, mom's doing great. All the tests have come back negative, there's no evidence of anything residual, and she doesn't need chemotherapy, radiation, or medication. We're hopeful it's gone for good, though one can never be certain. My brother and I never doubted her recovery because we trusted his messenger, though we took the surgery seriously, and knew it would be taxing.

We didn't arrive here overnight. The clues were spread over decades, nearly a lifetime, right from mom's childhood. To step back and see the pattern is big. Spirits helped us connect the dots because that's what they want to do for everyone. Our lives are much richer for it. If this is something you humbly seek, you will find it. Embrace the mystery and magic of life and you too will be embraced.